COUNSELING
THE
ALCOHOLIC WOMAN

WITHDRAWN

Joseph F. Perez, Ph.D.

ACCELERATED DEVELOPMENT INC.
PUBLISHERS
MUNCIE, INDIANA

Counseling the Alcoholic Woman

Copyright 1994 by Accelerated Development Inc.
10 9 8 7 6 5 4 3 2 1
Printed in the United States of America

Technical Development: Cynthia Long
                          Marguerite Mader
                          Janet Merchant
                          Sheila Sheward

Cover Design: Coleen D. Ahern

Library of Congress Cataloging-in-Publication Data

Perez, Joseph F. (Joseph Francis)
    Counseling the alcoholic woman / Joseph F. Perez.
        p.   cm.
    Includes bibliographical references and index.
    ISBN 1-55959-055-6
        1. Women alcoholics--Counseling of.   I. Title.
HV5137.P47   1994   94-914
362.29 ' 286 ' 082--dc20   CIP

LCN:94-914

ISBN:1-55959-055-6

Order additional copies from:

ACCELERATED DEVELOPMENT INC., Publishers
3808 West Kilgore Avenue
Muncie, Indiana 47304-4896
Toll Free Order Number 1-800-222-1166

DEDICATION

To the Deweys
Dan, Kathy, and Daniel Christopher (my grandson)

ACKNOWLEDGMENTS

A book like this could not have been written without help. I am especially indebted to five women who gracefully consented to share their alcoholic experiences in candid and moving autobiographical sketches. These will be found in Part II.

My especial acknowledgments go to Lucia Sullivan who typed the manuscript. Throughout that long trying period of rewriting she always responded calmly, cheerfully, and gracefully both at home and at work to my anxious, flustered intrusions. Then again, that's Lucia, a rare person who melds impressive competence with a warm and gentle disposition.

PROLOGUE and PREFACE

Ever since I can remember I've known that there was more status in being a boy than in being a girl. As a child I heard girls say that they wished they were boys. I never heard a boy say that he wanted to be a girl. What it has taken me a long time to recognize is that if I had *more* status than a girl just because I was a boy then she had *less* just because she was a girl. The injustice, unfairness of that was never part of my conscious ken. Only recently have I come to see that all those little girls of my childhood were victims of a socialization process, the effect of which was to enhance the boy and demean the girl.

Remarkably, many women, I think most, adapted to the victimization. Some did it by regressing into a narcissistic-like existence, some by becoming robot-like conformists. Most of them just denied it and inevitably paid the price—a low self-esteem. Some of course did not deny or adapt to the madness, to the reality of being a victim and being told, "it's not true." "There's something the matter with you." "It's all in your head." These last women tried to escape—via alcohol. To tell the stories of some of these last women was why I wrote this book.

This book is divided into three parts. Part I treats the **dynamics** of a woman's alcoholism. Treated here is (1) a comprehensive theory liberally sprinkled with writings of recovering alcoholic women, (2) the process of socialization and personality development of the woman in our society, and (3) the alcoholic woman in the family. Part II addresses the **effects** of alcoholism. This is done via describing and explaining the progression, recovery process and the constant anxiety of relapse. The stories of recovering alcoholics also are included in this Part II. In vivid fashion, these cases illustrate what happens to a woman and those close to her when she drinks alcoholically. Part III deals with the **theory** and **practical concerns** of counseling the alcoholic woman both individually and in a group.

Like most college professors, my first concern in writing this book was that it have academic and professional respectability.

The number of citations (100) give it that respectability. My second and very real concern was to make it readable and authentic. A disproportionate number of alcoholism counselors are themselves recovering alcoholics. The experience of their disease has made them cynical and not a little suspect about any heavy intellectualized tome about an illness they know first hand. What they demand are reliability and honesty. As will be seen, the autobiographical sketches in Part II, **Effects**, provide a riveting read precisely because of their authenticity.

This is a basic text for therapists of alcoholic women. I am confident that practicing alcoholism therapists and those new to the field will profit, considerably, from a studied reading.

TABLE OF CONTENT

LIST OF FIGURES

PART I
DYNAMICS

FACTS & FIGURES *
WOMEN and DRINKING

Although women drink less than men, the number of women who do drink is significant. Estimates indicate that of the 15.1 million people who abuse alcohol or are alcohol-dependent, 4.6 million are women. That means that roughly one-third of alcoholics are women.[1]

Women who drink heavily or are alcoholic are more likely to become victims of the alcohol related aggression of others, such as date rape.[2]

Drinking varies among women of different racial or ethnic backgrounds. African American women were more likely to abstain from drinking alcohol (66.9 %) than White women (52.6 %) during the month prior to their interview.[3]

Hispanic women drink infrequently and are more likely than White or African American women to abstain from drinking; however, this may change as they enter new social and work arenas. Abstention rates are greater among Hispanic women who have immigrated to the United States than among younger, American-born Hispanic women.[4]

Marital status influences drinking habits. Single, divorced, or separated women are more likely to drink heavily and experience alcohol-related problems than women who are married or widowed. Unmarried women who are living with a significant other are most likely to develop drinking problems.[5]

*(Excerpts taken from *Prevention Resource Guide: Women* by U.S. Department of Health and Human Services, Public Health Service. Alcohol, Drug Abuse, and Mental Health Administration, MS433. October 1991.)

Despite their relatively low consumption levels, women account for nearly one-half of cirrhosis deaths among American Indians.[6]

Women are more susceptible to alcohol-related liver damage. They develop liver disease in a shorter period of time and at lower levels of consumption. The number of alcoholic women who develop alcohol-related liver disease is higher than among alcoholic men.[7]

The impact of alcohol appears to be greater upon women than men.[8]

Repeated or sustained episodes of alcohol intoxication may suppress hormonal activity in women. Studies suggest that a higher prevalence of menstrual dysfunction and an accelerated onset of menopause among alcoholic women. Other problems such as obstetrical disorders and gynecological surgery also are more common.[9]

It is estimated that the number of women in the United States who drink has increased significantly over the last 40 years and that heavy drinking has increased among young, employed women. As many as 16% of these women may be consuming three to five drinks per day.[10]

1. Williams, G.D., Grant, B.F., Hartford, T.C., & Noble, B.A. (1989). Population Projects Using DSM-III Criteria: Alcohol Abuse and Dependence, 1990-2000. Alcohol Health & Research World 13 (4), 366-370.

2. Fillmore, K.M. (1985). The Social Victims of Drinking. British Journal of Addictions (80), 307-314.

3. National Institute on Drug Abuse, Division of Epidemiology and Prevention Research Triangle Institute, "Alcohol: Ever, Past Year, and Past Month (1990) by Sex and Age Group for Whites and Blacks," National Household Survey on Drug Abuse: Population Estimates 1990, pp. 84-85, 1990.

4. Holck, S.E., Warren, C.W., Smith, J.C., & Rochat, R.W., "Alcohol Consumption Among Mexican American and Anglo Women: Results of a Survey Along the U.S.-Mexican Border, " Journal of Studies on Alcohol 45 (2): 149-154, 1984. Caetano, R., "Drinking Patterns and Alcohol Problems in a National Survey of U.S. Hispanics," Alcohol Use Among U.S. *Ethnic Minorities, pp.* 147-162,

1987. Gilbert, J., "Alcohol Consumption Patterns in Immigrant and Later Generation Mexican American Women," Hispanic Journal of Behavioral Sciences 9 (3): 299-313, 1987.

5. Heath, A.C., Jardine, R., & Martin, N.G., "Interactive Effects of Genotype and Social Environment on Alcohol Consumption in Female Twins," Journal of Studies on Alcohol 50 (1, 39-48, 1989.

6. Indian Health Service. (1988). Indian Health Service Chart Series Book. Washington DC: U.S. Government Printing Office.

7. Grant, B.F., Dufour, M.C., & Hartford, T.C. (1988). "Epidemiology of Alcoholic Liver Disease." Semin Liver Disease 8 (1), 12-25.

8. Fellios, P.G. (1989). Alcoholism in Women: Causes, Treatment, and Prevention. In Alcoholism and Substance Abuse in Special Populations. Rockville, MD: Aspen Publishers.

9. Hughes, J.N., Cofte, R., Perret, G., Jayle, M.S., Sebaoun, J., & Modigliani, E., "Hypothlamopituitary Ovarian Function in 31 Women with Chronic Alcoholism, "Clinical Endocrinology (12): 543-551, 1980, and Gavaler, J.S., "Effect of Alcohol on Endocrine Function in Post-Menopausal Women: A review," Journal of Studies in Alcoholism (46): 495-516, 1985, and Mendelson, J.H., Mello, N., Cristofaro, P., Ellingboe, J., Skupny, A., Plamieri, S.L., Benedikt, R., & Schiff, I., "Alcohol Effects on Nalozone-Stimulated Luteinizing Hormone, Prolactin and Estrdiol in Women, " Journal of Studies in Alcoholism (48): 287-294, 1987.

10. Malliday, A., & Bush, B. (1988). "Women and Alcohol Abuse." Alcoholism: A Guide for the Primary Care Physician, pp. 176-180.

Chapter 1

A FRAME OF REFERENCE

In the book, *The Alcoholic Self*, Denzin (1987) defined and explained "The Six Theses of Alcoholism." These theses provide the frame of reference for much of this book. As will be seen, when these theses are applied to the alcoholic woman they make for a most enlightening and comprehensive personality profile.

The six theses involve

1. the temporality of self,
2. the relational structures of self,
3. the emotionality of self,
4. bad faith,
5. self-control, and
6. self-surrender.

Women may abuse alcohol as a result of problems listed in Figure 1.1. Reprinted from "About Woman and Alcohol" with permission, copyright 1980, Channing L. Bete, Co., Inc., South Deerfield, MA 01373.

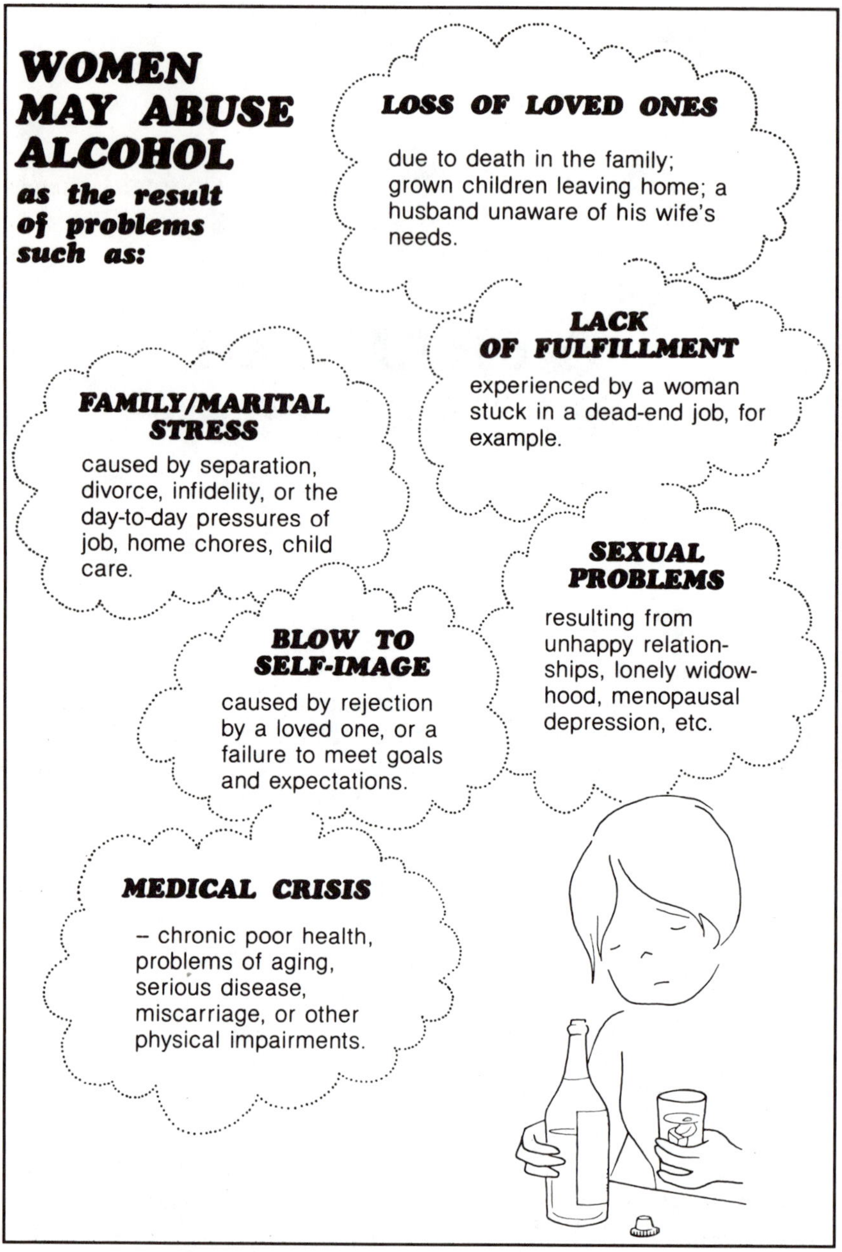

WOMEN MAY ABUSE ALCOHOL *as the result of problems such as:*

LOSS OF LOVED ONES
due to death in the family; grown children leaving home; a husband unaware of his wife's needs.

LACK OF FULFILLMENT
experienced by a woman stuck in a dead-end job, for example.

FAMILY/MARITAL STRESS
caused by separation, divorce, infidelity, or the day-to-day pressures of job, home chores, child care.

SEXUAL PROBLEMS
resulting from unhappy relationships, lonely widowhood, menopausal depression, etc.

BLOW TO SELF-IMAGE
caused by rejection by a loved one, or a failure to meet goals and expectations.

MEDICAL CRISIS
– chronic poor health, problems of aging, serious disease, miscarriage, or other physical impairments.

Figure 1.1. About women and alcohol. Reprinted from "About Women and Alcohol" with permission, ©1980, Channing L. Bete Co., Inc., South Deerfield, MA 01373.

THE TEMPORALITY OF SELF

An integral aspect of the alcoholic woman's personality is a warped perception of and relationship with time. When she drinks, her perception of time, both long term and short term, becomes confused. This confusion becomes incorporated into her sense of who she is and is not, what she can and cannot do. It is precisely this warped sense and understanding of time which structures for a baby-like view of it—to want, what she wants, when she wants it—now. This view is why deferred goals are an unfathomable mystery and a terrifying threat to her and why she seldom perseveres in striving to attain them. This view, too, contributes to her procrastinating ways, especially with meeting deadlines. More often than not, her conviction is that were she to meet the deadline (to *do* whatever) her efforts would be found wanting ergo, she would feel rejected.

Case of Hilda

Hilda is a recovering alcoholic who illustrates the alcoholic perception of time. Thirty-seven years old, she is a wife and the mother of two teenaged girls. Sober now for 14 months, she recently described for me how she typically spent her "normal" day.

On an average week day with Bob at work and the twins in school, I never had a drink before ten. Most days, I was able to do so because I kept myself busy. First I put a wash in, then I'd do the breakfast dishes and make the beds. Next I had a cup of coffee while watching T.V. The wash would be ready to come out and I'd put it in the dryer. While it was drying, I'd vacuum and pick up until the house was immaculate. By the time I'd finish ironing any clothes item that needed it, I'd take my first drink. Throughout the morning I'd check the clock after every single chore. I very quickly learned how long each one took. I got so I could make both girls' beds in three and a half minutes. Ours took two. I realize now that I was obsessed with clock watching because time hung so awfully heavy. It took forever to get to ten o'clock. I always felt like I'd accomplished something very significant, like winning a marathon race, when the grandfather clock in the living room finally tolled ten. My first drink, prepared at 9:45, was waiting in the refrigerator. Often I tried to hold off taking it until after ten. Doing that made me feel good about myself. The long and short of it was that in those days I saw time as my enemy, an enemy I had to kill.

So in order to kill time, and still feel good about myself, I'd look and find all kinds of asinine things to do, anything, even sweeping the front sidewalk, something that nobody on our street ever does.

Anyway at 10 A.M., or very soon thereafter, I'd take my first drink. And what I noticed by that act was that my frustrations evaporated, all my "nerves" weren't nervous and I'd quickly feel that I could easily handle all the things I was nervous about. Before I'd finished the first drink I felt serene. See, when I drank, time stopped. I guess I thought it was dead. I'd been successful. I'd killed it. On those days the clock did move, it moved very, very slowly. For some reason I always had to look at it every time that I poured a drink. Hindsight and sobriety tell me that despite my thought about it being dead I also thought of it as my anchor in reality, as a symbol of normalcy. Everybody, man or woman, alcoholic or not, abides by the same time.

If I took my first drink at 10:01, 02, or 03 it would not be 10:10 when I was refilling my glass. Between my first sip and my refill, I probably would have journeyed back to a happy incident in my childhood, or to one of my high school years, or to my wedding day—the happiest day of my life. I could take any one or all of those trips in less than six minutes!

Before noon I'd be glowing serenely and I'd have to eat. I usually ate a lot, I mean a lot. I did that because a very full stomach invariably put me to sleep and sleep killed more time. I didn't worry that I'd oversleep because when I made the bed earlier I always set the alarm for 2:20 P.M. See, the twins got home at 2:30.

A most informative point about this woman's story is her perception of time as something to be killed. Time for her was a threat, oppressively boring. It precipitated a lot of anxiety in her. Indeed, so much that she turned to alcohol to escape it.

Informative, too, is the fact that the time in which she could live better, quite obviously was not the present but the past. Healthy people live in the present.

THE RELATIONAL STRUCTURES OF SELF

According to Denzin an alcoholic can best be understood when she is able to discern the relational structures which she has constructed. The alcoholic woman lives in a world with real people like "normals" do but lives also with many people who, while figments of imagination, are people to whom she can and does relate. In these relations, both real and imagined, the alcoholic woman invests much emotional wherewithal. The whole kaleidoscope of emotions play a part in her relations—love, hate, envy, desire, jealousy, etc. They play and have very real meaning.

Case of Brenda

Brenda is a client of mine. She is 29 years old, a librarian and presently in recovery. I have been seeing her off and on for over three years. She wrote the following for me for inclusion in this book.

Like a lot of kids when I was little, I had imaginary playmates. The difference between me and most of them, however, was that there were times, lots of times, when they were not imaginary for me. They were real. In fact, they were realer than so-called real people for me.

Throughout my elementary school years my best friend was Jenny. Jenny was everything I was not. Jenny was blonde, blue-eyed and beautiful. Unlike anybody else in my life, Jenny let me talk to her about all my fears, anxieties, aspirations, and my joys too. In a word, Jenny listened. She never scolded. She held no expectations. I didn't have to perform for Jenny. And when I went to sleep Jenny talked to me, soothingly. Sometimes she sang to me. I loved Jenny.

Nobody ever knew about her because once when I was playing and laughing with her in the bedroom, my sister, Margie, the oldest of us kids, came in and made fun of me. She had two friends with her. They all teased me and made me cry. I was ten years old.

There were eight of us kids in the family and mom and dad. I was the youngest. I was also very lonely. That stuff about big families being happy families is just not true. Ours wasn't or at least I wasn't. Even though I had seven brothers and sisters I was lonely all the time, probably 'cause I was the baby in the family and six years younger than the next oldest. Anyway I wasn't lonely after Jenny came into my life.

After the incident with Margie I became much more careful. I didn't talk out loud to Jenny anymore. I didn't even whisper to her unless we were alone. Since there was always somebody around me, the only time I could talk to her was when I walked. I started taking long, long walks. Looking back now, I was unhappiest and loneliest when I was with my family or in school. I was happiest when I was alone with Jenny. So even though there never was a person in my life whom I could call a friend, I had Jenny.

It's only recently in counseling that, in creating Jenny and I can finally admit it now, I created my own Frankenstein. What I've finally come to realize is that Jenny was a kind of emotional two-edged sword for me. In dispelling my loneliness she also prevented me from learning how to act and relate to people. I know that now. Even though I can communicate pretty well like this by writing, I still can't talk to people. I made myself like that via Jenny.

Believe it or not there was a time I blamed Jenny for my being an alcoholic! Like most alcoholic rationalizations there's enough reality in it to make it all sound a little plausible. What I have to keep focusing on in my recovery is that it is I who created Jenny and not her me.

Brenda is most sensitive about her interpersonal difficulties. She feels quite inept making small talk. The reason for her interpersonal ineptness lies in the fact that she is still emotionally invested in Jenny. Right now she is involved in a kind of love-hate relationship with her. The love is of a nostalgic sort. The hate is founded in the fact that she recognizes too well that by "talking" and relating to Jenny for most of her childhood and teen years she stunted her emotional, interpersonal competencies. Brenda has much difficulty expressing emotion whether it be love, anger, humor, or whatever. She has comparable difficulty accepting it from others. A very quiet and sedate woman, she is quite bewildered when people are nice to her. For example, she spent much of a recent session explaining how embarrassed and uncomfortable she was when a professor at the university brought her some flowers because of the thoroughness of the computer search which she had done for him. She didn't know how to say thank you. What Brenda is finally coming to understand, albeit slowly, is that embarrassment, shyness, and discomfort with others stems from the fact that she has to learn, initially learn, just like a child does, that she has to emotionally invest in *actual* people. To do that she has to be and make herself available to others. She is starting to do that by attending group functions. Recently she joined a woman's political action group and a church social group. My sense is that with perseverance, and Brenda *is* a perseverer, she will become more interpersonally adept.

THE EMOTIONALITY OF SELF

The essence of this thesis is that alcoholism is an emotional disorder. The alcoholic woman has a veritable lost sense of self when not under the influence. A major reason she drinks is precisely to obtain, regain, her sense of self. Put simply, drink gives her an identity, an identity of feeling that she does not have when she does not feel the effect of alcohol.

The alcoholic is much better able to relate emotionally when under the influence. Alcohol lowers the emotional defenses. With this lowering, the alcoholic finds she is able to give love, accept it, vent frustrations and pent-up anger, even express jealousies. A not uncommon reason many women ingest alcohol excessively is precisely to rid themselves of the constant latent need to insulate their feelings. Such women have learned that it is bad to vent any emotion, positive or negative. When sober and with defenses up, they are able to maintain control. It is precisely when the pressure to release emotions becomes unbearably intense that the alcoholic woman gravitates to booze.

When cold sober, alcoholics such as these are very secretive about their feelings. They are aware of them but feel emotionally naked were they to display them. So they don't and are themselves literally offended when others direct feelings (positive ones included) toward them. Frequently, they become uncomfortable when they witness public emotional displays whether it be one they were obliged to view (crying at a funeral) or one they saw accidentally (two lovers kissing on the street). What makes the situation especially difficult for these women is that our society condones, even supports, the stereotypical idea that it's okay for a woman to be emotional. *And these women know it.* Still they can't easily emote naturally. It is why, too often, *they feel like freaks.* It is *a*, perhaps *the*, major reason their sense about emotions is so confused, another reason that the pressure to drink and vent emotion (which they can't when sober) becomes at time quasi-insupportable, another reason that they are unable to break out of their destructive cycle.

And so they drink and vent emotion, even accept it more easily (especially expressions of love). The most destructive effect of this cycle is that these women become psychologically acclimated to their emotions while under the influence of alcohol and are quite alienated even repulsed by them when sober. Put succinctly, *they become strangers unto themselves.*

Case of Nora

Nora, a clerk-typist, is a 33-year-old woman who had been married for 11 years. She was a member of an alcoholism counseling group which I facilitated.

Mark and I never had any children. We broke up because of that two months ago. The divorce will become final in about five more months. Actually I'm glad we never had any kids. He wanted them. I didn't. I never saw myself as a mother. I honestly don't think I'd know how to be one and frankly it's not something I have any interest in being.

14 *Counseling the Alcoholic Woman*

Dr. Perez asked me to describe my marital relationship. Actually Mark and I had a very, very good relationship during the first four or five years. We had the same aims and goals. We both wanted to own our own house and we both liked our work. We both worked hard. I did extra typing at home after working all day and he took a second job as a computer repairman.

We didn't see each other too much during the week but our weekends were glorious. We both loved to cook gourmet which we did together. Our meals were by candlelight as was our sex. I have to say Mark was a fantastic lover.

So what happened? What happened was that about five and a half years ago we got our house and right afterwards Mark wanted to start a family. Slowly, but surely we fell more and more apart. I tried real hard not to let it happen. Unfortunately the way I tried only made things worse. I bought more wine for our gourmet meals, and drank more—to loosen me up. In no time I was doing what I'd not done—I was drinking during the week, a lot, and liking it even more.

Then we started to fight and not just about having a baby. He started telling me all the time that he felt close to me only when we drank wine together. He also told me that I was too moody—either too high or too depressed. All of that was true and didn't hurt especially. What did hurt was when he told me that he didn't feel he knew me.

It took a long time of counseling, group and individual, to make me realize that Mark's words hurt because they were true. He didn't know me and probably because I didn't feel I knew him either. We didn't know each other.

Dr. Perez says that my problems have to do with feelings and getting in touch with them. Probably right. And God knows I'm trying. Anyway about my marital relationship? Mark and I are divorced now. It was a friendly divorce but the way we both saw it, if we didn't know each other after 11 years of marriage, neither one of us wanted to spend anymore time trying to.

What is definitely true about what Nora related is that she is indeed trying. She never missed a meeting of her alcoholism group and recently started seeing a colleague of mine in individual psychotherapy. About two weeks ago I met her in a shopping mall. Smiling and all aglow, she introduced me to her friend and new fiance. We chatted for a few minutes and when I turned to leave she kissed me on the cheek and whispered a thank you. I liked the kiss and remembered thinking that Nora was learning to vent emotion and even better learning to do it appropriately.

BAD FAITH

An alcoholic in a state of bad faith is one who is in denial of her alcoholism. Denial is a psychological defense and the defense which permits, facilitates the onset, and the development and maintenance of the alcoholic process. Denial permeates every aspect of body and mind. Thus, the addicted alcoholic refuses to acknowledge that her body craves the alcohol; that she feels she *needs* to have it; that she is preoccupied with its acquisition; and that alcohol is veritably destroying her social, vocational, and familial relationships. What compounds the whole problem of denial is that, despite its all-intrusive and transcending nature, the alcoholic at some level knows that she drinks uncommonly much but what she knows even better and most assuredly is resolved not to do, namely, is to give up her booze. This resolve, of course, is what keeps her alcoholic. This resolve does something else too, it permits her from avoiding a highly probable failure. Were she unable to stop drinking if she tried, her loss of "pride" in herself would be devastating.

Case of Darlene

Many of these dynamics are illustrated in Darlene's story. Forty-one years old, she is divorced and the single parent of three girls, all under ten years. Currently on some public assistance, she lives in a single home purchased when she was married and the home's upkeep is still maintained by her ex-husband. When able, she also moonlights as a cocktail waitress. A devout member of A.A., Darlene now has been sober for almost a year. She's been a member of my alcoholism counseling group for almost two years.

What I've learned is that my story is not especially different. I got married and became pregnant within two months. Within two years I had two more kids. Three years, three kids. For a husband I had a guy who only enjoyed making them. He had, still has, no interest in any of them.

My instructions in writing this were to explain why I think I became alcoholic and why I stayed that way for a long time. For a lot of us, those two questions are impossible to answer. Not so for me. I know. I learned in group.

What's a little different for me is that I didn't even drink until I was engaged. I can remember my very first drink—a Tom Collins. I didn't have any special reaction to it. I didn't like it or not like it. All I remember is that it was cold. I liked that because it was a hot day in July. My husband to be and I had gone to a wedding reception. Despite my indifference to the taste of it I had a second, and a third. I liked the way it made me feel, very relaxed and cuddlesome. My future husband liked my reaction too. He liked it so much that from that date on he made sure that we always had a few drinks, on our dates, sometimes more than a few. I'm not blaming him for anything. I'm not even suggesting that he had anything to do with me becoming alcoholic. I know very well that nobody ever made anybody alcoholic. We make ourselves so.

Anyway, I started by saying that I knew why I became a drunk. I began drinking like one when I found out I was pregnant with Nancy, my second. All my life I'd heard stuff like children are a joy and pregnancy is a perfectly natural condition. I heard it and I believed and digested it.

Tammy my first was no joy. She was colicky and she drove me crazy and she was all mine. My husband never got up once with her. Not once during the week. His explanation, that I bought was that he had to get up and go to work. On weekends his explanation was that he was too tired or that he simply didn't know how to feed or diaper. Weak excuses, right? Yes, but I bought them. I bought them because what I had digested growing up was not only that children were a joy but that the taking care of children is work for a woman, not a man.

The first eight months of Tammy's life are a blur for me and they are because they were a nightmare between her colic and my constant fatigue. When the nightmare began to end I found out I was pregnant and right there my alcoholism began. Without any ceremony, reflection, or concern I began drinking. It didn't matter what. My husband kept a well stocked liquor cabinet. I took and drank from it and I did it with indifference. My indifference vanished when my husband found his cabinet almost empty. He didn't get especially mad but he acted very surprised. That surprise made me feel a little queasy. It didn't really stop my drinking only my style. From then on I didn't do it openly, only secretly.

I noticed something. The more I did it on the Q.T. (on the sly), the more resentful and angry I became. Despite my anger I was very careful not to drink from his cabinet but only my reserve which I kept in my lingerie drawer.

I had my second baby drunk. And because I was, I almost had it in the taxi. I had so numbed myself with alcohol that I couldn't tell that my time for delivery had come.

With Nancy's arrival my drinking if anything picked up. You might wonder how I could take care of a 14-month-old and a new baby in a drunken haze. Personally I'm not too sure but I did. And I did it alone. My husband did nothing, contributed only his salary, no time and nothing of himself.

I was three months pregnant for my third before I knew it. What I've come to realize is that I functioned drunk for over two years and didn't even know it. I did everything I was supposed to do, and if I didn't do it perfectly, it didn't matter because I had no critics. My husband didn't care. And there was nobody else to care either.

Drunk or not I knew very well that nobody cared and I was in a fury about it. I've learned in group that alcoholics, especially women, feel like victims, that life has been unfair. The fury I felt was justified. I felt that way drunk and I feel that way now in my cold sobriety.

We women have been <u>conditioned</u>, and that's the word conditioned, to believe that we're <u>supposed to love</u>, to take care of babies, that we're <u>supposed to love being mothers</u>—and, if we don't, then there's something the matter with us. Well, I never enjoyed being pregnant. I know that and can admit it to myself and anybody else. I never especially enjoyed the diaper routine either. There's nothing enhancing about a soiled diaper and I was bent over three of them forever. What I blame me for is believing, accepting the propaganda that because I'm a woman I should enjoy nurturing. And if I don't, then I'm perverted, sick or at least very odd.

I take responsibility for incorporating such crap into myself. I've come to terms with my motherhood now and I've come to terms with myself. I'm never going to deny who I am, what I am, especially about what I <u>feel</u> about my kids and about me. The price I paid for that denial cost me and my kids too much.

Quite apparently, Darlene is one alcoholic who has learned not to deny who she is, what she is, and what she feels. She writes convincingly. She discloses sans inhibition.

My impression, from her interaction in groups, especially with men and her employment as a cocktail waitress, is that she is much interested in developing a meaningful long term relationship with a man. Once a member of a group, a woman, alluded to this interest, quipping about Darlene's sexy way of dress. Darlene's response was long and articulate—all of her words were delivered on an affect which could be fairly described as very warm, if not angry.

Her response makes me think that Darlene may still be operating with Bad Faith in some areas of her life.

SELF-CONTROL

The addict by definition is not in control of herself. Her addiction will not permit her to make choices freely. She finds herself manipulating, lying, deceiving in order to get control of her immediate environment and the people in it. More often than not she does any and all of these to get her booze, ingest it, and/or hide it.

The sociopathic behaviors and the preoccupation with control are, of course, a response to her own lack of control of self. When her efforts fail and more often than not, they do, the alcoholic finds solace in booze. In the hazy, nebulous inner world of drink, no one challenges the fact that she's in charge.

Case of Margaret

The alcoholic woman's problems with self-control are illustrated in the following story. Margaret is 61 years old and just retired from a small computer manufacturing plant where she worked on production line. About 5'4" tall she looks to weigh close to two hundred pounds. My impression from her comments in a counseling group is that she's been overweight throughout much of her adult life, if not all of it. This was a woman who thoroughly enjoyed being a member of a group. Indeed, she admits unabashedly that it was precisely in group that she was able to get a view of herself that she never had had. The following is edited from a tape.

I'll be forever grateful to the group because I learned a lot about myself in it. I always knew nobody liked me. It wasn't hard to know that because I never had any friends. I tried very hard as a teenager and as an adult with all kinds of people but somehow they never stuck.

I remember in elementary school giving kids candy so they'd play with me. They took the candy, played awhile, and disappeared.

In junior and senior high I wasn't so obvious in my need for friends. I lied. I lied about my parents. I remember as a junior in high school telling the guidance counselor, a woman, all kinds of fairy tales; that my mother was a great cook and that I had to be home for dinner every night at six because my father was very strict and gave me a lot of chores to do around the house. The truth was my mother was a lousy cook even when she was sober and most of the time she was drunk. Most of the time we ate separately even if she had prepared something. What I ate mostly, I swear I grew up on them, were T.V. dinners and junk food. Alone all the time, nothing else to do, I became addicted to them. It's probably why I got fat.

As far as my father is concerned about what we ate or when we ate it, he could have cared less. He was a T.V. zombie. He had his own set which he kept in the cellar. He'd come home from work and went right downstairs to it. Once in awhile he'd say hi to me and Mom on his way down. Most of the time he didn't. He had the cellar all to himself. On one side of it, he had the T.V. with a big easy chair and a coffee table on which he ate. In front of and on the other side of the coffee table he had a workbench with carpenters tools. I don't remember that he ever made or worked on anything. He had a refrigerator where he kept his beer and snacks. Oh yes, he never told me to do anything. He never told Mother either. He just didn't care what I did or what Mother did. My mother didn't care about me either. What I once said spontaneously in the group was about the truest thing I ever said about my upbringing—I grew up in a house of indifference. Neither of my parents cared about me or each other. They were both alcoholics. They didn't care that they themselves were. They didn't care that the other was. They didn't care that I became one. And I became one early on. Before I graduated from junior high school I was drinking pretty steadily and I was not yet 15 when I graduated. Oh yeah, I always had money as a kid. Both my parents gave me plenty, I guess to stay away from them. I did with drink what I did with food: I consumed it alone.

My way of relating to people was to lie. I never realized until I was in the group that lying is a chief symptom of an adult child of alcoholics. With two parents alcoholic, it was a symptom I was bound to get along with the disease. For me, telling a lie was as easy as telling the truth even when I didn't have to. The habit, and that's what it is, is so ingrained that I have to continually work at breaking it today every time I talk to somebody. Even though it's embarrassing, and it is, I have to correct myself continually when I'm telling a story because I embellish it so. Embellish, if you don't know, is a euphemism for lying. I don't have much of a vocabulary but I know that word. Interesting, eh?

Anyway what I learned in the group is that I don't have to lie. I don't have to lie to make people like me. I can't get people to like me by lying. In fact it's lying that keeps people away. Nobody likes a liar. Took all my life to learn that. Dumb eh? Dumb but true. [Margaret started to cry and stopped.]

You asked me to tell you an incident that stands out about my lying. It happened with my guidance counselor that I was telling you about before. I was a junior in high school and I used to see her a lot. I guess I kind of haunted her office probably because she was the only person in my life who gave me any attention. Anyway I was pretty fat even then and we talked about it. I remember telling her that I couldn't really do much about being fat because I had a glandular condition and it really didn't have anything to do with my eating or overeating. Then I really "embellished" the story. I told her I had to take a special medicine. I bought a dozen little brown bottles and put all kinds of flavored brandies in them and told her that the doctor's orders were that I had to take them every couple of hours. She believed me and wrote a note for me to show to all my teachers. The note said that I could be excused at anytime to take my medicine. That got me a lot of attention, and a lot of sympathy. The sympathy came only at first, only until I was found out. And I was found out by a student, a girl who went through my desk in homeroom. The guidance counselor was very indifferent toward me after that. See, I had made her look like a big jerk because she wrote out a note for me, because she believed me.

Believe it or not, I didn't feel all that bad about it all. I didn't feel that embarrassed or anything because nothing was really changed anyway. I was still alone, like always.

The problem was me. What I didn't see because I didn't want to was that my lying and deceiving kept people from trusting me. And trust as I finally learned in the group, trust is what you have to have in someone before you can ever like her.

Margaret is one woman whose prognosis for continued recovery is very good. Her new found realization that lying distances her from people has altered her interpersonal style. Where once her talk seemed totally unreflective and made one think of a rattling machine gun, she now speaks slowly and with very apparent premeditation, albeit with animation. And yes, she corrects or qualifies a statement if she thinks she's given the wrong impression. However, these are not the most important reasons for my optimistic prognosis. Rather it has to do with Margaret's new interpersonal stance. Her discovery that truth engenders trust and in turn engenders love and friendship has made her interesting, warm, approachable, and, most importantly, authentic. She came into the group a loner, she terminated with a lot of friends. I've seen her at a couple of retirement get-togethers, which I attended to socialize with graduates of the Employees Assistance Program. Quite apparently, she is now feeling very good about herself. It shows in the weight she has lost and in how she chats and mingles with both men and women.

SELF-SURRENDER

This thesis is derived from the first step of Alcoholics Anonymous program, "We admitted we were powerless over alcohol—that our lives had become unmanageable." The philosophical and psychological premise of this step is that the alcoholic is a narcissist of the first order who believes that she is the center of her universe. Until she comes to emotionally appreciate that she is not, she can not progress toward recovery and health.

The critical elements of alcoholic narcissism are a sense of omnipotence and defiance. That the alcoholic is in total control of herself, of her environment, and of those in it is a delusion she needs to hold onto. It is precisely when she feels she might be losing control internally or externally that she will act out alcoholically or withdraw with a defiant, latent, and sometimes blatant manner.

Self-surrender occurs, albeit too rarely for too many alcoholics. The whys of this are not difficult to fathom. Self-surrender involves not just an insightful dawning about the delusion of narcissistic omnipotence. It involves much more. Critical are a veritable reorientation and understanding of each of the preceding five theses, i.e., of her sense and relationship to time, of who she is and what enhances and demeans relationships, of learning to emit and accept the kaleidoscope of emotions, of giving up the denial defense and learning the true meaning of control, and of being in control means to have choices.

According to A.A. an alcoholic has to hit bottom before true surrender of self can occur. Hitting bottom refers to the alcoholic's total loss of self-control and influence over her environment. "Bottom" varies in meaning from person to person. It almost always involves "loss" —of status, a job, spouse, etc. In most cases the bottom is reached when the deprivation of an integral aspect of the alcoholic's life makes that life intolerable.

Self-surrender involves a profound introspection. The alcoholic who gives up "the alcoholic ghost is one who dons the mantle of humility." Such a mantle involves three components. First, an admission of powerlessness, of failure to live life. Second, an acceptance of one's humanity, that is, one's congenital penchant for failure. Third, a serene acceptance and internal integration of these first two components.

This last, serene acceptance, is the component which requires not only a constant vigilant awareness but must be translated into behavioral terms. The alcoholic can do this if she attends A.A. meetings, serves as a mentor for a fellow alcoholic, and/or generally involves herself in recovery work. Ideally, the alcoholic will at some point want to translate her sobriety into sharing her story with an A.A. group.

Surrender of self for the alcoholic, then, is premised on the notion that by surrendering one's self she surrenders her alcoholism. Complementing this surrender of alcoholism is that part of the self which is enhanced by doing for others.

Case of Martha

Martha is a 35-year-old woman who has been in recovery for almost six years. Last year she addressed my college alcoholism class. I asked her to tape her comments on surrender of self.

I attend at least one A.A. meeting per week as a consumer. It keeps me thinking and aware of my alcoholic self. At least once a month I go to a meeting where I tell my story. Once there were enough centers in the immediate vicinity (50 miles) that hadn't heard me, where I was a stranger and new. So for several years I didn't have to travel much. I drove to all these locations and the trips were easy and comfortable.   They certainly weren't inconvenient.   They've become so.   But then again, love is inconvenient. And these trips that I take now by both rail and plane I take and do out of love, love for what I call my spiritual ego. By telling my story I feed that ego.

In the Prayer of St. Francis of Assisi there are lines which I have found which capture the essence of what life should be about. In any case these lines provide the rationale for why I travel so far to tell my story—

> *"not so much to be consoled as to console*
> *to be understood as to understand*
> *to be loved as to love*
> *for it is in giving that we receive..."*

Anyway I try to live my life according to these words.

What I've learned is that when I'm able to put my love into action (I do that by traveling and telling my story), I surrender completely the egotistical part of myself—I surrender it to God. I do that a little bit when I listen and take in another alcoholic's story but I feel I do it more completely when I tell my story. That's why I travel and am inconvenienced, and spend money to tell it. I used to think that there was an element of egotism in doing that. I realize now it's not so much egotism as self-caring. I have to care for myself and give to myself. It's all I have to draw upon when I give to others.

The only appropriate comment to append to Martha's story can be summed in one word—Amen.

DANGER SIGNALS

As can be deduced from reading the cases written by women who have been alcoholic, causes and behaviors often vary from one woman to another. However, the danger signals generally can be identified. Figure 1.2 contains a list of 14 danger signals.

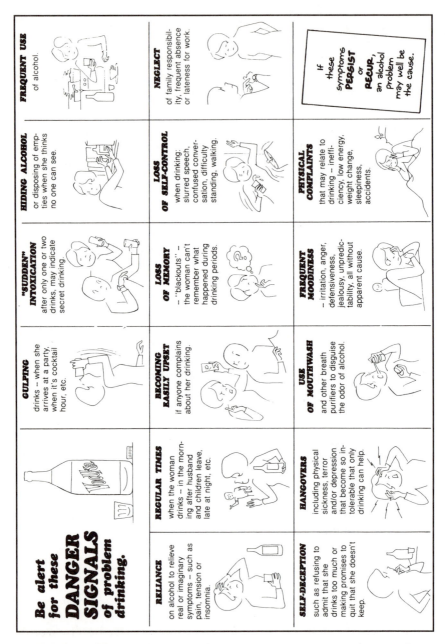

Figure 1.2. Danger signals of problem drinking. Reprinted from "About Women and Alcohol" with permission, copyright 1980, Channing L. Bete Co., Inc., South Deerfield, MA 01373.

SUMMARY

The six theses of alcoholism involve (1) the temporality of the self, (2) the relational structure of self, (3) the emotionality of self, (4) bad faith, (5) self-control, and (6) self-surrender.

Temporality addresses the alcoholic's warped perception of and relationship with time. This warped sense and understanding of time structure for a puerile like view of it, an inability to defer goods and procrastination.

The relational structure of self has to do with the alcoholic's inability to find a normal reward in interactions with actual people. In order to fill up her interpersonal life she may indeed create imaginary people. By doing so she inhibits her interpersonal competencies with people in the real world.

The emotionality of self deals with the fact that finally alcoholism is an emotional disorder. The alcoholic woman has a lost sense of self and drinks precisely to emit better and to accept her emotions. With alcohol too, she is better able to unwrap the insulation in which she has placed her feelings.

Bad faith refers to the alcoholic's need to deny her alcoholism. Denial of alcoholism permeates every aspect of body and mind. Even worse, denial feeds her resolve not to give up her booze.

The aspect of self-control focuses on the fact that the alcoholic is not in control of herself. Lack of self-control can precipitate various kinds of sociopathic behaviors, i.e., manipulating, lying, deceiving, and cheating. Such behaviors inevitably alienate the alcoholic from others and exacerbate her disease of alcoholism.

Self-surrender refers to the A.A. notion that the first step to recovery is to recognize one's powerlessness over alcoholism. To continue to move on the road of recovery the alcoholic needs to give up her delusional notion that she is at the focal point of society, that people exist to serve her. It is by giving and learning to find reward in giving that she can sustain her recovery.

FOR REVIEW AND REFLECTION

1. If you were asked to put these six theses in a hierarchy of importance, which one would you put first? Last? Why?

2. Can you validly rank these theses in a hierarchy? Why? Why not?

3. Which of the stories you read did you find the most moving? Why?

4. Is it ever healthy for a recovering alcoholic to want to kill time?

5. Can an alcoholic, budding, recovering, or wet, ever be enhanced by a figment of her fantasy?

6. Explain why appropriate expression of emotion invariably attracts while the inability to do so usually distances.

7. Why is self-pride of such critical importance to an alcoholic?

8. What do lying, deception and an acute need to manipulate reflect about one's self-perception?

9. Do you, alcoholic or not, accept the A.A. notion that a woman can better maintain her sobriety by sharing her story with the A.A. group? If not, why not?

10. Do you, alcoholic or not, accept the notion that one has "to hit bottom" before one is ready to recover? If you accept it, why? If not, why not?

SOCIALIZATION OF THE ALCOHOLIC WOMAN

The dynamics of alcoholism involve three phenomena: perception, conscience, and defenses. While these three phenomena exist for both men and women, particular qualities and aspects of each are markedly different by gender.

PERCEPTION

Perception is the foundation upon which we build our personality. How we perceive others determines how we interact with them. Our interactions provide us with experience, precipitate various meanings. These meanings, in turn, provide a constant source of feed-back for our perception. Personality development can be understood as the product of this constant cycle. This cycle is schematically shown in Figure 2.1.

Now, the more rewarding, enhancing the interaction, the more positively people perceive themselves, the more optimistically they come to perceive their environment and the men and women in it.

That men and women perceive differently is shown in a delightful and insightful book by Deborah Tannen (1990), *You Just Don't Understand.* In it she has shown how very much the

PERSONALITY DEVELOPMENT
THE CYCLE

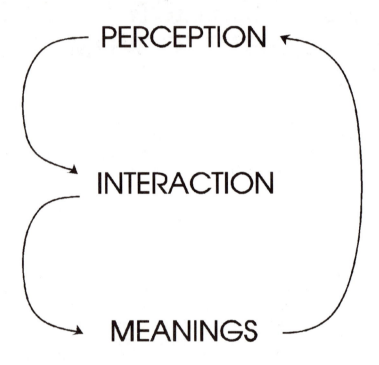

PERCEPTION

INTERACTION

MEANINGS

Figure 2.1. Schematic illustration of how personality develops.

sexes vary in their perceptual concerns and styles. In a very entertaining and cogent way, Tannen illustrated how women differ from men in their perception of self, in their perception of men, and in how they approach problems.

This variance of perception between the sexes seems to be determined in considerable measure by the masculinity/femininity concept. This concept can and is made up of a number of criteria. Among the most frequently employed are dependency-submissiveness/leadership-dominance; susceptibility to social influence; confidence/self-esteem; cooperativeness, concern for others and affiliation; expressiveness; narcissism; strategies for power; and aggression. Using these criteria Baldwin (1984) tested male and female college students to assess changes in their perception of what constituted masculinity and femininity. What he found was that neither men nor women altered their perception of each other or themselves over a ten year period. Indeed, the perception of men and women as determined by the average score difference remained pretty much the same between 1952 and 1980.

What this study shows is that perception and interaction between and among the sexes continues unabated according to learned stereotypes. Men and women have come to understand that which sex you are not only determines how you should interact but what meaning you are supposed to get from the interaction.

By and large the meaning which most women get from their interactions in our culture is that they should be dependent and submissive. Bernice Lott (1987) explained that women in America grow up expecting that they will be taken care of. Besides dependence and submissiveness women are expected to be nurturant, caring, soft, family oriented, passive but supportive, good at cleaning house, sewing, cooking, etc., etc., etc. The list is endless, mindless, and quite apparently, and by any standard, unfair. These so-called feminine qualities are learned early, indeed as early as two and three years of age. (Kuhn, Nash, & Brucken 1978).

Self-esteem has to do with feelings of self-worth. A socialization process which promotes dependency and passivity quite apparently can not elevate such feelings. And the research shows this. For the most part women do not think much of themselves particularly when they are pitted against men (Lott, 1987; Stake, 1983). Morgan (1980) found that women perceived themselves as less competent than men in virtually all their activities. She found that women did not find that they were as well adjusted to marriage as their husbands. Lips (1993) in a more recent work found that despite today's greater awareness and sensitivity to women's issues in politics, in the world of work, and in the media in general, women continue to devalue this work and themselves.

The problem for most women seems to be that their self-esteem is simply not enhanced by their stereotypical role in the family. Home and family, they are taught, are the prime (in some parts of America the *sole*) source of ego satisfaction. "Get your happiness from cleaning your house and being a devoted mother and wife or you'll never know what happiness is." This has historically been and continues to be the constant, basic message to the American woman. Ample research shows that the women who can not adapt and adjust to this message will be hurt emotionally. Gove and Tudor (1973) found that the woman who does not derive satisfaction from domestic endeavors and family life will suffer emotional problems. Israel, Raskin, Libow, and Pravda (1978) found that women who deviated or didn't behave according to feminine stereotypical standards were thought to be less responsible, less feminine than those who did. This finding was reinforced by a study by Tilby and Kalin (1980) who found that women whose behavior was not in the traditional mode especially regarding work, family, and sexuality were noted as maladjusted. What is more than a little bit disturbing is that the sample of the last two studies were not of middle-aged people but of male and female college undergraduates. What this suggests, of course, is that the stereotypical view of the role and function of women is not changing too readily.

Now, what about those women who do fill their feminine and cultural role, who do nurture, clean and function dependently and who project an image of enjoying it all? These women are especially at risk emotionally according to Bart (1971). Indeed, according to her, the woman most likely to feel useless and to become depressed is precisely that woman who excels at her housework and in fulfilling her motherly chores; put succinctly, functioning as a supermom does not bode well for one's mental health.

Trying to function happily in a role that is perceived stereotypical can indeed take its emotional toll. This is seen in a study done by Butterfield (1986). This researcher sampled Harvard men and Radcliffe women twenty-five years after graduation from college. The women showed themselves to be far more frustrated with their stereotypical "uncareered" lives than were the men who had fulfilling careers. More often than not, frustration such as this can lead to depression. This is especially true when the woman adheres and falls into the traditional feminine categories (Elpern & Karp, 1984). When such adherence endures into the middle years the result may well result in depression (Tinsley, Sullivan-Guest, & McGuire, 1984).

Doubtless many women learn to live with the depression effected by being steeped in a sexual role of low status. Many do via tranquilizing medication. Many do so by ignoring or denying the fact. And many do so by becoming alcoholic. Luepnitz (1988), in her fine work *The Family Interpreted*, pointed out that within the American family there are millions of women functioning alcoholically. In an earlier work Bepko and Krestan (1983) suggested that alcoholism may indeed be the route that many women take in order to escape the madness of trying to put on a happy face when feeling like a nothing.

A common denominator in the alcoholic personality, both male and female, is the self-view that many hold; namely, that they are victims. People in general chastise alcoholics about this self-view. Many well intentioned therapists attempt to help "rectify" the view, holding of course to the notion that objectively speaking it is unrealistic, paranoid, and basically untrue to feel that one has been victimized by life. What all the foregoing research cited should make transparently clear is that in the case of women *it is true*. They have been victimized. They've been victimized by a society which attempts to mold them into a role system which in too many cases is unfulfilling and for many, destructive. Worse still, after being so molded a woman is expected to like her mold and if she doesn't, she's told that she's crazy. It is precisely to escape this unjust molding and the unrealistic expectations of fitting the mold that so many women turn to alcohol. For such women sobriety is not a viable state because the sober world is too threatening. Such women feel they have to drink if they are to cope with the madness of their lives. A case in point is the following story.

Case of Naomi

Naomi is 45 years old, and recently divorced. She never had any children. A former client of mine, she assented readily when I asked her to write some of her thoughts about the frustrations which effected and related to her alcoholism. She has been in recovery for almost two years and has just opened a dress shop.

I married Bart the week after I graduated from college. My major was elementary education which I never put to any use because I never taught and I never had any kids. I never taught because Bart was opposed adamantly to the idea and I never had any kids because he was sterile.

I was married to Bart for twenty-two years. He was a lawyer, still is. He was also a dictator. I'll bet he still is that too. He wanted me to stay home and told me very frankly that he believed that it was the woman's place. He delivered a long lecture on the subject whenever I raised the subject of going to work. The gist of it was that most of the problems of society stemmed from the fact that women had left their homes to go out to work, and they had learned to like it so much that they never had children and when they finally did they were unable to supervise them. Home, he used to say with conviction was the "natural" place for a woman. In time I came to hate the word natural. It came to have an almost obscene connotation for me.

When we found out we couldn't have children, he assumed it was my fault. I did too. And I did for a long time. Even now I think about that fact a lot. It was thinking like this which fed his arrogant, condescending, and presumptuous attitude toward me. Those three words—arrogant, condescending, and presumptuous—sum up how he saw me, how he related to me, and what he thought about me. Any problems between us or even those I tried to tell him about that I had with someone else, Bart always saw as my fault.

He had a very rigid view of me and my functions. Neatness and cleanliness were among his obsessions and he praised me when the house sparkled. When it didn't, he raged. He also felt strongly that I should go to mass every morning. So I did. Whenever I didn't, he didn't rage but he let me know he was very disappointed. Of course, I felt guilty. I read once that Hitler summed up the role of woman in three words: children, church, and kitchen. In Bart I had my own little Hitler.

What I learned since my divorce is that our sex life wasn't much either. He was very prudish about it. We always had to do it in the pitch black dark. We did it only at night and pulled down the shades to shut out even the street lights. Bart gave new meaning to the word proper and to the word prim and prig too.

To the best of my recollection I didn't start drinking alone until about five years ago. My bout with alcoholism lasted about three years. And I contributed a lot to the reason. What I now understand is that I grew up to believe that I did not have to take responsibility for my life or for my behavior. My father did it first for me and then my husband did. I understood that. I believed that. I accepted that and worst of all I fed into it! Today whenever I think of Bart, I feel like I was screwed and I'm not referring to anything sexual.

CONSCIENCE

Carol Gilligan (1982) in her authoritative and professional best seller, *In a Different Voice*, pointed out that women in our society are taught to put more emphasis than men on caring, attachments, and relationships. Her findings were generally supported by the work of Ford and Lowery (1986) who found that women were more emotionally invested in concerns about caring than were men. From the earliest years, little girls are taught to cultivate personal traits to develop these qualities. To care and get close, to nurture, to cuddle, to show caring by kissing, and to give gifts are all characteristics for which the little girl learns that she will be rewarded. She displays them early and incorporates these and comparable qualities into her personality. Before she begins kindergarten, she has learned that her greatest dividends will be derived from emotional investment in people. A, if not *the*, critical function of her life is to get close to people. Via this function is how she develops her conscience.

People, especially those who engender and reward trust, are the source of all conscience. Conscience comes from other people; without trust in people, conscience, as we understand it, would not exist. Certainly there would be little need for it. Genuine, meaningful, and long-term relationships are anchored in trust and these develop conscience. When we are involved in such relationships, we love.

We are able to love, then, because we have trust in people. Trust erects conscience and is crucial for its maintenance. Trust comes from positive, enhancing experience with people. Only people can create trust. Trust invested in another and rewarded (another way to put it; love given and returned) expands and strengthens conscience, and, in turn, expands investment in people. This dynamic cycle of conscience and development can be depicted as shown in Figure 2.2.

As noted previously, women are taught to put more of their energies on the development of relationships than are men. With the expenditure of such energy, there is a natural, necessary complementary growth in conscience. Put simply, women develop a different conscience than men, one that focuses on other people. Thoma (1986) found that women not only are indeed different than men in conscience issues, but they also understand moral issues better and are able to reason more accurately about them.

In sum, the conscience of the woman is quite unlike that of a man. In general it is more focused on giving or meeting obligations, duties, and responsibilities especially when they involve the feeling reactions of others.

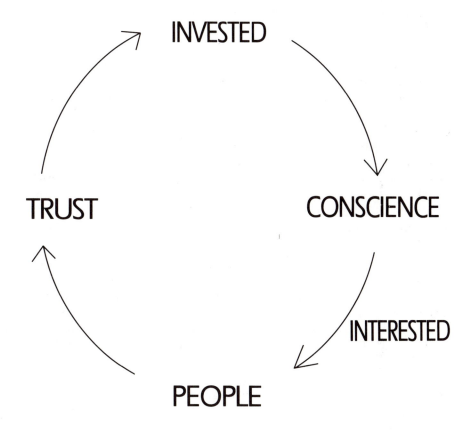

Figure 2.2. The dynamic cycle of conscience development.

As noted in a previous work (Perez, 1992, p. 16) "a person without a conscience is one who engages in antisocial behavior and feels no guilt. Such a person has been termed a psychopath." Many male alcoholics retreat into a psychopathic state when they drink to drown the guilt precipitated by their conscience. When in a sober state, such men revert to a scrupulous interpersonal stance to compensate and atone for these feelings.

In general, the alcoholic woman, even when drinking does not retreat into a psychopathic state. Her conscience won't let her. She is too aware, too exquisitely sensitive to what society says and feels about her drinking. Turnbull (1989) found that the social stigma attached to alcoholic women was so intense that it inhibited them from seeking treatment. Kress (1989), in a study published very shortly after, obtained comparable results as did Lorraine Smith (1992) who also found that employers and courts are less likely to refer alcoholic women than men for treatment. What these studies show is that to be female and alcoholic in our society is to structure for being mired in guilt.

This innate guilt is compounded by general social reactions and even more by the latent attitudes of professionals who treat women in psychotherapy. For example, Mary Lee Smith (1980) found that counselors and psychotherapists perceive women negatively. Schaefer (1984), a renown trainer of clinical psychologists, admitted that male psychotherapists tend to "idealize unhappiness with women." Thompson (1978) concluded that "women quite generally are perceived as weak, dependent creatures who needed to be reassured, supported, patted-on-the-head." Thompson's conclusions were reiterated the following year by Whitley (1979) who found that therapists are as likely as non-therapists to perceive the female client stereotypically. Study and reflection of all these findings about the alcoholic women become especially troubling when one examines a recent work by Tarasenko (1990) who found that two very important conditions for success of treatment of alcoholic women were (1) a positive image of self and (2) conviction that one's social image has not been greatly damaged. As the reader has learned, in those precise areas of self and social image are where the hide-bound guilt ridden woman of conscience is most vulnerable.

DEFENSES

Defenses are an innate and necessary aspect of the human personality. For the most part unconscious, they feed the ego and protect us from perceived threat.

Via defenses healthy people are able to perceive selectively, that is to perceive what they want to perceive and to ignore what they want to ignore. They create and maintain situations, events, and interactions that are satisfying, rewarding, and often personally enhancing.

With alcoholics, both male and female, this whole and very human process of defense becomes diseased. Their perceptions become not so much selective as distorted. The effect is to make situations, events, and interactions unsatisfying, and, too often, demeaning.

As noted in the concluding statement under *Conscience* the alcoholic woman is guilt-ridden and most vulnerable emotionally. In the initial phases of counseling especially, this is reflected in her unsureness and conflicting statements. A major task of the counselor is to help this woman rebuild and reinforce a defense structure that helps her to perceive herself and others more realistically, more accurately. Only when she has done that will she be able to deal more effectively with the host of problems with which she is beset. Besides deep seated, unrealistic guilt and lack of self-esteem, the alcoholic woman is gripped by a paralyzing fear to try alternative health treatments and an unfortunate resentment toward any and everybody who offers to help her. Not infrequently, this often includes the counselor. In any case, the same defenses which were once self-defeating and kept the alcoholic woman in the throes of despair, now have to be redirected and restructured to help her sustain her sobriety.

Explanation and illustrations on how to redirect and restructure alcoholic defenses are provided in Chapter 7 under Practical Techniques.

The only defenses treated here are those most commonly used by the female alcoholic. These are the following:

> denial,
> displacement,
> fantasy,
> projection,
> rationalization,
> reaction formation,
> regression, and
> repression.

Denial

An explanation of denial was given in Chapter 1 under Bad Faith. As noted there, it is the defense which permits, facilitates the onset, and enables the development and maintenance of the alcoholic process. Denial prevents the recognition or admission of any alcoholic addiction.

Displacement

The ventilation of hostility on a person or animal, engendered by neither, is displacement. An example might be the single parent mother struggling in her recovery who beats on her son because she was hounded all day at work by a supervisor.

Fantasy

This defense may be defined in one word, daydreaming. It is a favored defense by most alcoholic women. In Chapter 1 the story told by Hilda in "Temporality of Self" illustrates the fantasy defense. Without being clinical, what she communicates is that this defense provides much solace especially when the alcohol is first taking effect. For Hilda it provided a kind of nirvana to which she retreated to escape boredom and frustration. For others it may be the time when the alcoholic becomes expansive, overly generous, emotional, etc. In the world of fantasy a woman not only can soothe real or imagined hurt but also can imagine what she never is, the focal point of attention. In fantasy any number of ugly ducklings, actual or imagined, have become graceful swans. For most addicted women, alcohol becomes the catalyst which precipitates and facilitates the creation of a synthetic reality, one far more rewarding than the real world, indeed so rewarding that the alcoholic woman feels compelled to return to it again and again.

Projection

Motives which a woman harbors herself and attributes to another person or persons are referred to as projection. This defense develops invariably when she distances herself from others. Such distancing invariably engenders feelings of estrangement and lack of communication both of which breed and feed this defense. Suspicion and a picayunish-like sensitivity to others, exhibited by a too-quick-to-take-offense attitude, are common manifestations of projection. An example might be the hostess and owner of a restaurant who becomes abusive toward two of her waitresses because she is convinced that they are ridiculing her mode of dress.

Rationalization

This may be defined as making up excuses for actual or felt inadequacies or behaviors. This defense is often a support for denial. An example might be the alcoholic woman who justifies her need for three or more martinis before supper every night as her only way of relaxing after a hard day at work.

Reaction Formation

Briefly, this defense has to do with behaving in a way which is directly opposite to the way the individual feels or is motivated. It will be treated more definitively below under *Rorschach Test* findings.

Regression

When a woman uses this defense she is said to display conduct which is unfeminine and immature. Examples of such conduct include temper tantrums, sulking, and pouting. Such conduct by the alcoholic, reflect child-like attempts to manipulate and/or control.

Repression

This term refers to the ego function of pressing the memory of a person, situation, or traumatic event into the unconscious because of the fear and threat imposed by remembering. The majority of an individual's repressions are generally made during the first decade of life when the person's still small and immature ego does not feel it can cope with the threat perceived. Quite probably, forgetting à la repression is the preferred reaction for many women. Little girls because of the stringent demands of the socialization process, particularly as it regards conscience development discussed above, are excellent candidates for repression. Tahka (1966) found that alcoholics are more heavily repressed than people drawn from the normative population. Extensively repressed people are generally more unsure of themselves than slightly repressed. The people developing children and adolescents saw and/or, for reasons whatever, were more sensitive to threat and conflict than others. They learned and became accustomed to living in their milieus of trauma not by dealing with them in any overt, active way but by repressing the frightening, demeaning, and acutely depriving people, events, and situations. For children of alcoholic families, repression can become a quasi-habitual way of reacting to any and all perceived threat.

Thus, if a teacher was especially anxiety provoking, they repressed him/her as quickly as they could after moving on to the next teacher. What is important to note here is that inevitably and most assuredly, the effect of repression is to diminish one's life experience, lower one's self-esteem, and decrease one's level of maturity.

PERSONALITY OF THE ALCOHOLIC WOMAN—RESEARCH FINDINGS

As noted previously, to build and develop relationships is a prime concern of the American woman. Healthy women do that. The alcoholic woman is not able to do so (Walter, Nagoshi, Muntaner, & Haerzen, 1990). More often than not the so-called friends of the alcoholic are nothing more than "drinking Betties," that is, superficial acquaintances. Relationships are developed in talk while ingesting alcohol together. Such relationships seldom have any warmth or solidity and almost never endure. For many, they do not endure because these women never had the opportunity to learn interpersonal skills (Gomberg, 1989).

PROJECTIVE TESTS

Rorschach Test

In a previous work the author reported on the results of Rorschach protocols administered to 44 alcoholic men ranging in age from 24 to 46 years (Perez, 1992, pp. 24-25). To determine if comparable common denominators were present in the personalities of alcoholic women a similar type study was performed with women. Accordingly, the *Rorschach Test* was administered to 23 women who were diagnosed alcoholic. Then the tests were scored and interpreted. Like the men tested, these women were all middle class and clients who were being seen in private practice.

As reported in 1992 the men incorporated these characteristics in their personalities:

a very rich fantasy life,

a moderate to strong need to achieve and to be respected,

an introverted orientation,

a moderate to high expectation of rejection, and

a prime defense of reaction formation, and

a weak self-esteem.

The results with the women were surprisingly comparable. Like the men, the women displayed:

rich fantasy lives,

an introverted orientation,

feelings of rejection,

a penchant for the reaction formation defense, and

a weak self-esteem.

The women gravitated, and too often retreated to the world of make-believe. Like the men, too, they did this because of the threat imposed by a sense of ordeal and hopelessness of trying to cope in the real world. The women's need of adulation was stronger than that of the men and in fantasy at least, they felt that ultimately they would learn methods to become the focal point of attention in their real lives. Indeed, becoming such a focal point in their real lives was a veritable obsession. The obsession was the catalyst for precipitating episodes of daydreaming and alcoholic-like drinking. The daydream served to maintain a narcissistic preoccupation with self and being served by others.

The tendency toward fantasy complemented and was complemented by a strong, introspective bent. These alcoholic women like their male counter-parts constantly examined their feelings and reactions to real and imagined hurts and slights by people they knew and in a few cases by people they didn't even know. These self-examinations of feelings made up much of their working days.

These women felt even more rejected than the men. Not only did they feel rejected but like the men they constantly expected rejection. And, like the men, they were surprised when anyone did something for them or were graciously accepting or overlooked faults and blunders. The most unfortunate aspect of expecting to be rejected involves one in a self-fulfilling prophesy of rejection. As noted, these women expecting to be unliked and rejected could not believe that people would overlook a deficiency. When people did they tended to test and demand more and more until people would give up in exasperation and reject them. The women's response invariably would be of course, "See, I knew you didn't like me!" Put simply, these women tended to destroy relationships more easily than to build them.

Interacting via the self-fulfillment prophecy is characteristic of the alcoholic man or woman as it is premised in a large measure on the alcoholic's paranoid projection which involves the projection defense discussed above under defenses. The self-fulfillment prophesy is also a function of the defense termed **reaction formation**. When they use this defense alcoholics are trying to protect themselves from perceived threat by behaving

44 *Counseling the Alcoholic Woman*

in ways that are diametrically opposed to how they feel. Thus, when someone behaves graciously toward the alcoholic woman, she is honestly afraid to show or express gratitude. If she did, it would mean that someone is genuinely kind which is totally inconsistent with her basic perception of the world. Too often, the world is a hostile, threatening place where people are out to con or bilk. She doubts, and mightily too, that there are, or could be, any nice people in the world in which she functions. Ergo, she continues to test their goodness and does so until they become exasperated. Their exasperation proves her conviction that nobody is really nice, that nobody really likes her, that everyone has his/her own secret agenda. Reaction formation is a major debilitator of an alcoholic woman's personality because it alienates her from her own self. When she responds immoderately via this defense, a woman does not know how she truly feels. She can't because reaction formation, like all psychological defenses, is unconscious.

Now when one is not in touch with her own feelings she is, has to be, *very unsure of herself,* in how she performs, in how she relates, in how she functions in whatever role. And this was true of all the women in this sample. All of these human elements—feeling, awareness, performance, interpersonal competence, and general role functioning—all have to do with, are all integrally related to, what we call self-esteem.

Every counselor of alcoholic women learns very quickly that they suffer acutely in self-esteem in virtually every aspect of their personality and in virtually every role that they feel obligated to fill. By remaining constantly aware of the client's self-esteem problem the counselor will be more appreciative of the why of the client's embitterment, excessive concern for self, and this pessimistic perception of the world to which she jealously adheres. Moreover, the counselor can better understand that the client's focus on gratification is nothing more than a puerile-like attempt to feed a badly impoverished self-esteem.

This author's findings regarding the self-esteem of alcoholic women is of course not especially startling and is corroborated in the work of Beckman (1978) who found that a principal reason that many women become alcoholic is precisely because of their inadequate self-esteem. In a later study Beckman, Day,

Bardsley, and Seeman (1980) found that if a woman comes from a family where a history of alcoholism prevails the probability is strong that she will develop important self-esteem problems which will facilitate her candidacy for alcoholism.

Carolyn Bersak, (1990) after a thorough examination of the case studies of female alcoholics, concluded that a very effective treatment mode would be to focus on enhancing the woman's self-esteem. According to this researcher, enhancing the self-esteem of the alcoholic woman does much to lower her craving to drink. In Figure 2.3 is an illustration of the self-esteem cycle of the alcoholic. The poor self-esteem contributes to the drinking which causes more depression and so forth.

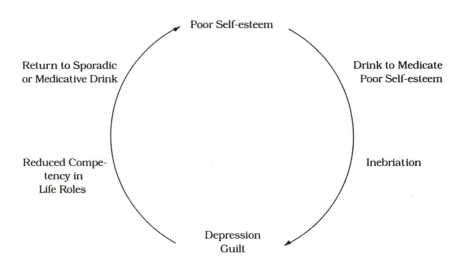

Self-esteem Cycle of the Alcoholic

Figure 2.3. Schematic illustration of the self-esteem cycle of the alcoholic.

Thematic Apperception Test (T.A.T.)

In the same way that the author compared the Rorschach findings of male alcoholics in a 1992 study to those of women alcoholics, the T.A.T was utilized to compare the personalities of women alcoholics to male alcoholics. With the help of four colleagues the Thematic Apperception Test, a projective test, was administered to sixteen women who were outpatients in a rehabilitation center. Unlike the Rorschach findings which showed the women to be remarkably comparable to the men in personality dispositions, these findings were more than a little different. Thus, in the study with the men, the author found the stories "were characterized by themes of (1) impotence, (2) inebriation, (3) dominance, and (4) hostility" (Perez, 1992, pp. 26-7).

The women's stories in this study were characterized by themes of (1) manipulation, (2) serenity, (3) serving and giving, (4) dependency, and (5) romance.

A recurring theme for the majority of women was a need to be in charge, to run things. Unlike the men's stories where there were few heroes, there were many, many heroines in the women's stories. Outcomes again and again had to do with their heroines successfully achieving and accomplishing their intended goals despite interpersonal problems and the wishes of others. The author interpreted this as a kind of compensating response by women who in real life were not too successful or who felt this way. At the same time, what this theme showed was a lot of strength, nerve, hope, and belief that ultimately they would rectify their unsuccessful lives.

These women were seriously interested in obtaining a peaceful, uncomplicated life. This need was seen as a response to lives which they felt were frantic, frenetic. What they sought were lives sans any conflict or pleasure. What they sought was an escape from the stress of their addiction, i.e., the acute need to ingest some alcohol.

The need to serve and give was very strong in every single protocol. This theme showed itself in every conceivable way, i.e., as a daughter taking care of a parent, as a wife, mother, lover, social worker, nurse, etc. Quite apparently, the need to nurture, though it may become latent in the alcoholic woman, is never erased even in women preoccupied with getting a drink!

At the same time, there was indeed a dependency streak in the personalities of these women. They wanted desperately to be taken care of. They were very tired of coping and failing. Most of them seemed to believe that were they able to establish the "right kind" of relationship their problems would be solved.

The romantic theme appeared in over 70% of the stories, including four with references to a knight in shining armor. Quite simply, these women were starved for affection. The romance theme was a response to lives barren of masculine attention, to feelings of interpersonal ineptness, and, in a few cases, to a belief of sexual ineptness.

In sum, these women's needs and concerns were quite unlike those of the men where the latter stories were laden with themes of needs of power, hostility, and inebriation. The women's stories, on the other hand, were concerned with the attainment of peace, nurturance, and finding a strong knight.

Not unsurprisingly, where the men and women were in comparable need was in the area of control. Here the women via the manipulation theme showed themselves to be healthier. They suggested in their stories that they had much hope that in the end they would obtain control over themselves and their lives. The men on the other hand, seemed resigned to a life of impotence, feeling that finally they did not have the emotional means to cope with the stresses of living.

Dorothy Hurley (1991) has drawn a profile of the qualities and dispositions common in the personality of the alcoholic woman. This profile is derived from a host of clinical and empirical studies reviewed by her. What makes this list of qualities especially authoritative is that each one is founded in the results of research.

This list was compiled by Hurley in order to show the remarkable similarities between the behavior and characteristics of the alcoholic woman and the woman victimized by incest. The list in total provides a comprehensive picture of what the alcoholic woman is like. The source used by Hurley is shown in parentheses.

The alcoholic woman is likely to:

1. *"feel stigmatized because of her alcoholism,"* (Sandmaier, M., 1980)
   As noted above in a couple of contexts an alcoholic woman is simply not viewed in the same light as is an alcoholic man.

2. *"deny and conceal her alcoholic abuse,"* (Beckman, L.J., & Amaro, H., 1984-85)
   For the same reason she is stigmatized the alcoholic woman does not talk about her alcoholism. Indeed, she is quite secretive about it. The secrecy promotes and structures many dysfunctional, destructive feelings and behaviors. Thus, it makes her feel alone, it makes her feel "different" and sick, it puts her under all kinds of stress i.e., not to buy liquor too often from the same store, where to hide the bottles, not to attend certain functions because of the duration, and so on, and so on, and so on.

3. *"seek treatment from health care professionals and not mention her drinking,"* (Beckman, L.J., & Amaro, H., 1984-85)
   The reason for this behavior has to do again with the stigma felt and of course, the feelings of guilt. The author in his own practice has encountered more than a few women in treatment for whom the presenting problem was one other than alcoholism. However, his experience is that once the trust which comes with rapport is established the client will indeed admit to a problem with drink. What he has learned is that in most cases it is alcoholism and not the stated ancillary reasons which generate self-referral.

4. *"have an alcoholic parent, most often a father,"* (Homiller, J.D., 1980)
   This finding by Hurley in her review and research has been much studied and is confirmed in a number of other studies (Nakamura, Takano and Iguchi; 1991; Harburg, Gleiberman, 1990; Luza, 1990; Orford, Velleman, 1990). Quite apparently, when a woman is steeped in an alcoholic family she learns to incorporate many destructive qualities into her personality.

5. *"perceive her mother as cold, domineering and rejecting,"* (Lindbeck, V., 1972)

What we can glean from this finding is that for some alcoholic women at least, their alcoholism is related to emotional deprivation which harkens back to their earliest years.

6. *"marry or be intimately involved with an alcoholic male,"* (Gomberg, E.S., & Lisansky, J.M., 1984)

The perception and interactive style of the alcoholic woman invariably, inevitably leads her into difficulty, especially in the heterosexual sphere. It is the author's conviction that she frequently gravitates to and becomes emotionally involved with alcoholic men precisely because she is unable and/or unwilling to get meaningfully close to a man. The dynamics of intimacy are a mystery to the alcoholic women as they are to the alcoholic man. Indeed, he too is unable, unwilling to get meaningfully close to a woman.

7. *"have a chaotic, disruptive and traumatic childhood,"* (Rathod, N.H., & Thompson, I.G., 1971)

Chaos and trauma in childhood breed an insecure disposition and quite generally make for dependency. The person who is reared in such an environment frequently seeks an emotional crutch. Sad but understandable then, is the female who is traumatized as a little girl and grows up to be dependent on alcohol.

8. *"experience loss of one or more parents during childhood,"* (Rathod, N.H., & Thompson, I.G., 1971)

Deprivation of a parent at an early age has to be at least bewildering, especially if there was any positive emotional involvement with him/her. Unquestionably, the effect is some lack of supervision, stability combined with an increase in tension and anxiety within the family construct. In any case, the loss seldom enhances.

9. *"experience fear and distrust of people during adolescence,"* (Jones, M.C., 1971)

It is during adolescence that we acquire important and significant interpersonal skills that help us to function successfully during adulthood. The alcoholic woman who fears and distrusts people during adolescence will tend to distance herself from them. The effect, of course, is that instead of skills she learns to become suspicious and distrustful. Such qualities block the ability for learning to emotionally invest in others, for developing meaningful relationships.

10. *"exhibit defiant behavior during adolescence (e.g., school difficulties, abusive drinking, parental conflict),"* (Sandmaier, M., 1980)

    Anger toward others occurs because anger has been engendered. The adolescent girl who is angry is so because she feels she has been emotionally deprived. Her anger very often is her way of calling attention to the fact of her acute need for attention and caring.

11. *"experience confusion surrounding her feminine identity,"* (Wilsnack, S.C., 1973)

    This is an especially debilitating problem. From this one issue a host of dysfunctional behaviors and attitudes which transcend, permeate the whole personality. It is one's sense of sexual identity which influences, if not determines, how we talk, walk, groom; whether or not and to what extent we are attracted to the opposite sex and to the same sex. Fairly or unfairly, rightly or wrongly, the reality is that the woman in our society who is unsure about her sense of womanhood will experience far more emotional pain than the woman who is secure in it. In short, a woman's sense of her feminine identity is the essence of her.

12. *"have low self-esteem and poor self-concept,"* (Beckman, L.J., 1980)

    An appreciation and understanding of the preceding quality make this one readily understood. A woman's low self-esteem and poor self-concept go hand in hand with a confused feminine identity.

13. *"experience serious depression and attempted suicide,"* (Rathod, N.H., & Thompson, I.G., 1971)

    A person who is suicidal almost always appears to be severely depressed. The suicidal person is also a very angry person. Suicide can be understood then, not only as a function of acute unhappiness but also as a function of anger, anger turned inwardly. The alcoholic woman's innate depression is exacerbated by the alcohol itself, as alcohol has a depressive effect, relieving control and defenses, sometimes releasing the built-up, intense hostility and directing it toward the self.

14. *"experience various types of sexual dysfunction and difficulty with intimate relationships,"* (Forrest, G.G., 1983) Again, an appreciation of the dynamics of qualities number 11 and 12 above make this particular dysfunction readily understandable. If a woman is unsure or confused about her femininity and has a low self-esteem she is most assuredly going to experience problems relating on the sexual level. If a woman at the unconscious level is not sure what it means to be a woman in relation to a man and at the same time has a low self-esteem to boot she will not easily be able to perform in a sexually responsive way. Self-esteem is a, if not the, critical determinant in all the activities in which a woman performs. Succinctly, if she thinks she's good, she performs well. If she doesn't think so, she doesn't. Quite apparently, this is as true of her competence sexually as it is of any other activity in which she participates.

15. *"turn to alcohol to overcome sexual difficulties,"* (Beckman, L.J., 1984) Such behavior is not especially surprising for three reasons: first, alcohol is understood to be the prime ingredient to facilitate heterosexual encounter; secondly it is readily available and thirdly, it continues to be a most socially acceptable way of medicating one's problems, both alone and in company. All these thoughts find support in a study by Wilsnack and Wilsnack (1991) who found that drinking problems and alcohol disorders among women were increasing. The increase was attributed in part to their need to project and maintain an image of social competence with "significant others."

SUMMARY

The dynamics of alcoholism involve three phenomena: perception, conscience, and defenses. Perception is the foundation upon which we build our personality. How we perceive others determines how we interact with them. Interactions, in turn, provide meanings that provide a constant source of feedback, continuing the unending cycle. Perception between and among the sexes continues as ever according to learned stereotypes. The meanings which most women get from their interactions in our culture are that they should be dependent and submissive as well as nurturant, caring, soft, family oriented, passive but supportive, etc. The research indicates that women suffer in self-esteem especially when pitted against men. It shows, too, that many women become alcoholic in order to escape the madness of trying to put on a happy face when feeling like a nothing. The idea that women alcoholics are neurotic and unjustified to feel like victims may be unwarranted because much evidence is available to indicate that they have been victimized in the socialization process.

Learning, caring, and emotional investments in people are the principal ingredients of the female conscience. In these three regards the female conscience is more focused and intense than that of the male. What studies show in regard to the conscience of a female alcoholic is that she is mired in guilt.

Defenses are an innate and necessary aspect of human personality. In the alcoholic personality the process of defense becomes diseased. The defenses most commonly used by the female alcoholic are denial, displacement, fantasy, projection, rationalization, reaction formation, regression, and repression.

The research indicates that the alcoholic woman has much difficulty developing relationships as she relates to people via alcohol and provides herself with few opportunities to develop interpersonal skills. The research with the Rorschach test done by this author with 23 alcoholic women showed them to have (1) rich fantasy lives, (2) an introverted orientation, (3) feelings of rejection, (4) a penchant for the reaction formation defense, and (5) a weak self-esteem. The T.A.T. findings showed that the women's personalities were characterized by themes of (1) manipulation, (2) serenity, (3) serving and giving, (4) dependency, and (5) romance.

Dorothy Hurley drew up a profile which incorporated 15 qualities incorporated in the alcoholic women. These included (1) a sense of stigma; (2) denial and concealment of alcoholism; (3) not mentioning her drinking to health professionals; (4) having an alcoholic parent, a father; (5) perceiving her mother as cold, domineering, and rejecting; (6) marrying or be intimately involved with an alcoholic male; (7) having a chaotic, disruptive, and traumatic childhood; (8) experiencing loss of one or more parents during childhood; (9) experiencing fear and distrust of people during adolescence; (10) exhibiting defiant behavior during adolescence; (11) experiencing confusion surrounding her feminine identity; (12) having low self-esteem and poor self-concept; (13) experiencing serious depression and attempted suicide; (14) experiencing various types of sexual dysfunction and difficulty with intimate relationships; and (15) turning to alcohol to overcome sexual difficulties.

FOR REVIEW AND REFLECTION

1. How would you characterize the self-perception of the alcoholic woman? In what important ways does it differ from that of the nonalcoholic woman?

2. How does the alcoholic woman perceive her world and the people in it?

3. Do you believe that the alcoholic woman is justified in perceiving herself as a victim? If so, why? If not, why not?

4. Naomi implied in her story that if she had learned to take responsibility for her life she would not have become alcoholic. Do you agree? Why? Why not?

5. Explain the relationship between caring and conscience.

6. Explain how people, trust, and conscience relate.

7. Of the defenses discussed, which one do you believe is the one that alcoholic women find most difficult to restructure?

8. A prime reason that alcoholic women have trouble developing relationships is because they never had the opportunity to learn interpersonal skills. What might be other reasons?

9. Male alcoholics fantasize much about power, women about being the focal point of attention. Does this make sense to you? Why?

10. Alcoholic women experience confusion about their feminine identity. Explain why this might be the core reason for their alcoholism.

Chapter 3

THE ALCOHOLIC
WOMAN IN THE FAMILY

Research shows that if alcoholic women live with family, then their addiction becomes familial and not just personal (Fletcher, Price, & Cook, 1991; Cook & Goethe, 1990; Gross & McCaul, 1990). Such women infect their families with their disease and then because of guilt or depression or both develop a disproportionate number of physical problems (Radomsky, 1992). These findings corroborated the conclusions drawn in an earlier study by Glenn, Parsons, and Stevens (1989) who found that living in an alcoholic family, while stressful for all its members, is especially so for women who, because of the nature of family culture and construct, are unable to hide their vulnerability to the adverse effects of alcoholism as well as men. Apparently, when a mother reduces her involvement within family because of alcoholism, everyone and especially she is aware of it. These last researchers found that alcoholic mothers in general are painfully aware of the emotional deprivation to which they submit their children. And such deprivation may have long term effects. For example, another group of researchers concluded that the emotional deprivation which a little girl encountered growing up with an alcoholic mother contributed to her becoming alcoholic herself (Beckman, Day, Bardsley, & Seeman, 1980).

Families, whether they be alcoholic or not, have emotional equilibrium just as individuals do. Such an equilibrium has been termed a "homeostatic balance" (Jackson 1957). This balance is achieved by how the family members perceive one another, by what they expect from one another, and by how they interact with one another. Each member has a role, and each plays a part in maintaining the equilibrium of the family. Examples include the husband who always drives home from a party because of the wife's inebriation, the adolescent who has learned to do the family's food shopping because the mother isn't feeling well—again, and the husband who serves as a scapegoat for the alcoholic wife's verbal abuse. Each member, consciously or unconsciously, has an emotional stake in maintaining familial equilibrium. What the author has learned is that when a member no longer wants to play (perform) the role, a change is effected within the family. The adolescent may rebel and refuse to do the family shopping, may refuse to accept the mother's protestation about not feeling well, and may, finally, confront the mother and father, too, about the mother's addiction. The crisis may effect a change to which the members must adapt or the family separates. The author remembers just such a case.

Janet, unhappily married for over twenty years, became so miserable with the quality of her life that she joined A.A. She stopped drinking and immediately afterwards, on the recommendation of a friend, referred herself to me. The presenting problem was not her long term drinking but her bad marriage. The husband was asked to join the counseling sessions but steadfastly refused. Janet was in counseling with me for over seven months and concurrently and faithfully attended A.A. and a supportive group for alcoholic women. What came out in the counseling was that Janet, who always had a penchant for passivity and dependence, had married a controlling, protective father figure. He had reinforced her dependency by tolerating her drinking and had kept the knowledge secret from their children and their friends. He even bought her booze. In a real, literal sense he had fed her alcoholism. When her drinking stopped, her need for a protective father figure also stopped and the family equilibrium changed. He could not adapt. Simply, he preferred and functioned better with an alcoholic wife. He filed for divorce.

Research data are available which show that the self-esteem of married couples drops as their consumption of alcohol increases (Konovsky & Wilsnack, 1982). Without a doubt, an alcoholic man can wreak emotional havoc in the family setting.

However, considerable research evidence shows that the effects of a woman's alcoholism are even worse. Curlee (1970) compared male and female patients in an alcoholic treatment center and found that once a woman took to drink, her problems and those of her family became more acute more rapidly than they did for a man and his family. Curlee's findings are supported by Nespor (1990).

The effects of female alcoholism on younger family members can be especially unfortunate. For example, two researchers found that students' reasons for drinking were positively related to the frequency of maternal intoxication (Harford & Spiegler, 1983). A male or female adolescent student's risk of becoming a problem drinker increased if he/she had been exposed to what the authors of the study called "maternal deviant drinking." In another study these same authors have suggested that genetic predisposition also may be a reason (Harford & Spiegler, 1982). Genetic predisposition not withstanding, there is little doubt that the negative impact of an alcoholic mother upon children is *dynamically* greater than that of an alcoholic father. This is probably because as was learned in Chapter 2, maternal alcoholism is not just less acceptable socially than paternal alcoholism but it is stigmatized.

THE ENABLER

More than just one star is cast in the tragic drama played on the alcoholic family stage. Costarring with the alcoholic mother and wife is the *enabler*. Usually her spouse is the enabler; however, anyone living with her—parent, child, uncle, aunt, or simply a live-in friend can be the enabler. Any person who unwillingly abets and promotes the alcoholic's addiction is an enabler.

Just as no two alcoholic women are alike, neither are two enablers alike. At this same time, certain common denominators are in the personalities of enablers which facilitates the alcoholic process in the alcoholic woman. Enablers are disposed to be

1. overprotective,
2. compulsive, and
3. worriers.

Overprotective Enablers

Overprotective enablers, like overprotective parents, are not loving but rejecting. The overprotective parent does not view the child as a separate and independent human being. The overprotective parent does not understand that the child's emotional health, growth, and maturity lie in making his/her own choices and decisions and in being responsible for his/her own behavior. In short, the overprotective parent perceives the child (regardless of age) as basically helpless and inept, which is more often than not the parent's unconscious self-view (projection defense). Both perception and defense are typical toward the alcoholic woman by this type of enabler. The overprotective enabler serves as a buffer between the alcoholic and the rest of the world. The rest of the world, please note, may include the rest of the family. Thus the enabler may lie, explain, and/or defend the alcoholic woman to children, parents, and, as well, outsiders. Most enablers in their zeal to protect, defend, and explain the alcoholic's behavior do not see that they are actually feeding and nurturing irresponsibility and immaturity. Indeed, their overprotectiveness creates a womb-like world for the alcoholic's mundane physical needs and insulates her from the normal, usual demands and anxieties of daily living. The alcoholic is excused from many family chores which she would ordinarily perform, from most social obligations, and usually from holding a job. Indeed, one might say that she is excused from life! A cocoon-like existence maintains the alcoholism and thereby accelerates her physical, intellectual, and emotional deterioration.

Overprotective enablers are people who need to control and manipulate. In the domineering type enabler, this need is easy to see in the arbitrariness, in the fits of rage, and so forth. In the submissive or more deferential type of enabler, this need is more covert but is just as, if not more, demeaning. In these latter types, it usually can be seen in the intense, inordinate interest which they take in their alcoholics' lives; in what they eat, whom they see, where they go, and where they are at that moment. Via this interest, complemented usually with this disposition to do, do, do for the woman alcoholic, the enabler is able to control her meals, social life, and virtually all of her movements. Overprotective enablers who find reward in achieving such control of another's life seem to fill an acute need for personal security.

The need for personal security is *a,* if not *the,* prime motivation for overprotective enablers. Simply, they can best be understood as being concerned primarily with their own selves. Why? Because their interest, conscious or unconscious, is to turn the alcoholic into an over-devoted and obligated companion. This is especially true of those who persevere in their enabling even after they become aware of it. These enablers seem to exist with a latent but constant anxiety that in the end they will be left alone. The irony is that often their enabling accomplishes precisely that, because enabling does nothing to engender loyalty.

Compulsive Enablers

Enablers tend to be *compulsive.* Their constant and most important mission, among many, is to solve any and all familial problems. They set up and implement schedules, not only their own but those of the rest of the family members, alcoholic or not. They tend to the myriad of family chores that need tending. If they cannot, for whatever reason, deal with a minor task themselves, they will bully or manipulate another family member into doing it. Then they will supervise to see that whatever was to be done was done to their satisfaction—meaning in letter-perfect fashion.

This obsessiveness with letter-perfect performance distinguishes the compulsive enabler from the normally efficient person. Some enablers acquire this quality of obsessiveness late in their lives; in others it seems to be positively congenital. Regardless at what point this trait is incorporated into their personalities, it is the one which is most evident and the one which precipitates arguments, fights, and stresses of all kinds in the family. This trait alienates children especially. Usually, because of this trait, children come to sympathize with the alcoholic woman, turn to her for closeness, which too often, because of her addiction, she is quite unable to give. *The enabler's compulsive ways may well be a prime reason that so many children of alcoholics become themselves alcoholic.* Many come to conclude unconsciously that it's better to be an easy going, relaxed drunk than a frantic, compulsive enabler.

Why are most enablers compulsive? The answer seems to lie in the alcoholic's withdrawal from the family. The enablers' compulsiveness in most cases can be understood as the response to that withdrawal. They feel that their compulsive ways bring order and sanity to the chaos and indifference which the alcoholic woman brings into the family.

Compulsiveness in the enabler is a response to something else too. Please note that compulsive people are usually people in constant motion—physically, intellectually, and/or emotionally. They are always doing something. Such constant, intense activity has an important benefit to alcoholic enablers as it distracts them from seeing the alcoholic woman's drinking. Such activity has another important benefit for enablers in that it prevents them from focusing on their inner selves and on how they continue to contribute to the family's alcoholic dynamics. In sum, compulsiveness helps enablers to deny the reality of their own and the family's situation.

Enablers As Worriers

Enablers are worriers who are unwilling or unable to see alcoholism or the insidious effects of it in the family. Like the alcoholic woman, worriers tend to see the drinking problem as being outside themselves. They see little or no connection between themselves and the problem. Despite this myopic view of their situation or perhaps because of it, they worry a lot.

The worry of many enablers comes in waves. Sometimes they feel inundated by it, at other times, free of it. When worried, they have to go into action—"do something" for the alcoholic woman or for another member of the family to assuage the constant sense of guilt with which they live. The guilt can be derived from the abuse they inflict upon others in the family or for the abuse others inflict upon them. Both worry and guilt seem to keep them on an emotional roller coaster.

These dependent enablers, both male and female, are sometimes physically abused. When that is the case, they usually develop the stereotypical male alcoholic-like view of being victimized by life and circumstances. Too often they develop a masochistic outlook and learn to suffer in silence. Occasionally these enablers develop a martyr complex much as if they are ennobling their suffering by doing so. They conclude that happiness of any kind, even a modicum of it, is not for this life but only for the next one.

What people think is of critical importance to enablers. Indeed, it determines and explains much about their behavior. Typical enabler thinking goes like this:

"What will people think if they find out my wife is alcoholic?"

"What will people think if they were to stop in when she's obviously drunk?"

"What if she drinks too much at the reunion, the wedding, the birthday party?"

"What will people think if she gets into an auto accident when she is drunk?"

This obsessive concern for appearances and propriety is a major reason enablers persevere in their enabling, a major reason they have so many worries.

ADULT DAUGHTERS OF ALCOHOLICS [ADOA]

A girl who grows up in alcoholic families, grows up emotionally deprived and tends to become manipulative and exploitative (Lyon & Greenberg, 1991). Sometimes she is reared in situations where the climate is explosive—temper tantrums, sudden and unpredictable happenings—seemingly for no reason. Here people scream, cower, and cry. Sometimes the climate is just the opposite. It is so undisturbed that the girl learns to live in an environment which could be fairly described as tomb-like; one where no talk or communication occurs and where members function in isolation and keep secrets from one another. Sometimes the climate is between these extremes. Even so, in these "middle climates" the children are often physically abused. If the children are not abused themselves they see other family members so verbally abused that they come to understand that hypercriticism and nagging are viable and legitimate ways of interacting. They learn, too, that promises are not necessarily binding as they may or not be legitimate.

Climates such as these promote insecurity. Climates such as these promote a sense of isolation and of never having been loved. Climates such as these promote a poor sense of low self-worth. It is for these reasons that *girls who grow up in an alcoholic home come to negate the worth of their own love and feel unworthy of anyone else's.* For many of them, the giving and taking of love becomes a mystery. The feelings of insecurity, the ineptness with love, and the low self-esteem are the major reasons that these girls as women exhibit a veritable host of debilitating personality traits. Chief among these are

1. a constant need for approval;
2. a low ability to persevere;
3. an inability to trust;
4. unreliability;
5. a tendency to lie and often for no reason;
6. an attraction to pain;
7. vacillation;
8. an inability to get close to others;
9. a tendency to become involved in relationships which are based upon pity, not love;
10. a terror of being evaluated; and
11. a frantic way of life.

Before proceeding, please note that the intention here is not to imply that daughters of alcoholics are all alike. Quite the contrary. Like their parent alcoholics and enablers they are seen here as all different from one another. The previously listed traits and descriptions which follow can best be understood as characteristics in their unique personalities. In some daughters of alcoholics, some of these characteristics are dominant, in others barely discernible, and in still others some of these characteristics do not exist at all.

Constant Need for Approval

Adult daughters of alcoholics tend to have an acute and constant need for approval. More often than not this stems from the emotional paradox in which many were steeped in childhood. They grew up in sharply contrasting emotional extremes. One parent (usually the alcoholic) was indifferent or rejecting. While the other one, out of misguided good intention to balance the emotional equation, was studiously over solicitous, if not overprotective. A worse situation (more common too) for such a person was to live a childhood where the same alcoholic parent(s) vacillate(s) between superabundant love, attention, and caring and icy indifference and/or hostile rejection. Behavior at both extremes of the emotional continuum is, of course, common among alcoholics as it is a function of the guilty conscience and inebriation.

The constant need for approval can be and often is channelized in doing for others. The gratitude and recognition they receive fuels them to continue to do for and to serve others through their lives. This is especially true among those who themselves never become alcoholic. They seldom, if ever, examine the why of their constant need to do and serve others. Their frantic activity is the alternative they choose to self-examination. It has a fringe benefit too. It salves their conscience, albeit never fully. Their conscience, in most cases, is oversized and is the reason they make so many decisions out of guilt and not out of choice. If this woman does not herself become alcoholic, she is the ideal candidate for the role of the enabler. As a result many do become so. They do because like most people they gravitate consciously or unconsciously toward those whose ways are familiar and which they feel they understand. If nothing else, potential enabler women do indeed understand the ways of the budding alcoholic. Therefore, they often marry one.

An unfortunate effect among those with an oversized conscience is that they feel guilty all the time. Their guilt may be such that they seldom take a stand on anything even if their integrity is involved. What they believe depends upon to whom they are talking. This is true especially with strangers. Such a submissive approach results inevitably in a loss of self-respect and the respect of others. The anger engendered in the daughter of the alcoholic by such submissiveness by those outside the family (and there is usually a lot) is often displaced upon family members. It is a reason why so much nagging, hypercriticism, and physical abuse occur in the alcoholic family.

Low Ability to Persevere

Adult daughters of alcoholics have a low ability to persevere in most activities, even those which they enjoy. In those activities which are unappealing or which are threatening their ability seems virtually nonexistent. As college students, their class attendance is at best spotty, and frequently downright poor. If they have chores at home, their style is to do them sporadically, not at all, or frantically. Most projects, even minor tasks, seem to be finished with little enthusiasm, often grudgingly. They change their jobs often and are the ones who suffer "burnout" most. In short, achievement and striving for success are not prime motivating factors in their lives. This is because many daughters of alcoholics are plagued by the latent but constant fear that they are going to fail whatever the endeavor, project, or work. This is especially true when they are confronted by new tasks and fulfilling obligations. Their response invariably is to procrastinate. Their emotional rationale seems to be, "If I don't try, I can't fail." Their inability to persevere and their penchant for procrastination can best be understood as a defense against lowering further their already pitifully low self-esteem.

Inability to Trust

Daughters of alcoholics are unable to trust. Trust is learned in a stable home, one where the child can predict with a high degree of accuracy what is going to happen. The alcoholic home, filled as it is with acute emotional vacillations and broken promises, quite apparently militates against such learning. The daughters of alcoholic families emerge from childhood distrustful and suspicious people. Their distrust costs them much. Because of it, they are unable to get emotionally close to others. As children, they are unable to identify with adults and peers and thereby lack a means to enrich their personalities.

This inability to identify with others is the reason that during childhood these girls appear so bland and apathetic in both appearance and disposition. The blandness and apathy seem to evaporate during adolescence and adulthood, but, in truth, are merely veneered beneath the social sophistication which comes with an increase in age. The core suspicions and distrust learned in childhood are very much present. These suspicions and distrust are the prime reasons for the poor quality of their interpersonal relations. The simple truth is that people can't get close to others if they can't trust. Daughters of alcoholics can't trust.

Unreliable

The daughters of alcoholics tend to be unreliable. This unreliability is a function of their low self-esteem. Self-esteem influences performance mightily, i.e., if we think we're good, we perform adequately. A disproportionate number of daughters of alcoholics believe that they are inadequate. Because of this self-view, they resort to the emotional rationale previously noted, "If I don't try, I can't fail". The result of these unfortunate cause and effect dynamics is that they present themselves as unreliable. Doing so is not of special significance to them because they grew up with unreliability. In most instances, being surrounded by one or more unreliable persons was an integral part of their childhood milieu. As adolescents and adults, they do like most people do. They mirror behavior with which they are familiar and which they understand. Also like most people, *they are far more concerned with maintaining some semblance of respectability in their self-esteem than they are in projecting an image of reliability.* In their view, they have to do that if they are to function at all.

Lie Frequently

Daughters of alcoholics tend to lie a lot—often for no reason. Several reasons exist for this. As children they spent much of their lives in fantasy to escape the chaotic, harsh reality of their real world. Many learn to find so much reward in their world of imagination that their fantasy lives become as important to them as the real world. For some, it becomes more important. For all of them *fantasy has become an integral defense for the harsh reality which daughters of alcoholics continue to perceive in adolescence and adulthood.* To mitigate that harshness, they invariably blend their fantasies with reality. The effect of all this fantasizing is to develop a distorted perception of self, and/or reality, and simply, of what's true. More often than not, they come to believe the reality which they perceive even though it is a blend of their own imagination.

For these reasons, daughters of alcoholics view their lies as "white" lies. If something is not exactly as they said it was, they feel justified in feeling and believing that it should be! Most of them are quite oblivious of the fact that when they blend fantasy with reality they are really telling themselves and others that reality and truth are really not important.

Attraction to Pain

Many daughters of alcoholics seem beset with an attraction to pain. The reason for this is not difficult to fathom if one keeps in mind the fact that conscience is a very real and major factor in the alcoholic family. It is usually evident, if not dominant, in all intra-familial interactions. More often than not, conscience is the critical determinant for making both major and minor decisions. In families such as these, conscience literally inundates the children with guilt—guilt which precipitates the need they have to punish themselves. They punish themselves with worry, useless anxiety, imaginary ailments, accidents, a constant scene of unworthiness, and so forth. Bizarre, but true, in the view of some of those reared and steeped in the crazy dynamics of alcoholism, such punishment is a kind of penance to atone for the original sin of being born into an alcoholic family. Thus, *daughters of alcoholics gravitate toward pain because they find that feelings of hurt salve their feelings of guilt.*

The most salient manifestations of their need to punish themselves are probably reflected in the harshness with which they judge themselves in all that they do and especially in the constant denigration of their physical looks. They are never pleased with how they look. If nothing else, this constant displeasure reflects the basic sense of self-loathing with which they live.

Vacillation

Daughters of alcoholics tend toward vacillation. This is not surprising because most were reared by role models who were indecisive, indifferent, and of low self-esteem. Most of these children became what they were exposed to.

Decision making for them is a painful experience, filled with much doubt and even more dread. They feel that making decisions reinforces their basic self-understanding that their judgement is terribly poor. If they do not make decisions, such reinforcement can not occur. So they vacillate.

What is ironic about vacillation is that it is both a product and a precipitator of anxiety. Thus, the vacillators who are too anxious about making a decision only increase their anxiety by not doing so when finally caught between the proverbial "rock and hard place." At that point, their anxiety is such that their judgement may indeed be poor and their decision faulty. In this way, they realize their basic self-understanding about their ineptness to make decisions. What also should be noted is that through this self-fulfilling prophecy they structure the anxiety for the next decision they have to make.

Emotionally Distant

The daughters of alcoholics find it difficult to get emotionally close to others. This is not surprising because the ability to get close and to love is founded on learning feelings of trust. Such feelings are learned best and most easily during the childhood years.

Now, if we are not exposed to closeness as children but to rejection and indifference, like children are in the alcoholic family, our sense of trust is developed poorly if at all. Why? Because when we let ourselves get close to others, when we love, we open ourselves up to potential hurt. We trust that our love will not be rebuffed but returned.

If the love we give as children is returned in kind or even more bountifully, we learn to trust. We learn to love. We learn to get close. Daughters of alcoholics learn early in life that they cannot trust because they never saw much love between their parents. More often than not, they themselves were the object of a love which was at best sporadic and unpredictable. In short, *what daughters of alcoholics learned in childhood was that the chance of being hurt was very strong if they got emotionally close.* Unfortunate but true, throughout their lives most of them are not willing to risk that chance.

Relationships of Pity

Many daughters of alcoholics, though unable to get close, still develop relationships with others. However, *these relationships are not based upon love but upon pity.* These relationships then are not relationships of give and take and are not peer-like, but are characterized by emotionally sophisticated condescension.

To be in a relationship where one is pitied is not threatening. One can feel kind and noble about oneself in such a situation and any demands made upon the pitied can or cannot be met without guilt. Love—especially peer love—is something else. Peer love necessarily involves not only the sense of trust, already noted, but also a healthy self-esteem, a feeling that one has something of emotional worth to offer the other person. Quite apparently, peer love means being loved and accepting the love of another. Such acceptance involves obligation, i.e., one has to pay love back. This is the critical rub for the daughters of alcoholics. They are threatened acutely by obligations of any kind. Paying back love is threatening indeed. *For daughters of alcoholics to obviate the need to pay back love and still feel that they are giving of themselves, they seek out, find, and relate to people whom they can pity.* In this way they are able to deny their inabilities to love in a peer and meaningful way.

Terror of Being Evaluated

The daughters of alcoholics live constantly with a terror of being evaluated. To most of them, being evaluated means to be demeaned, because they believe they will be found wanting. They go to extreme, sometimes self-defeating lengths, not to be evaluated. As college students, they are emotionally paralyzed by every test they have to take. They procrastinate about submitting papers on time and, thereby often have grades lowered. As workers, they tend to gravitate toward lower paying, fringe-benefitted, bureaucratic-like jobs which are not truly evaluated. They prefer such jobs to those where the compensation is higher but where productivity and competence are truly evaluated.

Although daughters of alcoholics seldom get into positions of prime leadership, responsibility, and accountability, they do sometimes rise into minor managerial type jobs. In such positions *they live with the constant dread that they will be found unsuitable if not inept.* To protect themselves from any such eventuality, they become clerks par excellence. They keep minutes of all meetings and then distribute the minutes immediately afterward if the agenda was not personally threatening. They distribute the minutes much later when memories have become fuzzy or blended if even the slightest threat to them was present. In these ways they are able to color what transpired and put themselves in a more favorable light. Of course, such behavior is not peculiar to the daughters of alcoholics but is indeed common in any hierarchial structure, be it industrial or governmental.

Nevertheless, *the need to protect one's derriere is an acute and compelling one for adult daughters of alcoholics.* However, doing so is not their only method of dealing with the constant threat with which they live on the job. *The other way is namely to not take a definitive stand, or any stand, where one might become the focal point of attention and possibly be wrong.* To be wrong to the daughter of an alcoholic raises the specter of being demeaned, disciplined, or dismissed. This is not as likely to happen if they never take a stand. So they don't. This elusive response to threat is learned from an alcoholic parent or enabler. A manifest purpose of elusiveness is to present a low self-esteem from being lowered further. Ironically it does just the opposite. More often than not, elusive people come to think less and less of themselves precisely because they don't know what they believe.

Ch 3 The Alcoholic Woman in the Family 71

Frantic Way of Life

Daughters of alcoholics lead a frantic way of life. The reason for this is a function of their oversized conscience and the super-abundant guilt which it precipitates. As we have noted in various contexts, love is a rare commodity in the alcoholic family. One of the unfortunate effects of that rarity is that children learn that if they are to obtain any at all, they must do, act, work, and contribute.

A grateful glance from a harried enabler mother or a bleary-eyed alcoholic father is usually enough to cause an emotionally deprived little girl to continue doing the dishes every night throughout her child life and to assume other duties far beyond her child-like competence. What these girls learn is that if they want even the tiniest crumb of emotional acceptance, they have to earn it. They have to do so with an undue expenditure of effort, too. Very often their efforts go unrewarded. Even the crumbs are withheld. Still they persevere, because they see no alternative. With the advent of adolescence, the indifference and the sporadic crumbs of the alcoholic and/or enabler take their toll. Their perseverance to contribute, indeed their perseverance for whatever, ends. Their constant frenetic activity does not. Productivity is not the issue for them anymore, just activity. In this way they are able to justify their existence to themselves.

Case of Linda R

This case exemplifies the insidious, destructive hold that alcoholic parents can have upon their children. The author dealt with Linda while a consultant in a school department. The reports which follow are the actual ones. Minor editing and name changes were done to protect the identity of the subject.

Linda was referred by her guidance counselor. She was reported as being out of contact in her classes. "Unreachable" was the word used most often to describe her class behavior. Linda was failing in all of her classes. She was suspected of drinking. A teacher had caught her in the girls' room nipping from a bottle of wine. Twice liquor had been smelled on her breath.

Psychodiagnostic Report

Name: Linda R

Testing Date: 13 Jan.

Date of Birth: 17 Sept.

Test Administered: Wechsler Intelligence Scale for Children (WISC),
Bender Gestalt Test,
Thematic Apperception Test (TAT), and
Rorschach.

Behavioral Observation. Linda is a short, slender, pale faced girl who wears glasses. She showed up for testing in a skirt and blouse which were clean but wrinkled and ill-fitting. Her shoes were well-worn and of vintage passé. Linda covered her mouth when she spoke or smiled to cover a missing tooth and a few badly crooked ones. Initially she was detached and shy but warmed up as the testing proceeded. Quite apparently, she enjoyed the attention she received from the testing session.

Test Results. Linda is currently functioning with a verbal IQ of 115, a performance IQ of 115, and a full scale IQ of 116. Scores such as these indicate that Linda functions in the bright-normal range of intelligence. Approximately 75% of the people her age score below her on this test. Linda has the ability to obtain A's and B's.

In the verbal sphere of competency, Linda functions best in general fund of information, vocabulary, and reasoning. In all of these areas, she functions like a person two years her senior. Her memory and ability to reason arithmetically are consistent with her general level of competency. She functions in the low normal ranges in social comprehension.

In the nonverbal spheres her ability is in the superior to very superior ranges in spatial relations but below average in both perception and social awareness.

The WISC findings seem to be substantiated by Rorschach findings. What we have here is a confused little girl who is growing up with glaring deficiencies in the social and interpersonal spheres. Linda is bewildered, shy, confused, and socially scared. She perceives a world filled with hostile or, at best, indifferent strangers. Such a perception has led to a general mistrust of acquaintances and teachers. (She reports she has no friends.) Quite apparently this is a girl who has been emotionally shortchanged during most of her life. She is in desperate need for attention of any sort. Her failing record can be understood as a function of her self-perception. Simply stated, Linda sees herself as a failure.

Recommendations. Home visits to assess conditions. Counseling at earliest possible time.

Joseph F. Perez, Ph.D.
Consulting Psychologist

Report of Social Worker

Linda lives on the one street of this town which could be accurately described as "slummy." An only child, she lives with her parents in a duplex house which sorely needs a coat of paint and the two front steps repaired.

I visited the home without benefit of an appointment because there is no phone and Linda was always vague and unwilling about helping to arrange the visit. I learned why when I got there. Both parents were home. I never got to see the father but I heard him only too well. He snored loudly in the bedroom off the kitchen throughout the interview. Mrs. R told me that he was sleeping off a half gallon of wine.

Mrs. R seemed oblivious to the untidy, even dirty, kitchen. The small living room was only a little better. Mrs. R told me she was 38 years old. She appears to be ten or fifteen years older. Her bleary look and confused speech convinced me that she too had had her share of the half gallon of wine.

The interview was a very short one because Mrs. R was uninterested and not a little embarrassed by my presence. I did learn that Mr. R is an unemployed welder who suffers from a "bad back." The family is on the city welfare rolls and has been for almost a decade.

What I saw in her house convinces me that Linda's problems are considerable. Both parents are alcoholics and oblivious to any problems Linda might have.

I concur with Dr. Perez. Linda should be in counseling. After seeing her mother and her home, I am not optimistic.

M. Corcoran
School Social Worker

Comments. After reading this report, the author arranged to see Linda on Monday mornings and Thursday afternoons. Our sessions lasted forty-five minutes each. Linda was so starved for attention that despite her suspiciousness and shyness, and perhaps because of our prior testing session, rapport was almost immediate.

Toward the end of the first session and continuing for many weeks she spent the entire forty-five minutes describing the utter deprivation in which she had been reared. The author still remembers some of her lines. "I was always alone. I don't even remember ever being held even... I saw the boy next door being spanked once for playing on the street. I remember going on the street to play. I guess I wanted to be spanked. My mother and father didn't even notice. They were both too drunk." Once after a particularly tearful session she confided her abiding fear that she would end up like her parents. Despite the defeatist attitude which threaded through her talk, Linda had an engaging way about her. The utter simplicity and candor with which she related the rejection and loneliness of her life was touching. So much so that the author stepped out of his counseling role and began to try to manipulate her life outside of counseling. He arranged through a dentist friend to have dental work done, her tooth replaced, and the others straightened.

He continued seeing Linda for the balance of that academic year and for all the next. Throughout he knew she had a crush on him. He used it and began to communicate his expectations about her school work. By the end of the first year of counseling,

Ch 3 The Alcoholic Woman in the Family 75

Linda was making first honor roll, had a part-time job, and new clothes. She began dating.

The following September Linda turned sixteen and never came back to school. She had obtained a full-time job at a local factory. She called the author at Christmas time of her sixteenth year to say that she was happily married and pregnant. The guidance counselor subsequently informed the author that Linda had never married.

Personal Note. Once while driving, I saw Linda coming out of her parents' house with a baby in tow. I stopped to talk. She never met my gaze but kept glancing away with a vague, defeated look. I had seen that look before, but never in anyone so young. It was the look of the alcoholic who has surrendered to life.

SUMMARY

If an alcoholic woman lives with family, then the addiction is a familial problem not just a personal one. Such a woman infects her family with the disease then psychosomatically develops a disproportionate number of physical problems.

Consciously or unconsciously, each family member has a stake in maintaining the homeostatic balance within family. Research studies show that a woman's alcoholism wreaks more havoc within family than does that of a man. Indeed, studies show that the negative impact of an alcoholic mother upon students of adolescent age is dynamically greater than that of an alcoholic father.

Co-starring with the alcoholic in the tragic drama of familial alcoholism is the enabler. Three types of enablers were considered: (1) the overprotective, (2) the compulsive, and (3) the worrier. Overprotective enablers are basically rejecting because they view the alcoholic as basically helpless and inept. The compulsive enabler is characterized by an intense need to solve any and all familial problems. The worrier enabler is one who tends to develop a masochistic outlook and suffers in silence.

A girl who grows up in an alcoholic family, grows up emotionally deprived and tends to become manipulative and exploitative. In addition to these two unfortunate qualities the adult daughter of alcoholics develops feelings of insecurity, ineptness with love and low feelings of self-worth. ADOA's may incorporate a number of debilitating personality traits. The following eleven were described: (1) a constant need for approval; (2) a low ability to persevere; (3) an inability to trust; (4) unreliability; (5) a tendency to lie and often for no reason; (6) an attraction to pain; (7) vacillation; (8) an inability to get close to others; (9) a tendency to become involved in relationships which are based upon pity, not love; (10) a terror of being evaluated; and (11) a frantic way of life.

FOR REVIEW AND REFLECTION

1. If the alcoholic woman lives in family, the addiction is a familial one, not just a personal one. Explain this.

2. Why should the effects of a woman's alcoholism be worse for a family than a man's?

3. Explain how an overprotective enabler is not loving but rejecting.

4. Discuss how the enabler's need to control is a response to a need for security.

5. How can an enabler's disposition toward compulsiveness engender stress in a family?

6. Discuss how the enabler's concern for propriety exacerbates the alcoholic woman's problems with herself and others.

7. Of the personality traits noted among adult daughters of alcoholics, which do you believe to be the most dysfunctional? Why?

8. Explain how an enabler's acute and constant need for approval can only increase an alcoholic woman's problems.

9. Vacillation in adult daughters of alcoholics is both a product and a precipitator of anxiety. Explain this.

10. A.D.O.A.'s are attracted to pain. How and what does this bode for relationships?

PART II
EFFECTS

Chapter 4

THE COURSE OF ALCOHOLISM

Alcoholism is a progression. Figure 4.1 contains illustrated acts which occur during alcohol addiction and recovery.

In 1951, E.M. Jellinek delivered a series of lectures which described the different phases through which an individual passes in the process of becoming addicted to alcoholism. Eight years later M. M. Glatt (1959) expanded and worked the substance of these lectures into a chart. The description of the four progression stages and recovering from alcoholism is derived from their work.

The following description is intended only as a general guide. Few alcoholics actually progress step-by-step through the four stages as described. Indeed, some alcoholics may become addicted with their first drink and touch on steps of the fourth stage in a matter of months or even weeks. Others might take decades to do so.

<u>Social</u> drinking

Stage One

Increases alcohol tolerance
Begins regular drinking after work
Drinks faster and more than others

—

Stage 2

Occasionally drinks at odd times
Sneaks drinks
Has guilt feelings about drinking
Begins memory blackouts
Projects blame for drinking onto others
Increases guilt

—

Stage Three

Becomes addictive
Has auto accidents, major and minor
Fails at attempts to stop drinking
Has acute resentments and anger
Increases social and vocational problems
Takes meals sporadically
Increases in blackouts

—

Stage Four

May lose job
Has indifference to physical appearance
May have family breakup
Decreases alcohol tolerance
May have onset of malnutrition
Begins having acute medical problems
May have death by accident

Alcoholism—The Progression

Figure 4.1. Schematic for alcoholism—progression and recovery process. Based on Glatt (1959).

Productive Life

Level Three

Begins to appreciate and like self
Reduces the need to drink to seldom if at all
Improves vocational life
Accepts others more readily
Increases self-esteem
Obtains a realistic self-view
Begins self-examination as a vital concern

Level Two

Solves problems satisfactorily
Diminishes the need to drink
Makes plans
Develops new interests
Increases self-confidence
Recognizes recovery as a definite possibility

Level One

Seeks alternative ways to cope with stress
Takes a more avid interest in grooming
Sleeps better
Takes meals with regularity
Seeks to put order & regularity into life
Seeks company of recovering addicts
Admits her addiction

Alcoholism—The Recovery Process

Figure 4.1. Continued.

Alcoholism—the Progression
(See Figure 4.1, Left One-half)

Stage One

1. May start with regular social drinking. The woman is uncomfortable when there is no booze at a party or social event.
2. Seldom leaves a party not high.
3. Increase gradually in tolerance for alcohol.
4. Takes a few drinks after work and/or before dinner.
5. Occasionally resorts to alcohol under pressure.
6. Drinks more quickly and uncommonly more than others.

Stage Two

1. Begins occasional drinking at odd times during the day.
2. Increases drinking under pressure.
3. Begins sneaking of drinks.
4. Delays eating to continue drinking.
5. Has guilt feelings about drinking.
6. Has onset of memory blackouts.
7. Begins to project blame for drinking onto persons, situations, or events.
8. Begins to find fantasy rewards in drinking.
9. Receives reproofs and chastisement by friends and family members.
10. Increases guilt. Attempts to stop.

Stage Three

1. Has psychological addiction with control over drinking at a very low ebb.
2. Receives speeding tickets and has auto accidents, minor and major.
3. Fails all attempts at stopping drinking.
4. Has acute resentments and anger toward friends and family.
5. Increase occurs in social and vocational problems.

6. Keeps problem hidden.
7. Is unable to keep up with household chores.
8. Takes meals sporadically.
9. Seeks out drinking "Betties."
10. Increases solitary drinking.
11. Increases blackouts.

Stage Four

1. Is beset by a constant stage of anger and/or depression.
2. Is unkempt, inappropriate in personal grooming.
3. May lose job.
4. Is interested, almost solely, in drinking.
5. May have family break-up.
6. Lives in an alcoholic daze or constant binge, drinking for days at a time.
7. Decrease may occur in alcohol tolerance.
8. May have onset of malnutrition.
9. Has overnight stays at a hospital.
10. Lacks concern in grooming and physical appearance.
11. Begins to have acute medical problems, i.e., liver cirrhosis.
12. May have death by accident.

Alcoholism—the Recovery Process
(See Figure 4.1, Right One-half)

The first step in the recovery process levels (admission of alcoholism) is a very personal and private matter. Why it does or does not occur remains a mystery. For some women it occurs in Stage One of the progression outlined previously, for others not until Stage Four, and for some, never.

The following three levels for the process of recovery, like that of the four stages for progression into alcoholism, is intended only as a general description. This process is not an easy, neat, and simple step-by-step movement, level to level. Indeed, the return back to a meaningful life is fraught with peril, anguish, temptations by the score and, occasionally, despair. In short, few alcoholics make this return with ease, but some do make it. The autobiographical sketches in the next chapter show that.

Level One

1. Admits alcoholism.
2. Makes a genuine request for help.
3. Learns about addiction, is willing to see it as an illness.
4. Seeks the company of recovering addicts.
5. Begins to find reward in a chosen form of therapy—individual, group, or recreational.
6. Seeks to put order and regularity into life.
7. Takes meals with regularity.
8. Sleeps better.
9. Takes a more avid interest in grooming.
10. Seeks to find ways to cope with normal stresses of living.

Level Two

1. Recognizes recovery as a definite possibility.
2. Has increase in self-confidence.
3. Takes a more active interest in others.
4. Develops new interests.
5. Makes plans.
6. Gets verbal rewards and encouragement from family and friends.
7. Has a decrease in the need to drink.
8. Deals with obligations through use of problem-solving skills, not always perfectly, but at least satisfactorily.

Level Three

1. Begins self-examination as a vital concern.
2. Obtains a realistic self-view.
3. Increases self-esteem.
4. Places guilt in proper perspective.
5. Reduces the need to drink to where, if a drink is taken, it is seldom.
6. Sees recovery as a life process toward a sense of fulfillment.
7. Accepts people.
8. Improves vocational life dramatically.

9. Begins to appreciate self and own productivity.
10. Accepts a life-long process of coping with guilt and confidence.

Alcoholism—the Relapse

Frequently, alcoholics who are in counseling and who have seemingly made an emotional commitment to stop drinking return to the bottle. For some it is because their commitment is something less than genuine. For others, it is because of the fear engendered by what they see in the self-examination process of counseling. For still others, it is because of the threat imposed by the realization that continued sobriety requires a radical change in self-perception, perception of others, and life-style in general.

The counselor should know that clients lapse back into drink also because of another reason. *They are testing the hypothesis upon which the whole process is premised; namely, that they are alcoholic.* Thus, they reason that if they are drinking they aren't really alcoholic and so don't really have to self-examine. In short, they don't really have to change. In their fuzzy way of thinking, their ability to drink is proof of their normalcy and of their health.

The relapse can be short term, protracted, or the pathway to death. In every case, the relapse is a classic illustration of the denial defense.

Symptoms of the relapse frequently can be found in sudden and new client behaviors. These fall into four general categories:

1. behavioral,
2. verbal,
3. emotional, and
4. body language.

Behavioral. The most obvious evidence of relapse is the *odor of alcohol.* Too many counselors (especially new ones) deny that they smell or think they smell liquor on their client's breath. They like to perceive the new gum chewing or peppermint sucking habit displayed by a client as a healthy alternative to booze.

If counselors think they smell booze, they should verbalize it to their clients, especially if the client is the one who never chewed anything before. The counsel's verbalization may be a blunt question or an observation toned facetiously. The style should gibe with the counselor's manner and personality. In any case, once the counselor makes the remark he/she should observe the response carefully and proceed from there.

Another possible evidence of relapse is *the client who comes in one day heavily perfumed or cologned.* The author's experience is that the client is trying to mask the odor of alcohol or is trying to redirect the counselor's perception. A remark by the counselor, pointed or subtle, is not inappropriate.

Being unusually early or late for an appointment is often a sign of a relapsed client. In the former situation, the client may be showing an inappropriate zeal for counseling (she protesteth too much). At the same time the client who suddenly starts showing up unusually early may be crying out that she is indeed on the brink of relapse.

Clients who suddenly start coming late for their appointment communicate that their motivation for counseling is on the wane. Often, such behavior reflects a client in or tending toward relapse.

Continued missed appointments because of "sickness" may well be a sign of relapse. Clients should always be asked about the absences. Again, their responses should be carefully observed.

Sudden weight gain is frequently a symptom of relapse. If the counselor one day observes that the client seems heavier, the counselor should inquire about it. In any social context and in other counseling contexts, this would be considered inappropriate. In alcoholism counseling, it is appropriate and a very worthy topic for discussion. Why? Because the simple truth is that when a client stops drinking, she ordinarily loses weight, or at worst, maintains it even if she increases her nutritional or junk food intake.

In sum, behavior by clients, which seems out of the ordinary, should be confronted by the counselor. The counselor's obligation is to let clients know that the counselor is sensitive to any and all changes which might be symptomatic of a relapse.

Verbal. The verbal manner of the client in relapse is different. The difference can be subtle, blatant, or somewhere in between.

Clients in relapse frequently *fudge their replies.* They suddenly seem unable to make a statement without couching it in qualifications, i.e., "Yes, I'm going to try to do that. That just might be a good idea you have there, doctor, and if I get a chance and if things are right, I might just do it."

Clients in relapse frequently *change the subject* especially if it even remotely borders on the possibility of their being in a relapse. Female clients especially seem to verbally flee from questions posed by the counselor and from subjects which smack of the client's attempted con of the counselor.

Clients who suddenly develop a new verbal style—launching into *long, rambling monologues—are legitimate suspects of relapse. This is a ploy used by the client who needs to control the counseling hour because of the fear of being found out.*

Discussions about former drinking associates delivered in almost nostalgic tones should be viewed suspiciously by the counselor. At its most innocent level, such talk should tell the counselor that the client has not yet learned to fill the time or social void provided by the client's prior drinking bouts.

A common verbal manifestation of relapse is the client's sudden *request for additional appointments.* Often what this means is that the client is in conflict and is crying out for help. If at all possible, such a client should be given the additional appointments. At the same time the counselor should make it transparently clear that finally it is the client's decision to drink or abstain and that the client's ego, not the counselor's, is the locus of control.

Emotional. The client in relapse always seems more nervous. Frequently a dramatic increase in the amount of tears shed in a counseling session occurs. This is true for women especially.

Client voices seem to be more strident and far less modulated. Unaccountably, client sentences seem to be punctuated inappropriately with nervous laughs, giggles, and chuckles.

Body Language. The client in relapse tells the counselor much with her body. The sudden onset or uncommon increase in each of the following signs may be symptomatic of a relapse:

> averting of the eye;
>
> fidgeting;
>
> nervous twitching, hand drumming;
>
> slight, almost indefinable eye glaze;
>
> facial puffiness;
>
> constant, latent, unaccountable glint of fear in her eyes, a vulnerable look, scared rabbit look; and/or
>
> client begins to sit at attention and seemingly listens too intently, or the vice-versa.

If any of the above signs were to be manifested with one or more of the others, the counselor should be especially concerned.

A point worthy of reiteration is that the particular *body language which communicates a relapse most clearly is that one which the counselor finds "foreign" and new in the client's personality.*

SUMMARY

The Jellinek lectures and Glatt chart served as the rationale for the description of alcohol progression and recovery. Progression began at Stage One with social drinking and continued into Stage Four with death as a possible outcome. The recovery process was explained as beginning with denial and continues lifelong.

Alcoholics go into relapse for a variety of reasons and manifest their relapse in a myriad of behaviors. These behaviors fall into four general categories: (1) behavioral, (2) verbal, (3) emotional, and (4) body language. The counselor should be suspicious of sudden, new, and inconsistent behavior by the client, as it may be a sign of relapse.

FOR REVIEW AND REFLECTION

1. At what point in Stage One of the Alcoholism Progression do you feel a woman should be concerned? Why?

2. Do you see any point at Stage Two of the Alcoholism Progression where a woman might be receptive to help? If so what might that be?

3. Can the alcoholic in the throes of Stage Four in Progression be helped? Why? Why not?

4. Why some alcoholic women admit to their addiction is a mystery. Do you believe some experiences could precipitate an admission? Why and what might they be?

5. What particular, specific life experiences could facilitate and/or accelerate recovery for an alcoholic woman? Describe them.

6. What elements make for a stronger commitment for a woman to stop drinking than others?

7. What fears specifically engendered by self-examination in counseling can precipitate a relapse in the female alcoholic?

8. Which of the specific signs of relapse listed under behavioral do you believe to be a "sure" sign that the alcoholic is drinking? Which of them do you think at best only a weak one?

9. Which of the verbal signs of relapse would you describe as subtle? As blatant? As somewhere in between?

10. Which combination of signs in body language would most likely communicate alcoholic relapse? Explain your feelings/reasons.

Chapter **5**

CASES:
WHAT IT MEANS
TO BE AN
ALCOHOLIC WOMAN

FIVE CASE STUDIES

The following stories explain as well as, perhaps better than, any research study or statistical chart what the cruel effects of being addicted to alcohol are.

Figure 5.1 illustrates the cycle of addiction. This cycle is found in each of the five stories.

THE CYCLE OF ADDICTION

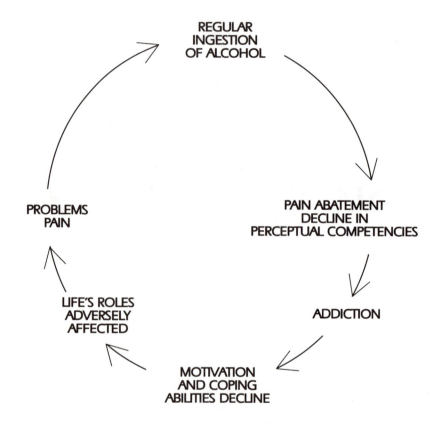

Figure 5.1. Schematic illustration of the cycle of addiction.

94 *Counseling the Alcoholic Woman*

Ethel

When I was asked to write this article I was nine years away from my last drink. The request produced a variety of emotions and I became very interested in exploring that part of my life.

A flash of a blond-haired blue-eyed 6-year-old girl on a rainy Saturday morning came to mind. She is much like other 6-year-olds: bright, precocious. Unlike most 6-year-olds on a Saturday, she is not watching cartoons. She has been in the kitchen making Kool-Aid. A great achievement most little people are proud of. She comes into the living room with her gourmet treat and makes a profound statement: "Drink this mommy, it won't make you sick like the scotch does!" It took six months and $6,000.00 in an alcoholic treatment center to make me realize that same simple truth—"Scotch makes me sick."

Truth is what I struggle greatly with these days, but in the days of my self-inflicted madness it was the thing I dreaded facing the most. Being confronted with the destructive effect that alcoholism had on my children is probably the most difficult truth I face today. The inescapable fact is that I did it to them. I reared them in an alcoholic setting.

At age 18 I had completed my mandatory education and supposedly was an adult ready to face the world. I didn't know what one searches for in an identity, because I was busy looking for a label: good, pretty, intelligent, loved, cared-for. At age 20 I had my first child followed by two other births of healthy babies. At age 28, I began full-fledged alcoholic drinking.

Having been abandoned by my own parents at age 2, I had no genuine role model of what a mother should be. I had the fairy tales and poems on Mother's Day cards. These cards said mothers were kind, caring, giving, and wonderful creatures; almost saintly and madonna-like—certainly, not drunk.

What stands out most vividly about my drinking days is how frantic they were. I was always dashing here and there, like a Keystone Cop going off in three directions at once. I'd have a sudden craving. A pizza, a sundae, an Italian grinder. I decided I wanted it. Decided I needed it and I had to have it. I got it.

I remember arguments too. Lots and lots of arguments with my children. I never could stand being contradicted and would never admit to being wrong especially with them. I learned in counseling that I did that because I had a "fractured self-esteem."

I remember being in bed "sick" a lot. I had migraines all the time. I realize now they were probably all part of my hangovers.

What my two younger children remember vividly is their older sister cooking meals and eating with them, taking them for walks and picnics in the backyard, and reading them bedtime stories in her bedroom. They remember Mommy "crying" and "hanging-on" to them a lot when she was drunk. I remember early in recovery being in a woman's therapy group where the topic was the inability of one particular woman to hug her child. With my ego and arrogance I stated, "Oh I hug my children all the time." The verb used by my children was "hanging-on." The reality is that in sobriety I had to learn to hug my child too. I still haven't digested the fact that I've never really been close to my kids. I'm still learning how. I'm still learning how to be a giver rather than a taker. Most women know motherhood is giving. In search for self with alcohol you become a taker of more than just a drink. Nothing is safe from your taking—friends, family, husband, or children.

If ever there was a model adolescent, my eldest child was. She was my greatest enabler. She didn't date, party, or act irresponsibly during her high school years. She was a care-taker, dependable. Always prepared for any emergency. Life in a home with an alcoholic mother is not secure and one never knows what is going to happen. She learned to drive at age 14, because one night when all the kids and mom went out to dinner, mother got drunk, backed into four cars in the restaurant parking lot and was unable to drive. My daughter could have called someone, but she didn't want them to know about her mother, so she drove home.

I awoke the next morning in absolute panic from the blackout. How did we get home? Were the children O.K.? If they were, who had gotten them ready for bed? What had happened? I struggled out of bed, inched down the hall, peeked into the bedroom. Thank God they were safe! Then down to the kitchen to get a drink to get rid of the awful feeling! One of many, many similar incidents. Yet, I remember telling my eldest daughter, "I'm an alcoholic and I'm going to get help." Her response was, "Mom you're not that bad, don't do that." I understand now her fear of loss of her role. Today at 25 she is in the Army, a very predictable, orderly place to be. She has had several short-term relationships with very dependent men and is beginning to want answers for why this keeps happening. I'm hopeful, for she wants answers not labels, as I did.

Being married to an active alcoholic can be very lonely, confusing, and frustrating. To compensate for this my husband took as his confidante and friend, our second child, our son. There was always a power struggle for this child's attention and affection between his father and me. It was a "no-win" situation for our son, so he chose to escape. He became involved in karate, little league baseball, basketball, and other sports. He made the All-Star team and won many trophies in karate. He developed a close circle of friends with whom he spent many hours. He did anything he could to spend time away from the rest of the family because it was such a painful place to be. At 18 he left home to live on his own. He has not been back. He is in a relationship with his high school sweetheart. From time to time in the last two years he pops in to see his mother. There is always a connection and always a distance. There is always a Christmas visit and gifts. Some years there is even a Mother's Day card, but it is not consistent. He will not accept a commitment because it may not be safe. Recently he was hospitalized for ulcers. He was told not to drink and he is finding this difficult to do. I have shared with him the fact that children of alcoholics are at high risk to develop the disease.

At 16, my third child (a difficult position even in a normal family) became heavily involved with drugs and alcohol. She dropped out of school. I was angry as hell. Not at her. My feelings were, "Come on God, we have had our share of alcoholism in this family!" I refused to enabler her. She had to move out. Her older sister, the great enabler, took her in. Two years later she hit bottom. Today she is home. Progress is slow. She lacks confidence and needs lots of support. Sometimes I wonder if that is a true statement, or my excuse to protect her because of guilt.

At 14, the youngest child had a serious suicide attempt. As I sat by her bed in the intensive care unit and listened to a machine beep out her heartbeat, I kept asking, "Why!" "Why!" The guilt was tremendous. I had had several suicide attempts during my heavy drinking and her early childhood. Months later after much therapy, I asked her why she hadn't shared her feelings with me. Most were feelings adolescents experience during this crucial time of growth. She answered with "I was afraid you would drink." At that time, I hadn't had a drink in six years!

After about three years of being sober, we were sitting at the dining room table and one of the kids said, "Mom, remember the time you were drunk and we were watching Peter Pan and you thought you could fly!" My heart sank, fear and guilt was my immediate reaction, but they continued the story. "You jumped off the couch. Hit your head on the beamed ceiling and fell down. You leaped so high and hit so hard you got a concussion. Boy, did you look funny flying through the air!" They started to laugh. I started to laugh. We laughed and laughed until tears came. It was the beginning of WE.

So how do you deal with all this? First of all "I" don't deal with it. "They" don't deal with it. "We" deal with it!

Alcoholism happened to me! The effects happened to us all; to our whole family. You see, the 19-year marriage ended in divorce after two years of being sober. Some damage can never be repaired.

Points to Ponder

1. This woman displays an uncommon concern with truth. How would you interpret this?

2. List and reflect on the defenses this woman discusses.

3. What are the implications for a child forced into the role of enabler?

4. Could you, would you label this woman courageous? Why? Why not?

5. Why do you think she was divorced after two years of sobriety?

Martha

When I seriously think about me and my being an alcoholic I can't believe it happened to me. I never really liked the taste of any of it—I had to "acquire a taste for it." But, oh boy, did I feel what it did to me—how it made me feel, and not feel!

I can't remember much about growing up, like little incidents or whole stages. I only can remember feeling afraid all the time but still having to cope, to perform, to do well. My mother had a vicious temper and no one knew when she would explode. No, she wasn't an alcoholic just angry all the time. My father was gentle and did little or nothing to protect me from my mother's wrath. So I lived in constant fear, I don't remember seeing and feeling much love—not at home, not in school, not in church, nowhere.

I remember feeling very secure and able to love when I was a junior in college. I felt very good about me—a lot of people admired me and praised me for my looks and brains. I began to believe in me. I met Marty and we got married. It was during the early fifties and we were busy having kids and acquiring a house, car, things. The thing for a woman to do then was to stay at home. So I did, and I let all my secretarial skills evaporate. We had three kids in three years so during the mid-seventies I had to go to work to help pay for our kids' college tuitions. My husband kept badgering me to get a job and the anxiety increased. The fear, the one that I'd had all my life, that I would never, could never, really succeed at a job began to gnaw at me. Constantly feeling scared, I couldn't sleep. So I began to have a glass of muscatel before going to bed. Then I needed a bigger glass before I could feel relaxed, so I switched to gin. God knows what happened after that. It's all a blur.

I remember being alone in the house and starting to shake. It was about 2 P.M. or so (or maybe it was 10 A.M.). Time was always a blur. The important thing I recall is walking into my bedroom at this inappropriate drinking time, dashing for the booze, gulping it down, and breathing a deep, relieving sigh when it hit me. I walked to the mirror, looked in it and said, "Jesus Christ, you're an alcoholic! Now how in hell did you get into this mess. Oh, my God, what am I going to do?"

I remember trying to stop and instead increased the amount I drank. I hid bottles everywhere. I drank morning, noon, and night. My kids (all three) were in junior high school and doing very well. I now had another baby and she was perfect. (I didn't have a drink, not one, during this pregnancy. All the public information regarding fetal alcohol syndrome was being ballyhooed on T.V., radio, etc.) After she was born I tried so hard to control the amount, the times, and the location of my drinking. Since I hadn't had a drink for nine months, I decided I wasn't an alcoholic. I drank again. I think in nine weeks' time I made up for nine months of sobriety. I helped to build a new house, moved into it, took care of three adolescents and a new baby and I was tipsy, drunk, or in a blackout all the time. My booze increased from a pint to a fifth to a quart bottle each and every day. Like a baby, I took a bottle to bed every night.

I remember one day about 1 p.m. I called A.A. and a man answered. I told him, "I'm an alcoholic." I cried saying those words. They meant I had no will power. They meant I would end up in the gutter. They meant I was less than human. I wept. The man asked me if I could come to the "center." I told him "no" because I had a baby napping. He then asked if he and another man could come to the house. I hung up. Two strange men coming to *my* house when I was alone confirmed my trip to the gutter. I definitely needed a drink to get through that one!! (Even as I write all this, I feel there is pain, a heavy weight, a feeling deep inside me, a lump in my throat. All the pain resurfaces and again I cry.)

I knew the older kids knew. Sometimes I saw it in their questioning glances. At times I felt guilty, at other times hostile and flaming angry, and at other times I just didn't care.

I went to soccer, basketball, tennis games, plays, teacher conferences. I did it all and I remember very little.

I had always been a very patient type of person. Suddenly I had patience with nothing and nobody. I couldn't, wouldn't put up with the least frustration. I refused to wait in lines or waiting rooms. I took to leaving my shopping cart piled high with food at the supermarket's checkout counter if I thought the line was too long. I walked out of the doctor's office if I had to wait more than a few minutes. Like it or not, sometimes I had to wait, for example at the bank to cash a check. Those times I would yell and make a scene. I remember ranting at bank tellers a lot and more than once at various bank officers.

Life was like that whenever I left the house, as if I had become infected by a mania serum. Suddenly I couldn't sit or stand still. I felt like I had to be in constant frenetic motion. The crazy frenzy left me as soon as I came back home, back to my sedative.

What finally pushed me to go to the center was a confrontation I had with Marty. I was to stop drinking or leave because, "you're drinking is ruining this family and I won't let that happen," he said. I went to a motel that night. The next day I returned home to get clothes and to plead with him. I told him that I had really tried to stop but couldn't. He told me he would do anything to help me. Right then I knew I had all the support I would ever need. I called the center.

The "center" was located in the worst section of town. I was definitely *not* from the worse section. I couldn't conceive of walking on that street, let alone into a building on that street. How strange my thinking was at that time. I didn't think anyone knew I was a drunk and, at the same time, I knew they knew. When I walked into the center, I wasn't saved. It took several months. Finally my non-drinking alcoholic counselor asked me to take Antabuse. I knew I couldn't get through one day without a drink so he asked me not to drink for at least eight hours. When I went that day, I lied and said it had been eight hours since I drank. He warned me that, if any physical symptoms occurred, he would rush me to the hospital. The one and only hospital in our small town. I knew if I swallowed that half pill and if I had to go to the emergency room, everyone in town would know that I was a drunk. I remember hesitating. Wanting to say, "Let me die." "Don't take me there." Instead I popped the pill and swallowed it. Immediately I wished I hadn't. I was a coward. I was sick and tired of living but very, very scared of dying. I felt like such a nothing that I didn't want anyone to know me. I'd rather be dead than to be known as a drunk. I broke out in a rash, I itched, I sweated, I had trouble breathing, I paced. I got through one day. I almost didn't make it through the night. No big physical reaction, just an overwhelming feeling of anxiety and dread. The center opened at 9 a.m. I flew there at 9:01 a.m. I paced... paced... paced. Day two passed, then day three and four.

What pushed me to finally stop drinking was a major confrontation with my counselor after one of my "slips." He said he knew I was still drinking and soon I would start drinking on the job. (I had gotten a job about three months previously.) I liked my job and the people I met there. One evening I began shaking at work. I couldn't wait to get to my car to have a gulp of gin and I knew my counselor was right. I couldn't keep it at bay any longer. It was a lion devouring me. I had to stop or kill myself. Nobody likes a drunk but everyone feels sorry for a suicide victim. The problem was that I was too scared to die!!

The hardest things for me were to drive by a liquor store and to live through the nights. I knew where every liquor store was located. I clenched the car's steering wheel every time I drove by one. About three weeks after practically living at the center, I drove by a liquor store and I didn't realize it was looming there in the corner of my eye. You know what I wanted to do? I wanted to stop the car in the middle of this busy street, jump out, and yell to the whole town, "Free at last! Oh, my God, I'm free at last."

About one year after I had stopped drinking I came home from work in a very silly mood. My elder 17-year-old daughter very cautiously asked if I was drinking again. I was furious with her, and it hurt inside me. This episode was a milestone. I realized I had hurt many other people and also that it would take a long time, maybe forever, for my family to forgive and to trust me. But it was my own doing that caused the suspicion. It may never happen, nevertheless it was worth trying to recapture their esteem and love.

Much of my life is forgotten. The early years were lost by fear, the middle years by booze. Perhaps the later years I'll remember because I'm loving again. I remember stating earlier that saying "I am an alcoholic" meant many negative things. Now I'm *mostly* glad that it happened. I'm a much better human being because of it. I'll tell you something though. I wish I could have learned from a dream instead of from a nightmare. I have been 11 plus years without booze. It just dawned on me, learning by living is the best.

Points to Ponder

1. What can you say about the relationship of emotional deprivation during childhood and the development of alcoholism. Why might it be true for some and not others? Are women more vulnerable to the relationship than men?

2. What is the significance of taking a bottle to bed?

3. What can you say about this woman's view that she had tripped to the gutter because two strange men might be coming to her home?

4. Do you think this woman's fear of dying was a boon or a detriment to her recovery?

5. Do you believe that this woman's views of herself are healthy now? Would you bet that she stays on the recovery road? Why? Why not?

Jane

I was married right out of high school. And I was married because I was pregnant. In those days a girl who become pregnant and wasn't married got married or committed suicide. In a town that was 50% Irish, 50% French-Canadian and 100% Catholic, abortion was not even a topic of conversation let alone an alternative. Good girls never got into trouble. And if they did, they got married, of course. That was the viable alternative because it was the only respectable one. Those were the 1950s. Life was very simple then. Black and white. There were no grays.

For 18 years I lived under my father's rule. Then I married John and lived under his. He was only 22 but he was responsible. He had to be. He insisted on marrying me. I don't know if everybody knew I was pregnant on my wedding day, but I sure thought they did, and if they didn't, they sure knew when Karen was born. It wasn't especially hard to visualize them all counting on their fingers with positive glee because she came about three weeks early and only six and a half months after my wedding.

What bothered me most about all of it was that everybody — my father, my mother, all my friends and even John, maybe especially John, made me feel stigmatized, like it was all my fault.

Ch 5 Cases: What It Means to Be an Alcoholic Woman 103

Nobody said that, of course, but they all communicated it with their arrogant know-it-all smiles—sometimes accusatory occasionally pitying and always condemnatory. I grew up expecting my wedding day to be the happiest of days, if not, the happiest of my life. It was something less than that probably because for every day preparing for it I had been literally marinating in guilt.

We were married. And while I don't want to belabor the point, but it needs to be said, because it was so unfortunate and so characteristic of the unfairness of the lives of women like me of my generation. It's this. John and I were never equals. He was always in charge of our relationship. And it was because of the guilt I felt and carried for being pregnant. I was subservient to him, and I, myself, felt like I deserved to be because I had not been pure enough morally, or at least, I had not kept rein on my emotions that I could have kept. The conventional wisdom in the 1950s, and that's the best way to put it, because everybody *knew* that girls were *different* from boys, was that girls were expected to keep a lid on their emotions. Emotions was the euphemistic word for "sex drive." Everybody "knew" that they could keep that lid on because, "they were made so that they could." "Boys were made different and couldn't help themselves." I can still hear our high school gym teacher saying those words, probably because she said them at least once a month for every one of the four years I had her. Every time she said them, she gave me the distinct impression that she would have taken it personally had I become pregnant. Sounds crazy, huh? Not so crazy, because she walked right by me with a mean stare when I was pushing my new baby in a carriage on Main Street. I mention all this because I need to remind myself that my reality was an accurate reality, that I wasn't crazy.

Anyway we got married and went to live with his parents. John had just graduated from college and went to work with his father who had a small insurance agency. We went to live with his parents, I was told, so that we could save money to buy a house. Money is another sore spot with me. All my life with my father I had it doled over to me. I got married and it was doled out by my husband. I never had it. He made such an issue about it that I was terrified to spend any, especially on myself. I've come to realize that money's important. I suppose it became an issue for me because it's more than a symbol of power. It's power. Like I said. I never had any.

My life before marriage and during never did much to make me feel good about myself, to give me any kind of a self-esteem. One of the things I learned in treatment is that a low self-esteem is common among alcoholics. Well, during my marriage, I had to be among the most common of the common. Sometimes I still get very angry about it all. I did then because I began to realize that a major reason for me thinking so little about me was because I never had a chance to do anything, learn anything, be anything, achieve anything in my own eyes to make me feel proud of me. I tried to express something about this once to my husband. He followed his usual verbal routine with me telling me first that I was crazy then trying to bolster my spirits by pointing out that I was married and lived in a beautiful house and had my own car, that *really* I had everything that I could possibly want. The problem with his method of bolstering was that he always finished up the same way, with the same line "And you never even had to work for it!" And there precisely was the rub.

Once I read that our society makes people on welfare feel inadequate and very guilty, that's exactly how I came to feel after living 24 years as a housewife and mother. Actually I didn't *live* during those 24 years, I only increased in chronological age. I certainly did not grow. I felt victimized.

If there's a reason I became alcoholic, it's because of that feeling of victimization. My nice, neat, respectable life had made me feel like a zero. As with most human phenomena there's probably a process in becoming a zero. For me it was positively insidious because, it was so gradual, it was imperceptible. Paradoxically, alcohol masked and, at the same time, facilitated the process.

Like most alcoholics, I didn't even know I was one until I was. I was 30 years old before I realized that I had any kind of a problem. I'd gone to the kitchen to get a drink when I found the vodka bottle empty. I looked at the clock. It was nine-thirty in the morning. Right then I realized what I had become and verbalized it aloud to the empty bottle "My God I'm an alcoholic!" My realization did not hinder or alter my activity, however. The only thing that my new found realization did was to make my drinking more secretive, my public drinking behavior more normal. I couldn't let anybody find out, anybody at all. My terror, my only terror, was that I would be discovered.

From that day on I was careful not to have more than three drinks at a party. I read where alcoholic types drank more quickly than others so I paced myself to sip my drinks more slowly. At dinner parties I refused wine with dinner. All this game playing didn't reduce my consumption of alcohol. Quite the contrary, it increased it. It increased because after we got home and to bed I'd wait for John to get to sleep and I'd get up and drink myself into a stupor. I did that for years without his discovering me.

There were times I thought I'd be discovered, like the time he took the trash out to the curb and found three empty bottles. When he asked me about them, I shrugged and explained that I'd been careless and let them collect in the liquor cabinet. He gave me a knowing grimace, me and carelessness, it said, were a close couple with which he was very familiar.

From that point on, I was super careful not to leave any tell tale signs. Even if I had, I doubt that he would have noticed. We notice what we want to and John had stopped wanting to notice long ago and in fact, right after our children moved out. It doesn't do too much for a woman's self-esteem when her husband doesn't show any interest in her. His lack of interest included moving out of our bedroom. He moved out of it and I moved in the booze. I turned the little shoe closet next to my bed into a bar and drank myself into a stupor every night.

Within a month from the day he moved out of our bedroom, he moved out of the house and, less than a week after that, I was served with divorce papers. The deputy sheriff handing me those papers was the act which precipitated my recovery from alcoholism and the beginning of my growth as a woman and as a human being.

That very night I went to my first A.A. meeting. There I met women who talked like I thought and who listened and who *didn't judge*.

Summer began the 21st of the following month and that's the day I began my college education. Today I teach English in a Community College.

From A.A., my therapy, and my brain I learned that my alcoholism was caused by a combination of many things not the least of which was the fact that until I was divorced I had been steeped in a life of no choices. When that deputy served me those papers, he served me the ticket to a new life.

Points to Ponder

1. Do you think Jane contributed to the problems of her marriage? If so how?

2. Could Jane have done anything to elevate her self-esteem? If so what?

3. Do you believe Jane was a victim? Explain.

4. What does secretive behavior do to one's perception of self? To one's perception of others?

5. Explain what you think Jane meant by being "steeped in a life of no choices."

Wendy

Joe Perez asked me to write this seven weeks ago. I'm doing it now, at last. I mention this only because that's part of me too, part of the syndrome or at least my syndrome, my procrastination. It's gotten worse over the past couple of years, of that I'm sure.

Let me introduce myself. My name is Wendy. (It really isn't; I prefer to be anonymous). Unlike my name, this story is true, tragically, pathetically true and at the same time very banal. Even so, in this very sober moment I want to share it. I want to see this in print. It's been a while since anything I've written has been published. The irony is that alcohol is the reason for that and it's about that that I'm writing.

I was introducing myself. I'm 42 years old and I'm single, never been married. I have a Ph.D. in political science. I was born and reared in northern Illinois, on a farm. My father was a farmer, still is. My mother could best be described as one too. She works just as hard as he does and both in and out of the house. No brothers or sisters. I was an only child, the only one they ever had or wanted to or could. I don't know the why of it. It wasn't ever the kind of thing they would or could or ever did discuss with me. Once as a little girl I asked my mother why I didn't have any brothers or sisters and if I was ever going to. She didn't reply, just gave me a look that combined surprise with embarrassment. I never asked her again. Right then I learned that any topic even remotely related to sex was verboten. Actually conversation was not the most common of commodities in our house. Work was. Both my parents worked all the time. Surprisingly, they never even asked me to contribute. From my earliest recollections, all I was ever expected to do was to take care of me and mine, my person, my clothes, and my room.

We met for supper every night, eight o'clock in the summer, five o'clock in the winter. Mother did all the cooking. In the summer she did it at night so she could work out-of-doors during the day. We'd have the meal the next day warmed over. Conversation was not a side-order. We ate in quiet. My father never commented on the quality of the food or the cooking. I never thought to. I still never think to when I eat today.

Growing up on a farm, a child is alone. The most exciting part of my life was school. I loved it. I loved it from the first day. I took to it naturally. What I really took to was reading. Life began for me when I learned to do it. I don't remember learning. It was early I guess. I read all the time. I came home from school with a new book every day. I had read virtually every book there was in our elementary school library before I had finished the sixth grade. The only time I remember pestering my mother about anything was about taking me to the library. I always took out the maximum number of books, which was five. I used the word pestering, actually I only had to do it for a short time, during the first week of summer vacation because, once I got them out, I could have them for only two weeks. After that there was a fine. My parents, especially my father would never have brooked paying a fine for a late book. Funny, he never said that but I knew it. As a very little girl I knew that. What kind of a man was, is, he? The words that best describe him are *taciturn* and *work ethic personified*. I never remember my father sick. I can't recollect seeing him ever in a horizontal position. My father worked *all the time*. He never talked. He did figure. He figured a lot. Most nights he sat in the kitchen and went over accounts. I can still see him bent over the table, brow furrowed, adding up long columns. Growing up I had the impression and again, not because of anything he said, because he never said anything, that he was always on the verge of losing the farm. He hasn't. He's still on it with my mother.

His whole life was dedicated to the farm. My mother's was too. At the same time, I don't have the impression that they were much dedicated to each other. We never had fun together. As a family we never went anywhere, not even church. I don't remember belonging to any church. On Sundays they worked, both of them.

No one ever came to visit us. Once some relative cousins did come. I remember them only dimly, probably because we never visited them back. My parents had no friends. And I never had any either, probably because I never knew how to make any.

As a child and as a teen my life was all about reading. I read *War and Peace* before I had finished fifth grade. All that reading helped me get straight A's in school, a National Merit Scholarship, free entry to the University and ultimately my Ph.D. Neither parent ever took much interest in any of my achievements. When I think about it, and I do, I always come down to asking myself why did they bother to have me?

They never beat me or abused me. They were just indifferent to me. Had I not had books I might have gone crazy or been like them. Actually, maybe I did go crazy. I am odd. I should feel very lonely. I have no friends, not even one, but I'm not, I'm not lonely. In fact I like being alone. Odd, eh?

I guess I am like them in that I like being alone. The one way I'm not, is that I like alcohol. They never drank. There was none in my house. Not that either one ever spoke against it or about it. They were indifferent toward it, just like they were toward me.

I had my first drink in college, at a mixer during my freshman orientation. And I loved it! It was a screwdriver. Actually I don't remember buying alcohol; I didn't drink seriously until I got to graduate school. Roommates do not permit for privacy and drinking for me is a private matter. In grad school I roomed alone and that's when I started buying my booze.

I drink alcohol every day, sometimes as much as a fifth of vodka, sometimes as little as a half of a cup. It all depends on what's going on professionally. I drink a lot more when school's not in session than when it is. Most people would say I'm alcoholic. I know Joe Perez thinks so. That's why he asked me to write this. *Alcoholic* is a term, a label. I refuse to be labeled. Like most human beings, I can't be because I'm too complicated. I enjoy alcohol and I'm not about to give it up. I do not *want* to. I see no reason to.

In therapy with Perez I examined my life. And I don't see where alcohol has hurt it much. We talked mostly about me being divorced from people, socially, and I am, but I was long before I ever drank.

I can't for the life of me see how drinking has hurt me. Alcohol may have cut into my publications production but the truth is I've had more articles published than any other member of my department and at 32 was the youngest woman promoted to full professor in the history of the school. Big deal. Who cares, really?

The one thing that alcohol might have done to me is to make me into a procrastinator. But what I've learned is that everyone procrastinates a little and a whole lot of people do a whole lot.

Anyway, I drink, and I'm not going to stop, at least now, because I enjoy it.

Author's Addendum

Wendy's story had to be transcribed by me as it was taped. The transcription was more difficult than most because she spoke even more rapidly than is her usual wont. The talk needed more editing than the other four stories combined as it was quite disjointed. My strong impression is that Wendy was more than a little under the influence when she taped.

Some points that Wendy did not include can be edifying. She was a self-referred client who saw me only four times in therapy and terminated. She is quite pretty. Auburn haired, round-faced, she's approximately 5'5" tall, slim and has a better than average figure. Wendy gives the impression of not being aware of her good looks, or, maybe like her parents, she's indifferent to the fact.

Points to Ponder

1. What are the most glaring indications that Wendy is indeed alcoholic?

2. Do you think that at some point she will want to stop drinking? Why? Why not?

3. What of the facts she related do you think were most conducive for structuring for her taking to drink?

4. What if anything do you read into the fact that she talked more about her father than her mother?

5. Wendy said she was not lonely. What do you think?

Betsy

My name is Betsy, I am an alcoholic/addict. For me there really is no difference between the two, I am addicted to ANY chemical that will change the way I feel. I make a distinction only to remind myself of that fact.

I grew up in an alcoholic home. My dad was a drunk, but it was not just my dad's drinking that was a problem. My family's reaction to it was probably more damaging to me. All my life I was taught to ignore problems, hide feelings, and never show anger. At the age of 11, my dad, whom I idolized, left us. Combined with the onset of puberty and my emotional turmoil this proved too much for me and I picked up my first drink.

From the first drink, I drank alcoholically; that is, I always drank to change the way I felt. There was never a time when I took a "social drink," in fact that never even made sense to me. I could never relate to anyone who left a half a drink on the table or went home before the bars closed.

My mother was, and still is to some extent, a person who "takes care" of others. I was the oldest child and the only girl and somewhere deep inside me is the notion that I am supposed to be like her, the nurturer and caretaker, and always putting my needs last. When I began to drink and drug however, my selfishness took precedence and I rebelled strongly against that attitude. In fact I tried very hard to be "one of the guys," I didn't cook or clean, I could fix cars and talk about sports, but most of all I could drink like them. Oddly enough, this attitude was a turn on for a lot of males, and consequently I was always involved in a relationship. Of course most of these men were as sick as I was, but I did not know that at the time.

In my early teens, my relationships were extremely emotional. I felt incomplete without a boyfriend. My drinking and drug usage began to escalate. I was using at least every weekend if not more often. I always felt different, scared, and alone.

At the age of 16, I found myself pregnant, and, after much debate, my mother finally talked me into an abortion. Although I see this in a different light today, at the time it was absolutely traumatic. I believed, as many inexperienced teenagers do, that having a baby would solve my problems and be the answer to my emotional needs. We went to New York where a saline was performed. When I got home, I began to rebel even more. I quit high school and spent all my time in Harvard Square getting high and selling drugs. I began to construct walls that imprisoned my feelings. My relationships began to reflect this in that I became more self-centered and, even though I still had to be in a relationship all the time, I no longer let myself become dependent or too involved. I did have a long relationship with a man who was "healthy," but eventually my disease got in the way and destroyed what we had.

In my early 20s, I began to experiment with cocaine. Although I had tried a variety of drugs, and would use whatever was available, my choices were alcohol, speed, and pot. At this time (early 70s) coke was just beginning to become popular but it was very expensive. My usage was limited by the price.

At the age of 23, I met a man and decided to get married. I then found myself pregnant again, so we eloped. His mother never got over this, and my relationship with her was never good. I had my daughter, we bought a house, and I even learned to cook! But we were both sick and we started to deal cocaine. I began to abuse it while my husband used other drugs. Our relationship began to deteriorate, but, before it reached any kind of climax, my husband was killed in a gun accident.

I was 25 years old with an 18-month-old daughter, a strong cocaine addiction already, and a huge insurance settlement. I was absolutely overwhelmed by my feelings of loss, anger, and guilt. Then I discovered that this tragedy was everyone's excuse for my behavior; I could do anything and be excused for it. This was all I needed to let my self-pity and self-centeredness take control. I began to use coke and alcohol daily for about the next two years. Finally one of my brothers came to me and said I needed help. I knew I did because I had run out of money. I went to a 12 step program where it was suggested that I stop drinking as well as drugging. At the time this was impossible for me to comprehend; after all, I just wanted to learn how to control my drug usage, not become a saint!

My only solution to my problem of no more money was to start dealing again, which I did. I also learned how to freebase (smoke cocaine) and this was the beginning of the end for me. For about two more years I was doing about $2,000 worth of coke a week. My life became totally insane; all I did was buy, sell, and do drugs. I neglected my daughter and my house, I lived with weapons and my associates were all drug addicts or criminals (mostly both). I could not see that there was anything wrong with

Ch 5 Cases: What It Means to Be an Alcoholic Woman 113

the way I was living. Eventually, I got to a point where I knew I would die but I did not care. At least I would die high.

By now my daughter was 5 years old and I was not even attempting to hide anything from her. She called my mother-in-law and told her that "mommy was doing drugs and needed help." Luckily my mother-in-law did not try to handle me herself. At this point I probably would have tried to hurt her. Instead she called my family and my mother came to my house. I remember her walking up the stairs and standing in the doorway; she told me it was time to do something. I can't explain what happened except that I felt an overwhelming relief and a desire to change. I went to the same treatment facility that my dad had gone to. At the time of admission, I was addicted to cocaine, alcohol, and valium.

That was January 14, 1986; through the grace of God I have been sober ever since. I believe that is because of my willingness to do whatever was necessary to stay sober especially in terms of developing spiritually. I had to develop a concept of God that I could live with and trust in that power.

I have received many gifts from sobriety, including a relationship with someone I met in treatment and another daughter. I graduated from college and received a graduate assistantship to do a master's. Today I can set goals and accomplish them without drugs and alcohol getting in the way. There are still some things that I work on however. One thing I've discovered in sobriety is that the only role model I really had for how females should behave is my mother. As a result I often feel like "super mom" being all things for all people and often get resentful about it. Part of me wants to make up for all those years of selfishness but part of me sees this as a stereotypical role that I am probably grooming my own daughters for. This disease and these attitudes are being handed down from generation to generation and I want to break the cycle. It is hard to find that balance between rebel and doormat, but, I know that if I pray for the courage to change the things I can, it can be done.

Points to Ponder

1. Consider the effect of a father's desertion on the conscience development of an 11-year-old girl.

2. Why do you think that Betsy began to rebel even more after her abortion?

3. What can you offer as an explanation for Betsy's overwhelming relief and desire to change effective 14 January 1986?

4. What are some of the ingredients for Betsy's resentment about playing the role of "supermom"?

5. Consider, do you believe that this woman is grooming her own daughters for a stereotypical feminine role?

Part **III**
TREATMENT

118 *Counseling the Alcoholic Woman*

Chapter 6

THEORETICAL CONCERNS

THE THERAPIST

How effectively counseling proceeds will be determined in considerable measure by the therapist. The question has been raised as to whether or not a male therapist can function as effectively as a female therapist can with the woman client. Harriet Lerner has outlined the reasons a female therapist can function more effectively (Lerner, 1988, pp. 136-138). A summary of those reasons follow.

1. Openness, especially as regards sexual experience, self, and stereotypical feminine behavior.

2. Sexual involvement is obviated.

3. Enhancement for the client via identification with the female therapist's achievements, competence and skills.

4. "Women's Issues" are more effectively dealt with by women.

5. Unresolved issues of a maternal nature can be more deeply and richly explored with a female therapist and can be more effectively explored with a female therapist.

6. Acceptance and acknowledgment of one's worth by a female therapist can be especially significant and profitable.

7. Possibilities for sexual identification are increased with the same sex therapist.

Each of the above reasons for picking a female over a male could just as easily be the reasons for picking a male over a female. Thus:

1. A woman may feel more comfortable discussing sexual issues with a man rather than a woman.

2. A woman may feel that "sexualization" of the relationship facilitates rather than blocks learning.

3. A woman who has anxieties about her own achievements may indeed be threatened, even feel inadequate, precisely because of the female therapist's achievements, competence, and skills.

4. A woman who has concerns about "women's issues" and feminine role may be just as easily hurt as helped by the female therapist who has her own concerns and agenda in these areas.

5. A woman may be just as easily blocked as facilitated on issues dealing with "mother" by the female therapist precisely because a woman in the role of therapist can facilitate being perceived as a mother.

6. A woman feeling acceptance by another woman is sometimes not as important as her feeling acceptance by a man.

7. For the woman who has sexual identity problems, a male therapist may facilitate resolution of her anxieties in relating to the opposite sex.

This author's conviction is that how effectively counseling proceeds will be determined by the *competence* of the counselor. Competence, quite obviously, is not a function of gender. Lerner herself noted that "...being male does not condemn one to tunnel vision or to a rigid and unexamined adherence to patriarchal attitudes. Nor does being female guarantee one's freedom from unconscious biases and prejudices against women" (Lerner, 1988, p. 139).

Sex bias of women clients by male counselors in counseling does occur. Of that there is little doubt and has been so researched and observed (Smith, 1980; Schaefer, 1984). Professional hand-wringing and soul-searching will accomplish little to rectify it. What will accomplish more is to research what qualities make an effective alcoholism counselor. These were outlined in a previous work by the author (Perez, 1992, pp. 115-138). The qualities considered were personal and professional and were found to be melded together.

Personal and Professional Qualities

1. The motivation to grow and learn

2. The ability to find reward in serving another person

3. A healthy perception of alcohol

4. An optimistic expectation of client success

5. A penchant for nurturance and truly liking others

6. A disposition for empathy

7. An exquisite ethical awareness of personal conduct with clients

8. Self-awareness as to competency, attitudes, prejudice, and limitations

9. Maturity, flexibility, respect for clients, and intuitiveness

10. The ability to listen and communicate

A TRAINING PROGRAM

To be an effective counselor with the alcoholic woman, a counselor needs to have training. Effective programs are those which include both theory and practice. In addition, potential applicants should be assessed to determine their current levels of functioning. Even for very well qualified counselors an assessment period would be ultimately beneficial to both the trainee and the institution he or she serves. Criteria and length of training would be determined by needs of the setting. Ideally the program would be counselor centered and its curriculum and length determined by the counselor's performance.

Stage One—Theory

Readings, discussion, and assessment in the following areas:

- Personality Theories—Freud, Jung, Adler, and Rogers
- Abnormal Psychology
- The Alcoholic Personality: Male and Female
- Sound Psychology with the Focus on Women's Issues
- Selected Themes and Techniques of Counseling
- Women and Mental Health
- Group Dynamics

Stage Two—Practice

This period could begin concurrently with Stage One or many weeks after the onset of Stage One. The variable would be the entering level of trainee sophistication in Stage One.

Purposes of Stage One are two-fold:

- To increase the trainee's own sense of awareness
- To teach her/him counseling skills

Accordingly, at Stage Two experiences would include:

- Doing individual counseling via videotape. If this is not possible, then by tape recorder. Recordings would be discussed with a mentor supervisor.
- Role-playing with a mentor supervisor. The trainee would alternate roles between the alcoholic client and the counselor.
- Working as a co-facilitator with a staff member experienced in group dynamics.

SOME THOUGHTS TO THE NEW COUNSELOR OF ALCOHOLIC WOMEN

Counseling is a very personal and private enterprise. To a very great extent it is a function of personality. How it is done finally is up to you, the particular therapist.

The foregoing research findings, theoretical positions, and explanations are presented for your critical examination. What implications they have for you and your counseling is dependent upon you. Quite apparently, they can be accepted and injected into your developing counseling system or they can be rejected out of hand—your choice. The ultimate criteria for what you accept or reject has to be what fits and works for you. For in your counseling, *you are the ultimate technique*. This is a heavy responsibility because for your client, at least, you are the personification of the counseling process.

To live up to your client's expectations and more importantly, to your own, you will need to strive for excellence. Striving for excellence in counseling is a life-long process and it involves constant self-examination. If you are going to strive for excellence in your work, you will need to operate from a solid frame of reference so that you will be able to articulate to yourself and, if need be, to others your philosophy of counseling process.

The following list of questions are intended as guidelines to help you develop a general philosophy of counseling not only to work with the alcoholic woman but others too.

1. What is your definition of counseling?
2. How would you define your role as a counselor?
3. What are the most important functions of a counselor?
4. What are the personal qualities that make a competent counselor?
5. What makes a counselor's excellence? What distinguishes a mediocre from an outstanding counselor?
6. What are your central values? How do they influence you as a counselor?

7. What are your beliefs and attitudes about
   a. the contemporary woman?
   b. abortion, marriage, alternate lifestyles?
   c. neglect of children, the aged, and addictions (not only alcohol)?
8. How can your position on any of the items in Number 7 help or hinder your work?
9. How would you define or describe "the good life"?
10. What needs do you meet as a counselor?
11. How do you view your level of functioning? Why do you think you can be of value assisting others in resolving their emotional struggles?

As noted, the effective counselor is the one who finds reward in serving another person. Unfortunately this valuable quality sometimes becomes warped in the new counselor by a Florence Nightingale—like zeal and expectation that he or she will cure all clients.

If you are a new counselor, be informed that *no cure* exists in any treatment program for alcoholism. However, a recovery process is available via counseling. Recovery is possible, however, only if the alcoholic woman stops drinking. *Stopping is done by the client*, never by the counselor. Two basic truths in alcoholism counseling are

1. no one ever made anyone alcoholic, and

2. no one can make anyone stop drinking alcoholically.

The reality of sobriety is that it is a function of *choice* and choice can be determined only by the client. Lectures, badgering, condescension, brilliant logic, and/or emotionally charged pep talks by the counselor will not make a woman stop drinking if she is not ready to do so. Finally, she will stop only if she chooses to.

As many reasons exist as to why alcoholics stop drinking as there are alcoholics. All these reasons, however, have a common denominator. They are all born out of a sense of desperation.

THE "BOTTOM" — THE BEGINNING OF TREATMENT

In Chapter 1 under *Self-surrender*, the phenomena of the "bottom" was defined. The reader might find a quick rereading of that section helpful here.

The bottom can be understood as occurring at different levels—*high, middle,* and *low.* A woman "bottoms out" when she finds that a drink no longer provides any solution for her desperation. At this junction most women perceive only two alternatives—death or treatment. At this point is when some women will attempt suicide, in most cases half-heartedly, via overdoses of prescribed medication or in a few cases, violently, i.e., wrist slashing.

Each alcoholic arrives at her "bottom" differently and for different reasons. For example, the middle class housewife and mother who is still very much intact emotionally and still has much materially may find a sarcastic comment about her excessive drinking by a close friend to be the catalyst that precipitates self-referral into treatment—a "high bottom."

The "low bottom" may be exemplified by the woman who came into treatment with me via the state hospital, where she had awakened in a detoxification ward, "loaded up" on thorazine because she had been violent on admission. June was 38 years old and a former teacher who had lost her job because of her drinking. In the course of her journey into the snake-pit of alcoholism, she had lost her spouse, her children, and all her material possessions. She's been in recovery now for almost five years.

While the level and nature of the "bottom" varies with the woman, it always embraces her entire dynamic system. Perception, defenses, and values are always affected. Despite these variances a common denominator prevails for all women at "the bottom"—it is the beginning of treatment.

Only when alcoholic women experience their private "bottom" (please note, not all do) can they appreciate their own cry, "Help me!". It is only when the woman says to the counselor "help me" with emotional conviction and commitment and when the counselor is able to believe her emotionally and cognitively, only then is she able to start the psychotherapeutic journey to sustained recovery.

Some women are not good candidates for psychotherapy. These include

- the hard core sociopath who is incapable of trust (The socialization process makes for very few of these);

- the person afflicted with Korsadoff's syndrome, i.e., a psychosis that is usually based on chronic alcoholism, and which is accompanied by disturbance of orientation, susceptibility to external stimulation and suggestion, falsification of memory, and hallucinations;

- the woman who is so deficient intellectually that she cannot retain cognitive or affective meaning from session to session; and/or

- the psychotic woman.

Such women are the exception. This therapist's experience is that "bottomed out" women can profit and mightily, from emotional self-examination via psychotherapy. How effectively this self-examination is conducted will be a function of the counselor's technique and skill. Chapter 7 addresses these concerns.

GOALS

Goals have traditionally been the basic issue in counseling. Wolberg (1954) believed that they are critically important because the process of failure of the counseling can be assessed only in terms of the understood objectives. Patterson (1963) believed that the general goal of counseling is for the client to become "responsible, independent, and self-actualizing." Rogers (1961) believed that the prime purpose of counseling is to help clients become "more similar to the idea which he/she has chosen." Kanner (1963) believed that the goals which best served children in counseling were those designed to "relieve, relate, release, relearn, and relax." On reflection these last seem especially appropriate for the alcoholic woman.

Primary Goal

The primary goal in counseling for the alcoholic woman is maintenance of her continued sobriety. The code word in this statement is *continued.* What needs to be borne in mind is that the woman has stopped drinking and you, the counselor, must know it—not only in your head but in your heart, too. If you have any doubt, confront her. If after confrontation you still are uncomfortable with her, you should consider termination of treatment. Why? Because to continue to see a client in alcoholism counseling who is still drinking is to be sucked into her dynamics of alcoholism. You, the counselor, become part of her problem because you the counselor have become her enabler. If she is drinking and seeing you, she can rationalize her drinking to herself, to others, even to you the counselor. "I'm doing the best I can. I'm seeing my counselor!"

In addition to the primary goal there are secondary ones. These are important because they facilitate the process toward the primary one and equally important, help the woman adhere to the primary goal.

Secondary Goals

1. *To help the woman learn as much as possible about alcoholism.* For the motivated client this is achieved fairly easily because the objective is primarily cooperative in nature. Regular attendance at A.A. meetings is basic of course. Readings, discussions with the counselor and others, lectures, and seminars are helpful.

2. *To help the woman restructure her perception both of self and of her environment.* The focus of this effort would be to help the woman understand and come to grips with her sense of victimization about her womaness, to support her view that there may indeed be much truth, much reality in her feeling put down and demeaned by people, events, and situations in her life. The counselor can help her

Ch 6 Theoretical Concerns 127

become aware that she may herself have contributed to her sense of victimization by her own attitudes, values, and behaviors. Once she comes to appreciate emotionally that you the counselor can empathize with her, she will naturally move on to understand that finally, *sans alcohol,* she is and can be in control of her life. She doesn't have to be a victim anymore, of alcohol or of society either, if she chooses not to be.

3. *To help the woman structure her life so that she may learn to find reward in sharing and giving.* This counselor usually has found this goal to be the first one achieved. Women, probably because of the socialization process, can and want to give and share. Indeed, alcoholics, men included, almost instinctively seem to find that their future health and well being lie in giving to others by sharing their stories of alcoholism with them. Much complementary support to achieve this goal comes from A.A. Indeed, this is the very premise upon which it is structured.

4. *To help the woman gain insight into those defenses which slow down, impede her full recovery, or tend to slide her into a relapse.* Most often these include denial, rationalization, projection, and intellectualization.

5. *To help the woman evaluate her self-esteem by helping her to come to appreciate emotionally that failure is part of the human experience.* This evaluation is ongoing. An important aspect of it involves helping her to structure her life for vocational and interpersonal experiences where there is a high probability of success. The cornerstone of the alcoholic woman's self-esteem is continued sobriety and she knows that. More often than not with that knowledge, because of it, she lives with a constant, latent anxiety that she will relapse.

Periodic Reevaluation of Sobriety

The best way to deal with this anxiety of relapse is to help the client discuss feelings and symptoms indicative of the alcoholic woman's latent but constant emotional nemesis, the phenomenon termed BUD, **B**uilding **U**p to **D**rink. These discussions must be interpersonal and concurrent with the pursuit of secondary goals if the primary goal is to be achieved and maintained. The symptoms of BUD often come in combination and are as follows:

- periods of silence in the usually talkative and cheerful woman;

- machine-gun like monologues by the woman who usually speaks deliberately, slowly, quietly;

- uncharacteristic irritability and/or hypomanic-like movements and activity;

- unexplainable, acute fatigue;

- listless, apathetic behavior in the usually active person;

- focus and perseverance on depressed talk; and/or

- euphoric-like overconfidence in the client's talk about how she is adhering to her sobriety.

If the client is unwilling to admit or to discuss these symptoms when the counselor sees her, the client invariably lapses into drink. What this counselor has observed is that symptoms usually become even stronger after the alcoholic begins drinking. In most cases, however, the lapse can be obviated if she is helped to discuss symptoms, both those apparent to the counselor and those felt by her.

The reader might want to complement his/her reading of this section with a rereading of the section entitled Alcoholism—the Relapse, which is in Chapter 4 of this book.

Two Illustrations of Goal Setting

The following two illustrations exemplify approaches to counseling the alcoholic. The first is termed **directivist** and the second, **nondirectivist**. Both counselors are vitally concerned with the client's achievement of sobriety and both leave the responsibility of attaining it to the client but there the similarity ends.

The directivist is assertive, confrontative, at times harsh, and quickly responsive to the client's rationalizations and denials. At times she or he seems even harsher in his or her attack upon those defenses.

Counselor as Directivist.

CO=Counselor   CL=Client

CO: *Oh, Mary, good to see you. Come in, come in and sit.*

CL: *Thanks. I'm sorry I'm late.*

CO: *You were the first time we met, Mary. Are you nervous about seeing me?*

CL: *Maybe, a little.*

CO: *I do appreciate that but being late doesn't make me go away. I presume you still want to see me?*

CL: *I guess.*

CO: (chuckles) *Not sure, eh?*

CL: *I want to see you.*

CO: *There's still not an awful lot of conviction in your tone and I know I'm not the most agreeable of persons. I can be abrasive at times. But I'm here for you Mary and my job is just one, to help you stay sober. You want to stay sober?*

CL: *I wouldn't be here if I didn't. God, I have to.*

CO: *Your words are good words. Important words. But if you were on time, maybe even a little early even, that would show me, more importantly yourself, that you really mean them.*

CL: *I got held up at breakfast.*

CO: (replies softly) *You were late getting there, Mary. You were coming in when I was leaving. Please let's not play any games with each other. As I said yesterday all my cards are on the table. If we're going to make any progress, you and I, yours need to be too.*

CL: *You're saying you want me to be honest.*

CO: *Yes. Did you go to A.A. last night?*

CL: *I did.*

CO: *How much did you read of the book I gave you?*

CL: *About a hundred pages.*

CO: *Very good.* (The counselor asks her questions about the reading.)

CL: *How come all these questions. Don't you trust me?*

CO: (smiles indulgently) *Among us alcoholics, Mary, trust does not come on faith in the person, only on experience with her, and even that's a little of an anxiety trip.*

CL: *Not exactly heartwarming.*

CO: *Mary, it really doesn't matter much if I trust you or not. What matters is that you trust yourself to do all the things you have to do to stay sober, A.A, the readings, sharing with me, and working on the weekends as you are supposed to do.* (Counselor laughs.) *And speaking of trust it would help us both if you trusted me.*

CL: *Why do you badger me?*

CO: *Not badgering. We call it bird-dogging in this center. I'm going to be bird-dogging you 'till you don't need me anymore.*

CL: *I can't conceive of how bird-dogging as you call it is going to help me. That's been my problem all my life. First my mother, then my husband, then my boss, everybody badgers, in fact, everybody shits on me!*

CO: *If they shit on you, it's because you let them. People treat you the way you let them. Mary, it's up to you how they treat you.*

What we saw in this brief excerpt is a very polite but firm counselor who makes it clear to the client what her goal responsibilities are and will be with respect to meeting time, A.A. attendance, readings, and self-disclosure.

Counselor as Nondirectivist. The nondirectivist is verbally reserved. She or he does not give advice, believes rather that the client should decide her own way. The counselor approach is to help the client come to her own realization about the nature of her distorted perception and the futility of feeling abused and of reveling in a sense of victimization. The counselor's focus is on being an emotional helper and on developing a healthful positive relationship.

The reader will decide whether the preceding illustration ("Counselor as Directivist") or the following one is more effective. Which is so perceived will be determined by which one fits with the counselor's personality. Not uncommonly, a counselor incorporates aspects of each approach into his or her counseling.

CO: *Ah, Alice good to see you.*

CL: *Sorry I'm late.*

CO: *Only a few minutes. It happens. These first few sessions make most people a little anxious.*

CL: (Nods) *They do?*

CO: *So what do you want to talk...*

CL: *I went to the meeting. I really enjoyed it. Listening to that speaker made me realize a lot.*

CO: *Tell me.*

CL: *Well, for one thing I've been a bitch to a lot of people for a long time.*

CO: *Haven't we all?*

CL: *What do you mean?*

CO: *Just that all of us from time to time are selfish, petty, we lie, cheat. Those sins aren't peculiar to you.*

CL: *No?*

CO: *No. What matters is where we go from here. The past, Alice, is a canceled check. What matters is the future.*

CL: *I don't see too much of a future; I don't even have a job anymore.*

CO: *You'll get one.*

CL: *I know, but will I be able to keep it?*

CO: *I don't know that. Only you do. Only you can determine that.*

CL: *That scares me. I just don't have any faith in myself for anything, leave alone getting and keeping a job. I mean what am I going to tell them when I apply, that I'm a drunk?*

CO: *You don't want to tell them your a drunk?*

CL: *Heavens no!*

CO: *Hmmm.*

CL: (Laughs) *But I have to, huh?*

CO: *Your decision.*

CL: *How do you tell somebody you're a drunk?*

CO: *Didn't the speaker do just that last night?*

CL: *Yeah, but that was A.A.*

CO: *In front of what, forty, fifty people?*

CL: *Yeah, I get your drift. If she can do it with so many, why can't I with one?*

CO: *You already have. You told me.*

CL: *You knew about me.*

CO: *But this is the first time you actually said it.*

CL: *This is different, you're supposed to understand. It's your job. Besides, you're an alcoholic yourself. How does it make you feel to tell people?*

CO: (Laughs) *Honest. It makes me feel honest.*

CL: *I never feel like that.*

CO: *Well?*

CL: *I should try it, huh?*

CO: *Your choice.*

CL: *Don't you ever give advice?*

CO:(Shakes his head) *Not usually. Life's hard enough without living it according to somebody else's opinion.*

This counselor while he alludes to goals, gives minimal direction, preferring to let the client carry the counseling ball. His focus, if you examine the excerpt, is the relationship and letting the client choose her own way.

RAPPORT

Definition, Research, and Discussion

As in the French language from which the word rapport is borrowed, it, in general, has to do with accord and affinity in a relationship. In counseling, rapport means that warmth and trust exists between the counseling participants, an emotional give and take, critical to counseling. Two researchers found that its establishment inevitably facilitates the resolution of interpersonal problems. At least two studies concluded that if rapport cannot be established, then the client should be referred (Cheng & Hsin, 1973; Katsuhiko, 1969).

Qualities that make for an effective therapist, included previously under the heading "The Therapist," facilitate the establishment of rapport. A rereading of that part of this chapter might be profitable. Axelson (1967) found that the counselor's quality that establishes rapport most quickly and effectively is an *empathic disposition*. Although the word empathy has been used in other contexts a number of times, perhaps taking a closer look at it might be profitable because of its close relationship to rapport. Empathy is derived from the German Einfuhlung which means "feeling into." One of the more complete explanations of the meaning of empathy in counseling was given by Arnold Bucheimer (1961) in an address to the American Personnel and Guidance Association (Name changed July, 1992 to American Counseling Association). In this he described five aspects of empathy.

1. **Tone**, which has to do with harmony and mutuality with which the counselor and client interact;

2. **Pace**, which has to with the timing with which the counselor leads the client;

3. **Flexibility**, which has to do with the counselor's ability to adapt to new climatic moments and ignore and discard previously thought out procedures;

4. **Frame of reference**, which has to do with becoming attuned to and gaining an understanding from where the client is coming and then rephrasing, reflecting, and getting at the essence of what the client is communicating; and

5. **Repertoire of leads**, which has to do with the counselor's ability to respond to both verbal and nonverbal contexts of the client's consent.

One, then, can rightly conclude from Bucheimer's (1961) thoughts that the counselor's ability to establish rapport is closely allied with his or her ability to empathize effectively.

When the client comes for the initial contact, the emotional climate may be strained. This strain is understandable. The client is meeting a stranger with whom she is obligated to share thoughts and feelings which until that moment have been viewed as supremely private. Add to that all the characteristics associated with the alcoholic personality as outlined in Chapter 2 together with the sense of shame and the inhibitory traits acquired via socialization and it becomes transparently clear why the initial moments may be strained. The counselor has the obligation to relax and retrieve the initial strained moments. Some counselors believe that the best approach is to open with a neutral topic like the weather. Others believe the neutral topic approach is a waste as does this author. Counseling finally is not a social chit-chat. Moreover chit-chat sometimes leads to even more tension if the counselor has not developed a more communicative approach. In his or her opening remarks the counselor should focus on why the client is in the counseling office. After the initial greetings and amenities, the counselor may make these kinds of comments, "I'm glad you're here, tell me how I can help." "I'm your counselor. This is your hour." "The fact that you're here tells me that you want to start back to something better."

More often than not the counselor has access to client records regarding background and family. These data should be examined before the first session so that the counselor can ask open-ended questions. Questions about work usually are appropriate, i.e., "I understand you're a nurse practitioner. Tell me what it is like." "I understand you were just promoted to supervisor. How is it different than being on the line?" "You're a teacher, I understand. What is it like?" When delivered with a casual appropriate tone, comments and questions such as these facilitate communication. They are meaningful questions to the client because they are about her and unlike social chit-chat they are forthright because they focus on the reality of the client's presence.

At the same time, recognize clearly that rapport is more than just relaxing a client and getting underway. It transcends the whole process of counseling. It is constant. It continues from initial contact to termination and is characterized by cordiality, confidence, and cooperation. The working relationship between counselor and client is and needs to be unique, far different from most other relationships the client has.

The author asked a directivist and a nondirectivist to express their views on the subject of rapport with an alcoholic woman. Both responses were tape recorded.

Directivist Views of Rapport
Edwin—Male, Forty-one Years Old, Eleven Years an Alcoholic Counselor, and a Recovering Alcoholic

What can I tell ya? I think rapport is important, man or woman. Who would say otherwise? But to be honest with ya, I don't myself focus on it. I focus on the purpose, the goal— sobriety. Rapport has to do with being liked. To be frank with you, I don't care whether my patients like me or not. I'm not running a beauty contest. There's one issue and one issue only —the patient's sobriety.

When a patient, man or woman, comes in to me that first day I tell him or her plain and simple, **"I'm not your nurse maid, I'm not even your friend. I don't know you yet. I am your counselor. I'll help by listening and if asked, I'll answer**

straight forward. I expect the same." I don't like patients who make like they're Spanish athletes, ya know, throw the bull. Only one way a patient can make progress and that's if she is completely honest, right to where it hurts her and hurts badly. Before my patient can do that I gotta' do the same thing. So I do it. I tell him and, if it's a her, I tell her, too, about me and my booze. By the time I'm through, takes about three sessions, I usually have my rapport. At least they know me. And that's where it's at in this game. If you want rapport, patients have gotta feel they know you, before they can trust you. And in this business trust is where it's all at. Once patients trust you, they will let you take the first step with them down that awful long road back to life.

Nondirectivist Views of Rapport
Marietta—Female, Thirty-two Years Old,
Six years as a counselor, the last three with alcoholics,
M.A. in Clinical Psychology

Rapport is critical. It is the foundation of the whole process. Without it, you have no counseling, you can't because you have no trust. Prior to my coming here I worked with mentally handicapped, retarded children. Rapport was so easy with them. They loved me immediately. Even those who had been hurt and abused trusted me almost immediately. But then again, they were children. These are not children, at least not in age. Alcoholics are a jaded and a very clinical lot, both men and women, women especially. What so many women feel today through all this consciousness raising and awareness is that to be a woman is to be used, not just by men but by institutions, by employers, by society. More and more normal women, by that I mean nonalcoholic women, feel like that. Let me just say it, *I* feel like that! Well a woman diseased by alcoholism feels like that ten times over. She's simply just not going to trust a stranger just because he's a counselor. They've learned that they can't trust people in their own families how can they possibly trust and bare their souls with a stranger, man or woman? Anyway, I think it's harder for a woman to trust because of feelings of being used than it is for a man even though, like they say, women need relationships more than men do. It's that need for relationships that finally gets them to trust, I think, to give them a sense of rapport. Once rapport is established they move very fast, faster than men. I think they do because, and I'm not sure of this, but my sense is that when women do bare their souls, they do it even so more profoundly than men because, when finally they come to trust, they trust all the way.

Obstacles to Establishment of Rapport

Some obstacles effectively can block the establishment of rapport. These include

- a lack in counselor's ego strength,
- unmotivated client,
- client's negative perception of counselor, and
- personality clash.

Counselor's Ego Strength. Deficiencies in the counselor's ego can interfere with the establishment of rapport. In counseling she or he does need to have an ego that is strong — strong enough to focus, attend, and adhere to the client. The counselor should be disciplined enough to prevent and block irrelevant and distracting thoughts from interfering with the ability to meet client's needs. In short, when doing therapy, the counselor should be able to keep personal life compartmentalized, and the healthful ego should be in total control of his or her personality.

Unmotivated Client. Sometimes the counselor finds himself or herself with a client who genuinely is not motivated, a client who has not "bottomed out," but who is at best conflicted in his or her self-referral, or, worse, who has been mandated into the therapy, a not uncommon phenomenon, especially with recent drinking and driving legislation.

To establish a meaningful productive rapport under a mandated referral is especially difficult, if not impossible. The length of time for counseling usually is fixed and the client, of course, knows it. More often than not, such clients present themselves as victims. Not uncommonly, they are resentful, hostile, and sometimes do not even try to hide their boredom. At best, such clients attempt to manipulate the counselor by putting on a deferential, even submissive, manner so that they can fulfill their obligations, "serve their time," and get the note for the judge which will let them drive and drink again. Counseling under these conditions is an exercise in futility.

Client's Negative Perception of Counselor. Rapport establishment is often difficult when the client perceives the counselor negatively. This negative perception usually has nothing to do with the counselor's competencies or credentials but has to do with the needs and perception of the client. For example, the counselor may be years, decades, even a generation younger than the client. Under such circumstances the client's view might be, "What can a counselor who's young enough to be my son or daughter do for me?" Or again, the client may be well aware of the fact that some available counselors are recovering alcoholics and such clients are convinced that you, the nonalcoholic counselor, can't help them. Then, of course, as was alluded above under "Nondirectivist Views of Rapport" some women have inordinate difficulty trusting because of feelings of being used. Then again, a woman who has been sexually abused or victimized by incest could have inordinate difficulty relating to a male counselor. The competent, knowledgeable counselor must learn to take situations in stride. Even so, the recommendation is that the counselor should hold several sessions with these women if for no other reason than to assess the situation. If in good conscience the counselor feels rapport establishment will take inordinately long, then the client should be referred to another counselor.

Personality Clash. Sometimes rapport cannot be established because of a personality clash. For the counselor this should be a very rare occurrence indeed. The truth is, however, that counselors also have their own idiosyncratic dynamics. As a result, each counselor will find she or he has difficulty in working with some clients for whatever reasons. Even so, the counselor should be perceptive and honest enough to know the potential for an ineffective relationship by the end of the first session—certainly by the second. Then, after discussing the problems honestly and kindly, the client should be referred. To delay referral will result in communication of a personal rejection later—something no alcoholic needs. Just as bad, delay may result in little or no progress in the counseling.

Counseling Room. The conclusion can be drawn from research that physical setting influences how people perceive each other. In a study by Maslow and Mintz (1956) and another by Mintz (1956), people perceived more optimistically when the room in which they were situated was more attractive. Conversely, they perceived more pessimistically when the room was shabby. On the basis of these studies, time, energy, and money should be invested in making the counseling room attractive and comfortable. Pictures and draperies should be hung, rugs laid, and flowers or plants added. The validity of such efforts is reflected in a study by Chaikin, Derlega, & Miller (1976) who found that the more positively a client perceives the room, the more positively she or he will relate to the counselor. In short, a room decorated with care can only enhance the counseling process.

Haase and DiMattia (1970) did a study to determine what kind of seating arrangement counselors and clients preferred most. The arrangement they found to be the most popular was the one which is used most, the client sitting at the side of the desk. Widgery and Stackpole (1972) found that the position of the desk influences the counselor's credibility. Those clients who were binding much anxiety rated counselor credibility higher when no desk was present. Those with low anxiety rated it higher when a desk was present.

Space. The effect of space upon the counseling process has been investigated. Haase and DiMattia (1976) have found smaller rooms tend to inhibit the length and duration of self-reference talk. In another study, Haase (1970) found that which sex a client is does not influence the distance preferred between counseling participants. Both males and females indicated that between 30 and 39 inches was about right. Research in social and familial settings indicates that this is the distance preferred by spouses and by intimate friends. Interestingly, clients feel that the same kind of distance is best for counseling.

COMMUNICATION

In a previous work the author (Perez, 1979) explored a system of communication which he turned *Avenues of Communication.* What the author has learned in the intervening years is that his approach to an understanding of communication is especially apt for describing the interaction of the alcoholic woman in general and especially within her family. The system, revised and modified in light of his experience, is presented here.

The avenues of communication common to the alcoholic are

1. condemnation,
2. submission,
3. indifference, and
4. congruence.

Condemnation

Condemnation is characterized by an interpersonal stance that is generally demeaning with common aspects of nagging, hypercriticism, and belittling. It is the way of the woman who feels threatened, of the woman who perceives a hostile, threatening world. It is the way of the woman who seeks to distance herself from others. It is the way of the woman who becomes emotionally divorced from her environment. It is a way common to the alcoholic woman.

Women who utilize this avenue a lot have self-esteem problems. Their emotional rationale is that, "I get bigger if I make them smaller." Their interpersonal demeaning style becomes constant and inured, a veritable core aspect of their personality.

Alcoholic women who travel this road are usually rigid. People, problems, and situations are perceived in black and white. The are quite unable to tolerate grays. Even though they have a strong penchant for argument, they will brook little from others.

Such behavior can be understood as defensive, a reaction formation to a loss of control. Among the harsh realities of addiction, to the alcoholic woman the harshest has to be the loss of control over her life. By travelling this avenue of condemnation and engaging in its ancillary behaviors they are able to feel that they are in control of others, of their environment, and of themselves.

Submission

The personality trait most salient among people who relate submissively is guilt. Alcoholic women are usually laden with it and so are enablers. More usually still, people so laden have an acutely low self-esteem just like the condemner types. The reason submissive types communicate in a diametrically opposite way is that they are beset by an insatiable, all-consuming need to be liked. So insatiable is this need that they have surrendered to their environment. More often what they believe, indeed their very convictions, are fleeting and transitory—a function of whom they are talking to at the moment. For them being liked is the issue, not convictions. The effect of such an interpersonal stance only reinforces and confirms low self-esteem.

Manifestly, "nice gals," submissives, seem also to be givers and enhancers. When asked to give of time or money they cheerfully give far, far more than asked of both. The inevitable effect of such giving is that it alienates people because it makes them feel obligated. The resultant wrong is that the submissive's all consuming basic motive is totally confounded. People don't like them. People stay away. More ironically still, such behavior by others only fuels the submissive alcoholic's and/or enabler's perception that people do not like them!

The final wrong and the saddest has to be that women inclined toward submissiveness frequently find and marry condemner types. The why of this might be that one or both perceive what the other is like or can be and want the relationship. It might be simply that they meet each other's perverted needs at the outset or, again, that they cultivate and unconsciously nurture each other's potential disposition. Whatever the reason, condemners and submissives do seem to find each other, and, in the alcoholic milieu, the problems of each are only exacerbated.

Indifference

Among the avenues of communication, indifference is one to which alcoholic women gravitate and adhere. Aloneness and emotional distancing fit with their need. Among the avenues of communication, indifference is the most unhealthy because it communicates total unconcern, if not meanness. Unfortunately, it is used most often with those to whom alcoholic women are closest, i.e., family or persons with whom they work, because it is most effective with them.

Indifference can never enhance but only demean. It is precipitated by hostility, fear, and the abiding alcoholic's need to manipulate.

Indifference can be communicated in different ways. One is silence, another might be termed quasi-indifference, and a third way is by avoiding behaviors.

Quite apparently, one can communicate anger or any other negative emotion by simply not talking—***silence***. The anger can be communicated even more apparently if, at the same time, the non-talker slams drawers, cabinets, and glares. Such behavior can be long or short lived, its duration being dependent upon the intensity of the hostility or the reason for manipulation. Sometimes alcoholic women and/or enablers especially are silent because they just don't want an emotional scene. Not infrequently it's because of embarrassment precipitated by guilt. Probably the most common reason among them is the most obvious, the simplest—they don't care.

Quasi-indifference refers to a method fairly common in alcoholic homes. For example, the alcoholic woman who has not uttered 50 words over the course of a week dutifully brings home her paycheck, leaves it on her husband's checkbook, and goes another week not uttering 50 words.

Avoiding behaviors involve talking in flat monotones, without affect and without looking at one another. If forced into interaction, for example at a meal, the topics are always safe ones, i.e., the weather, current foreign news events. Everyone scrupulously avoids being together for no reason. If three rooms are in the apartment, each of its three inhabitants manages to stay most of the time alone in their respective one.

Congruence

This is the healthy avenue of communication. The object of counseling, be it individual or group, is to help the client to learn to travel this avenue of communication.

One communicates with congruence when words, emotions, and behaviors all meld. One communicates with congruence when soft words ride on soft tones and facial and body expression fit with both. Similarly at those rare times when anger is in order, angry words are expressed in tones and with a face and body stance which match.

People who communicate by this avenue say and emote what they mean and do so comfortably. While they are able to express what they feel and usually when they feel so, they are able to do so tactfully. Tact, they have learned, is a function of the tolerance derived from their healthful levels of security, acceptance, and self-esteem.

Via Body and Emotions

DeRivera (1977) is one who believed that emotions and body are very much woven together. His work has led him to conclude that emotions affect the body and mirror its condition. This view is comparable to one expressed earlier by the noted psychiatrist Thomas Szasz (1961) when he wrote that most of our bodily symptoms are no more than "cries for help." The alcoholic woman who when sober, is complaining constantly of headaches and a variety of ailments may be saying only, "Help me, I'm in trouble." "I want to talk about me." Unfortunately, what she wants to talk about are physical ailments. Note that these ailments can indeed be a starting point for what should be the focus—the emotional dysfunctions which have precipitated the client's addiction.

Communication occurs in a variety of ways, with words, with tones, with behaviors. When these are congruent, the message is simple, clear, and direct. Communication becomes garbled, however, when words, tones, and emotions do not jibe and they do not often with many alcoholic clients. "No I wasn't hurt, at least not that much, when he called me a drunken slob," she says wiping her eyes.

Levels of Communication

Human communication is too often complicated. Communication becomes especially intriguing when it occurs on different levels, the unconscious as well as the conscious. Freud (1949) was the first to point out this phenomenon. He explained in a convincing way that at times people let their ego relax, give vent to id striving, and by the verbal slip, memory loss, or behavior let their true feelings come forth. Such emissions are unconscious but should be taken seriously as they have the greatest meaning.

Resorting to unconscious messages is of course a sad commentary upon human interaction. That people do so, however, reflects the frustration, intense need, and determination which all people have to reach out, express themselves—in a word communicate. Nowhere is this seen better than in alcoholic women. Most of them feel that their messages are not received, that no one is listening, that no one even cares to listen—ergo alcoholism. Their alcoholism can quite rightly be understood as a message—a message that they have given up and surrendered to a cruel environment.

Via Double Messages

The confusion and fear which alcoholic women experience in trying to communicate are due in no small part to the lack of learning and mislearning they underwent during the critical childhood years. Many of them never learned how to communicate in a congruent fashion (words, tones, behavior jibed) because they weren't exposed to such communications in their families. They were exposed rather to double messages, i.e., "Of course I love you darling and you know how much I do too. But I'm really, really sorry I just can't come to the play this morning. It's that awful migraine again. I'll make it next time. Promise. Come, give Mother a big kiss. Hurry now, or you'll be late for school." Messages such as these have a devastating effect upon a child. They split her emotionally. Which message does she accept? Desperately she wants to believe and accept the words of love punctuated with a kiss. Yet there's the other message, too—a message of rejection brutally exemplified in an absent mother with the perennial migraine. The conflict for the child necessarily becomes more acute, especially when the child begins to learn that gin is simply not an appropriate medicine for migraine. The conflict and confusion inevitably result in a latent, constant depression when the child begins to feel (children simply don't intellectualize) that Mother loves booze more than her. In any case the home where a pattern of double messages is the communicative style is a home that breeds confused and too often uncommunicative people.

Via Body Language

The body is a prime vehicle for communication. How a client takes care of it, spaces it, and uses it tells the counselor much about the client.

The client who comes in looking impeccably groomed simply does not have the same self-view of the world as one who comes in looking unkempt. Quite apparently, the former communicates a strong concern for self, perhaps for counseling. Conversely the latter person is on the skids and doesn't care. Self-care is a reflection of self-love and self-esteem and is demonstrated physically in one's appearance.

This author has found that having at least a couple of alternative chairs available for the client is useful. Where the client sits in relation to the counselor also reflects something about her interest and motivation to communicate. Accordingly, this counselor makes it a point to sit in his chair first and lets the client choose her seat, one being farther away from the counselor (about five feet) and the other (about three feet). The distance a client sits from the counselor affects process as has been supported in research data. Knight and Blair (1976) for example, found that the distance between counselor and client affects client comfort. Stone and Morden (1976) found that when clients sat too close or too far from the counselor, they were more inhibited about their self-disclosures than if they sat at an intermediate distance.

The language of the body motion has been the topic for research and discussion now for almost three decades (Ekman & Friesen, 1969; Kendon, 1972), and quite rightly so. On the whole, a relaxed person sits casually. In the protected, emotionally charged climate of counseling, most clients display their feelings by their bodies, on their faces usually, or with a leg that swings, a hand that drums, or a general shifting and reshifting of their bodies. Even the immobile, stone-faced clients are telling the counselor something — they are hide-bound by their denial and/or intellectualization defenses. In sum, the perceptive counselor is one who is sensitive to the body movements of his or her clients. If appropriate, the counselor will react and deal with them.

Via Defenses

The clinical roots of communication are found in psychological defense. Another way to understand the communication system of the alcoholic, then, is to approach it through her defense system. The most salient defense in the alcoholic's repertoire is denial. Rationalization, intellectualization, and projection are used too, usually to support denial.

Denial. The refusal to acknowledge one's behavior and the effects of it upon oneself and others invariably engenders guilt. Not uncommonly the guilt effects changes in the alcoholic's personality, i.e., submissiveness or passivity; or again the guilt may precipitate behaviors at the other end of the behavioral continuum—fits of anger or temper tantrums. One of the more insidious aspects of denial is that too often it seems to infect others close to the alcoholic. They too begin to deny. They joke about the alcoholic's drinking, tolerate it, even protect her in it. Not uncommonly, after a time they begin to see drunkenness as part of her general personality. Communication, if at all, focuses on irrelevancies. Any occasional attempt by a friend or family member to confront or even broach the subject of drink seems futile. Compounding the problem further is the fact that often the alcoholic becomes positively creative in thwarting such attempts. This response to what is perceived as an attack upon her denial may be a humorous quip, indifference, anger, or worst of all, a stony silence.

Rationalization. Communication with rationalizers is almost impossible. They neatly justify what they do, even what they themselves think. Rationalization is an important prop for denial. Alcoholic rationalizations are all too familiar. "I only drink white wine, never the hard stuff." "I never drink before noontime," or again, "Only on weekends," "I just don't drink that much, less than a pint of gin a day just isn't that much, besides I haven't missed a day's work in almost two months."

Intellectualization. Often a prop for the alcoholic's denial is intellectualization. With the highly intelligent person, intellectualization is especially difficult to break down. The reason for this difficulty is that the intellectualizer talks and seems to function as if she has no emotions. She behaves as if joy, rage, and despair are not part of her emotional ken. This lack of emotion combined with a refined ability to think, reflect, and analyze makes any meaningful communication difficult.

The best way to deal with the intellectualizing alcoholic woman is precisely not to intellectualize, not to duel with her intellectually with logic, or with analyses. The weak link in her armor is emotion. She refuses to acknowledge her own emotion, and she is more often than not befuddled if not terrified by the emotion, scorns it, or reacts indifferently to it, because she does not know how to deal with it. Accordingly, the counselor's responses should be inflected with feeling tones and all comments and questions should focus on the client's emotions. The following illustrations might prove helpful.

Counselor as Directivist.
Illustrative Excerpt of Intellectualization

CO: *Now let me get this straight. You mean to tell me that your husband had half of your pay legally attached and deposited in his account? He actually did that?*

CL: *Yeah, he did that.*

CO: *Wow!*

CL: *I do owe him a lot of money. Actually, I can understand him doing that.*

CO: *Okay, you can understand it, but explain to me how did it make you feel? I mean in your gut? How did it make you feel?*

CL: *Well, to be honest, I'm not sure. What was important was what to do. I thought about it and went to my lawyer.*

CO: *Agnes, weren't you angry, upset?*

Counselor as Nondirectivist.
Illustration Excerpt on Intellectualization

CO: *Your husband had your pay attached.*

CL: *Yes.*

CO: *How did that make you feel?*

CL: (Shrugs) *I'm not sure. I did check with my lawyer. It was legally appropriate.*

CO: *Did the legality assuage any possible feelings of anger you might have had?*

CL: (Pause) *To be honest about it, I'm not sure.*

CO: *You said your drinking increased dramatically after the attachment.* (Pause) *And what might that tell you, Agnes?*

Both counselors are following their convictions about the approach. The directivist is himself more emotional. The nondirectivist, it should be noted, gets into a little dueling with the client, manipulating her, almost trapping her into admitting she had to feel anger at the attachment. Both counselors, however, focus on the real issue, the intellectualizer's apparent alienation from her feelings about the matter.

Projection. Communication with alcoholic women who project stretches a counselor's patience to the limit. The essence of the problem is that projectors perceive people as being basically hostile or selfish or unconcerned with them. People don't like them. (These feelings, of course, are ones which they harbor about themselves.) In any case what projecting alcoholics do is test people. They make demand upon demand until people react negatively thereby confirming the alcoholic's basic perception that people don't like them.

In conclusion, problems are considerable. As has been observed, the essential ingredient for counseling to proceed is rapport founded on trust. The projector finds this intolerably difficult. Testing of the counselor may take a variety of forms, i.e., late appointment, self-disclosing little bombshells a few moments before the end of the hour to extend it, cynical comments about counseling, and so forth. The most effective way with this client is firmness and adherence to agreed upon ground rules. For example, if the client comes late, she gets only the balance of the scheduled hour, cynical comments are ignored. The counselor cannot permit manipulation by this type of client for a moment. Rapport will not be obtained in a relationship where there is manipulation.

TRANSFERENCE

Transference is the process of redirecting feelings and desires, especially those unconsciously retained from childhood toward the therapist. Briefly, the transference occurs because of two dynamic phenomena—repression and identification. The client who was exposed to parental rejection in childhood and/or was not permitted to express her true feelings toward her parents represses these feelings. These repressions stultify emotional developments and invariably debilitate her ability to develop relationships especially intimate ones.

In the emotionally sheltered climate of counseling the client who develops rapport with the counselor identifies with him or her and inevitably goes into transference; that is the client attaches feelings repressed in childhood toward the rejecting parent. The parent figure and the therapist unconsciously blend for her and they do so even if the rejecting parent figure and the therapist are of different sexes.

The transference can be positive or it can be negative. Whichever, it is dependent upon the nature of childhood repression. Thus, if in childhood the client was too terrified to express dissatisfaction or hostility, then in the transference (negative) the client will vent these feelings upon the therapists. If as a child the client was not able to attach feelings of love, then the transference is characterized by these kinds of feelings for the therapist.

By working through the transference with the counselor, the clients gains insight into the cause of the problem. The alcoholic gains insight into her true feelings about herself and others, the counselor included.

The reader should know that transference is a phenomenon dealt with by the psychoanalyst. Many, perhaps most, counselors do not deal with it as the lead-in to insight but treat it lightly, if at all. Three of the most renown among these are Carl Rogers, the exponent of client-centered therapy; Albert Ellis, the exponent of rational emotive therapy; and Joseph Wolpe, the advocate of conditioning therapy.

Manifestations

Whatever one's position may be on the issue of transference, the author believes that the counselor who is oblivious of its nature will be at a disadvantage in dealing with his or her client. To obviate this disadvantage, some manifestations of transference are outlined.

Positive Transference.

1. The positive attitudes expressed by the client increase, e.g., "I like you. I feel you really understand me," and so forth.

2. The client begins to ask questions about the counselor's personal life, e.g., "Are you married? Are you from around here?" and so forth.

3. The client begins to sit closer.

4. The client may seek to touch the counselor.

5. The client who initially arrived a little late for appointments begins to show up promptly, even early.

6. The client may bring small, "cute" gifts, even expensive ones, to the therapist.

Negative Transference.

1. The client begins to express negative attitudes, if not about the counselor then about the counseling, e.g., "I think this is all a lot of foolishness. I'm not sure you're helping me. Did you really have to go to school for this?"

2. The counselor may focus on those aspects of the transference which seem especially pertinent to the client's life now or which threaten to thwart progress already made. For example, if the woman feels she is in love with the counselor, the counselor may feel that an explanation of the dynamics might be in order. This author feels that such an explanation would be prudent. Without such an explanation a client could interpret the counselor's responses as being cool, uninterested, and essentially rejecting. Interpretations such as these would probably terminate the counseling at a critical juncture.

3. The counselor could pursue an analytic approach seeking to work through the transference by probing with questions focusing on the client's childhood.

COUNTERTRANSFERENCE

Definition

A countertransference occurs when the counselor attaches repressed feelings to the client. If the therapist does, then *she or he is in danger of destroying the therapeutic relationship.* When countertransference occurs therapists fall prey to their own feelings. They become overwhelmed by the client's emotions and demands and their own. They lose the ability to listen and interpret the true meaning of the client's feelings. Their perception becomes so clouded that the person of the client becomes major for therapists, the alcoholism minor, or they become unable to distinguish between the two at all. To meet the therapist's needs, (perhaps justify the feelings of supposed love for the client), the counselor often lets himself or herself be sucked into the client's psychological defenses, denying or rationalizing the client's alcoholism. Under circumstances such as these, the therapist's perception becomes so distorted that she or he loses sight of the very purpose of the counseling—to meet the needs of the client. In sum, therapists in countertransference risk losing their integrity both as therapists and as persons.

Symptoms of Positive Countertransference

The obvious symptoms of countertransference may include one or more of the following. The counselor

- is attracted sexually to the physical aspects of the client;

- is obsessed in off-hours about the client;

- fantasizes and looks forward to sessions with the client;

- spends more time in physical grooming for the sessions than typical;

- probes, during sessions, into aspects of the client's life and habits which are at best only tangentially related to the alcoholism problem; and

- does for the client what she or he ordinarily does not do with others, e.g., helps the client on and off with coat, offers coffee, brings doughnuts, and so forth.

The symptoms of a positive countertransference are transparent. The reader should know that too often they are not so to the counselor who is suffering it. The ethical, competent counselor suffers it indeed. A few years ago this author received a call late on a Friday night from a colleague, a 37-year-old single woman with a flawless reputation for both competence and ethics, who counsels in a local clinic. She was very distraught and wanted to talk. She came to this author's home and told him that she had agreed to a date for the next night with a 45-year-old divorced client, who was in her professional judgement a recovered alcoholic. She had had five sessions with him once a week for the past five weeks. The woman, who dated seldom and who could fairly be described as "average looking," when queried about the client, described him as a handsome and once successful lawyer who was practicing again. When asked why she had come to talk, she replied embarrassedly that she wanted confirmation that the date she'd made was okay, wasn't it? The author who felt pompous, even sanctimonious doing it, told her he felt it was inappropriate, even unethical, and that she was in a classic countertransference. She left, kept the date, went through a stormy love affair with him, which terminated recently. She is still a practicing counselor. The lawyer is still sober and still single.

What the reader should conclude from this is that a countertransference can happen to the very best of counselors. No guaranteed way can be given to prevent one. The best, the only, prescription to minimize its happening, is for the counselor to know what his or her weaknesses are with respect to other human beings.

Symptoms of Negative Countertransference

The symptoms of a negative countertransference are easy to detect but even more easily rationalized. The counselor

- is irritated by client's speech, manner, dress;
- discusses the client with other colleagues in a disparaging way;
- dreads sessions with the client;
- is uninterested, inattentive, and bored during the sessions;
- forgets an appointment, cuts it short, even cancels appointments; and
- will be making minimal progress at all.

A negative countertransference can happen but should happen very rarely. Again, the best prescription for its prevention is a strong counselor sense of self-awareness.

INSIGHT

Many counseling theorists believe that achievement of insight is an indispensable requisite to the whole counseling process. Sustained change toward a more healthful life is not possible without insight achievement. Some counselors disagree with this view. Skinner (1956) in one paper and Hobbs (1962) in a later one have both questioned the importance and significance of insight in bringing about change.

Definition

What actually is insight? This author defines it as an intellectual understanding and an emotional appreciation of the why of the problem(s) which led the client to seek counseling. Both the intellectual and emotional levels of appreciation are critical. An intellectual understanding without concomitant feeling is simply not enough. This counselor has sat many times with alcoholic women who explained, analyzed, and interpreted the why of their own behavior. They sounded positively insightful in doing so. Then they went out and got drunk. Intellectual understanding is not enough.

Importance of Insight

When both an intellectual understanding and emotional appreciation about the why of drinking exist, the question remains, can a guarantee be given that the alcoholic woman will achieve her sobriety? The answer is no. Guarantees, as one chap put it, are found on boxes of soap powders. Simply put, none are in human dynamics. This too, must be said, however, that while the client may not stop drinking because she has achieved insight, she definitely will not stop drinking if she has not achieved it. In short, the counselor can conclude that helping a client to achieve insight has merit.

TERMINATION
Uniqueness in Counseling the Alcoholic

Ordinarily the counseling process has a period of time devoted to terminating. That period is considered important by most counselors. It prepares the client to integrate what she has learned about herself, to rid the self of any vestiges of dependency, and prevent any depression over the sense of loss about ending a unique relationship. Commonly, termination generates a measure of anxiety in the client.

None of these termination activities need to be true in counseling the alcoholic. The author's conviction is that formal terminating in alcoholism counseling is inappropriate. Even when a prolonged and healthful state of sobriety has been reached, the door should be left open for subsequent contact. No alcoholic is ever cured of the anxiety associated with taking a drink. This knowledge has led this counselor to do what he never does with clients suffering from other types of illness—he calls his alcoholic clients periodically to learn how they are doing. More than a few times these calls have resulted in added counseling sessions. The latent anxiety this counselor feels about terminating his clients is shared by other counselors. Goodyear (1981) in a provocative paper observed that termination is a loss experience for the counselor as well as the client. Counselors, he pointed out, often have anxieties about client competence and may suffer feelings of guilt and sadness when their clients are leaving. This counselor has experienced these feelings about his clients generally and about his alcoholic clients in particular.

SUMMARY

How effectively counseling proceeds will be determined by the **competence** of the counselor, not by gender. The personal and professional qualities which enhance counselor competence are (1) the motivation to grow and learn; (2) the ability to find reward in serving another person; (3) a healthy perception of alcohol; (4) an optimistic expectation of client success; (5) a penchant for nurturance and truly liking others; (6) a disposition for empathy; (7) an exquisite ethical awareness of personal conduct with clients; (8) self-awareness as to competency, attitudes, prejudices, and limitations; (9) maturity, flexibility, respect for clients, and intuitiveness; and (10) the ability to listen and communicate.

Effective training programs are those which include both theory and practice. Ideally the program would be counselor created and its curriculum and length determined by the counselor's performance.

To be an effective alcoholism counselor one must strive for excellence. Striving for excellence in counseling is a life-long process and involves constant self-examination and an ability to articulate to oneself and others one's philosophy of counseling.

Among alcoholics the phenomena termed high, low, and middle bottom exist. Each alcoholic arrives at her bottom differently and for different reasons. The level and nature of the bottom varies with the person and always embraces the alcoholic's entire dynamic system. Meaningful, effective counseling can occur only when the alcoholic experiences her private bottom.

Goals are basic issues in counseling. The primary goal in counseling the alcoholic is the achievement of **continuing sobriety**. The secondary goals are important too, as they facilitate the achievement of the primary goal. Periodic reevaluation of the client's sobriety is critical if it is to be maintained because most alcoholics experience the BUD phenomenon.

Rapport has to do with accord, affinity, warmth, and trust in a relationship. Tone, pace, flexibility, frame of reference, and repertoire of leads are all integral aspects of rapport. Rapport transcends the whole process of counseling.

The setting in which counseling is done can affect it. The size of the room and the seating arrangements bear important consideration. Time, energy, and money need to be invested in making the counseling room attractive.

Avenues of communication common to many alcoholics are condemnation, submission indifference, and congruence. Clients communicate also by body and emotions, on unconscious levels, by double messages, with body language, and by defenses.

Transference is a function of repression and identification. The transference can manifest itself both positively and negatively. The counselor can ignore it, focus on those aspects which are pertinent to the client's life, or can pursue an analytic approach.

As is the case with transference, countertransference has both positive and negative symptoms. The best prescription for minimizing the occurrence of a positive or negative countertransference is for the counselor to have a full appreciation of self.

Some believe that achievement of insight is an indispensable requisite to the counseling process. Achievement of insight by the alcoholic as to the why of his or her addiction is no guarantee that sobriety will be achieved, but the alcoholic will definitely not stop drinking if insight is not achieved.

Formal termination in alcoholism counseling is inappropriate because alcoholics live with a constant latent anxiety that they will relapse into drink. Accordingly, periodic check-ups by counselors of their clients is appropriate.

FOR REVIEW AND REFLECTION

1. What personal and professional qualities do you possess which make you a competent counselor? On which quality(ies) do you need to work?

2. Articulate your philosophy of counseling. Is it truly a function of your personality?

3. Why are some "bottoms" reached quickly (a matter of months) and some never?

4. What are for you the primary goals for your professional counseling?

5. Which approach has more merit for you — the directivist or the nondirectivist? Why?

6. What body language habits do you possess which facilitate and/or hinder communication with those of a client?

7. What needs do you have which may be conducive to a countertransference?

8. What is your definition and/or criteria for achievement of client insight?

9. How can counselor awareness and sensitivity to the transference phenomena help the client? The counselor?

10. Do you agree with the author that formal termination of alcoholism counseling is inappropriate? Why? Why not?

Chapter **7**

PRACTICAL
TECHNIQUES

The practical techniques which are explained in this chapter will be employed more effectively if the counselor has an understanding of the frame of reference, with which many alcoholics operate. By frame of reference, the author refers to where the alcoholic is coming from emotionally, spiritually, and intellectually.

A FRAME OF REFERENCE

Without doubt the organization which had been most effective in helping alcoholics to achieve and maintain sobriety has been Alcoholics Anonymous. A couple of recent studies have shown this: one with physicians (Galanter, Talbot, & Ballegos, 1990) and one with the general population (Kaufman, 1990).

For many a woman, the achievement and maintenance of sobriety are living and identifying with the *Twelve Steps of Alcoholics Anonymous.* More often than not these steps are her frame of reference and not uncommonly, provide initial topics for explanation and discussion in counseling.

The prospective counselor who is a recovered alcoholic knows the steps, has reflected, meditated on them, and lived with them.

The counselor who is not a recovering alcoholic may not be familiar with these steps. The author's conviction is that the effective counselor, recovering alcoholic or not, is one who knows what these steps are and is concerned with what they mean to the client. Quite generally, the counselor who has an intellectual and emotional appreciation of the twelve steps finds that rapport with the client invariably comes early. More importantly, once the counselor has learned how the client interprets these steps, the counselor has obtained an invaluable window into the client's system of thought and emotional life too.

These twelve steps are provided in the material that follows. For the first five the author has provided his interpretations. Hopefully, counselors, who are familiar with these steps and have developed their own interpretations, will find more food for reflection. Counselors who are not familiar with these steps are encouraged to explore other interpretations and finally develop their own subjective meaning.

Step One: "We admitted we are powerless over alcohol, that our lives had become unmanageable."

Taking this first step is critical if one is to change and redevelop her personality. The view here is that a healthy nonalcoholic personality can be built only upon a foundation of avowed human weakness. The woman who is not able to admit to a lack of control toward drink cannot expect to recover in any substantial way. A woman who is unable to attain a meaningful sobriety is precisely one who has not been able to admit to innate powerlessness.

Acceptance of this first step is excruciatingly difficult because it is an admission that she has lost control over her own self. Many cannot accept this first step because by doing so they feel that they have become "losers" in their own eyes. This first step can best be understood as an avowed, external admission of long time internal feelings of weakness and ineffectiveness. The denial and rationalization defenses have kept these internal feelings from surfacing. In most cases an acute sense of desperation is what tears them down. The process of restructuring and altering these defenses is an important focal point of the early counseling session.

Step Two: "Came to believe that a Power greater than ourselves could restore us to sanity."

This step is conducive to a restructuring of defenses. Why? Because with acceptance of this step, the alcoholic woman begins to perceive a whole new world. She comes to understand that physical and emotional energy need not be directed inwardly or focused upon personal inadequacies and failure but, rather, can be directed externally. By this step she comes to understand that investment in one's fellow human, in God (in whatever context or definition) or in the cosmos generally can reap rich and enhancing dividends. Implied in this step is that every individual must have an object upon which to attach faith. Without such an attachment, self-esteem and a continuing self-enhancement are not possible.

Implied, too, in this step is that the alcoholic woman who comes to accept this step, admits to an emotional life in shambles and a distorted system of thought. Simply, she admits to a life which has been lived insanely. Previously, energies have been channeled into maintaining that insanity. With acceptance of this second step she is able to return to a sane life.

Step Three: "Made a decision to turn our will and our lives over to the care of God as we understand him."

Steps One and Two lead the alcoholic woman away from an exaggerated concern with one's self and encourage physical and emotional energies externally. Both steps are meditative, reflective, and oblige only acceptance. Step Three obliges her to act on the acceptance of the first two steps.

The key to acceptance of Step Three is motivation. The alcoholic woman who is motivated toward investment in God will be successful. The definition and interpretation of God are left to the particular individual. For many women this definition is the fellowship of Alcoholics Anonymous. To this fellowship many submit their will and their lives.

By this step then, the individual woman becomes dependent on A.A. Such a dependence she comes to believe results in an independence of spirit and a more emotionally relaxed life. What this author has learned is that clients who have accepted Step Three develop a more optimistic perception of problem situations. More importantly, people are viewed more tolerantly and interaction with the alcoholic woman invariably becomes rewarding.

Step Four: "Made a searching and fearless moral inventory of ourselves."

The desire to fully achieve this step leads many alcoholic women into counseling. The traditional A.A. interpretation of this step is based upon an understanding and control of the basic human instincts. In the A.A. view, instincts unbridled are conducive to self-destruction.

The author has utilized the woman's interest in this step differently. Thus, the counselor has encouraged her to focus on those aspects of her personality which are of special concern. This counselor has found that general and basic psychological needs—security, love, self-esteem, and self actualization—have provided an effective framework in which to help her better understand her specific concerns and anxieties and those instincts from which they spring. What the author has found, too, is that the alcoholic penchants for excess, guilt, and mood swings stem from a lack of understanding of the basic human search for satisfaction of these needs. This Step Four seems to be best achieved by women when they come to have a clear understanding of what self-esteem means to them.

Step Five: "Admitted to God, to ourselves, and to other human beings the exact nature of our wrongs."

The A.A. view here is that "confession is good for the soul." Such a view not only promotes the counseling enterprise but may even facilitate rapport. The author's experience has been that alcoholic women who are strongly identified with this fifth step are positively eager to self-disclose. These clients seem especially eager to explain in graphic detail those incidents where they inflicted pain upon others.

For such women the counseling session is perceived as an opportunity for an emotional catharsis, and it is. Clients at the end of a draining session usually feel better. (A positive by-product is that rapport and the client-counselor relationship are almost always strengthened.) The counselor should be very much aware that catharsis, while beneficial, is not in itself the end-all of the counseling process. Catharses are at best temporary. Their value lies in precipitating insight and, in turn, change. Very often clients, especially alcoholics, have shared their most intimate experiences and conflicts and even convincingly explained to the counselor the why of their drinking. Then they proceed to engage in the same destructive behavior! In short, catharsis, even catharsis complemented with insight, is no guarantee of positive changes especially in the alcoholic client. Only when the client genuinely finds reward in change will she be and stay on the road to recovery.

NOTE: Steps Six through Twelve are reproduced verbatim for the benefit of those counselors who are not familiar with them. They were not interpreted because the author felt that their content was not conducive to any meaningful interpretation of the counselor-client process. The A.A. interpretations can be obtained from the manual *Twelve Steps and Twelve Traditions*, Alcoholics Anonymous World Services Inc., 468 Park Avenue South, New York, N.Y. 10016.

Step Six: "We're entirely ready to have God remove all these defects of character."

Step Seven: "Humbly asked Him to remove our shortcomings."

Step Eight: "Made a list of all persons we had harmed, and became willing to make amends to them all."

Step Nine: "Made direct amends to such people wherever possible, except when to do so would injure them or others."

Step Ten: "Continued to take personal inventory and when we were wrong promptly admitted to it."

Step Eleven: "Sought through prayer and meditation to improve our conscious contact with God, as we understood

Him, praying for knowledge of His will for us and the power to carry that out."

Step Twelve: "Having had a spiritual awakening as the result of these steps, we tried to carry this message to alcoholics, and to practice these principles in all our affairs."

REDIRECTING AND RESTRUCTURING DEFENSES

As noted in Chapter 2 helping the alcoholic client to restructure her system of defense is a critical task of the counselor. In many of the illustrations which follow, notably confrontation, the reader will be able to see that this process typically is woven together with other client issues. Examples which follow are simulated to focus specifically on the issue of defense. The counselor style depicted melds directivist with nondirectivist.

Denial and Rationalization

These two defenses are treated together because they often occur in tandem with rationalization as a support for denial. A common phenomenon among newly recovering alcoholics is the refusal to acknowledge their competencies. Such is the case in the illustration that follows.

Illustrative Excerpt: Counselor Shawn

CL: *I think I've decided not to take the office supervisor job.*
CO: *Oh?*
CL: *I honestly don't think I'm ready for it.*
CO: *I'm confused.*
CL: *Why?*
CO: *Yesterday you said you were going to take it. You told me you were looking forward to going back to it.*
CL: *I changed my mind.*
CO: *I was under the impression you were a supervisor for almost twenty years.*
CL: *I was and look what happened! I became a drunk.*

CO: *You became a drunk because you were the office supervisor?* (A hint of incredulity in the tone would not be inappropriate.)

CL: *Well, it contributed to it. People, women especially, are a bitch to work with. If I were a man, I wouldn't hesitate—women respect men more.*

CO: (Grinning) *It's because you're not a man that you can't be a supervisor at this time. You don't feel you command enough respect.*

CL: *You think I'm making excuses don't you?*

CO: *Aren't you? Janice, the reality is that you functioned for twenty years as a supervisor and the last five you were a drunk a good part of the time.*

CL: *And if I did it drunk, I can do it sober, eh?*

CO: *What do you think?*

What the counselor does here is to focus on the client's denial, repeating, and rephrasing. The counselor always is focusing on what the client is saying. This helps the client see her vacillation is founded upon the plain fear that she can't do what she's already done for a couple of decades.

Displacement

Occasionally, clients will ventilate anger. More often than not, this counselor's response has been simply an acceptance of the client and her feelings. To respond with anger is grossly inappropriate. The view is that the follow-up session to the ventilation, sometimes during the same session if clients are feeling remorseful, is the more critical point in the therapy. What the counselor has to communicate to clients is that while anger is a legitimate emotion, when displayed, it doesn't serve to enhance personality. What the counselor has to communicate, too, is that what angry clients usually feel is a function of other disquieting and troubling circumstances of their lives. More importantly, that they have to deal with those people and situations which have endangered that anger.

Fantasy

What clients daydream about, what they wish for are important. Fantasizing can be more than a simple escape from boredom or harsh reality. It can be a springboard to creativity. Certainly fantasy does not have to be destructive as it may have been for alcoholics during their drinking days.

Alcoholic women, particularly those who seek to share their fantasies, need to hear those ideas. When they begin talking about some of their wishes and dreams, the sensitive counselor will do more than listen. She or he should help clients to evaluate the feasibility of translating fantasies into reality.

Projection

The suspicious client is not easy to deal with and many alcoholics are very suspicious. Too often it is a major aspect of the alcoholic's make-up. The best counselor antidote for suspiciousness in alcoholic clients is reliability and trustworthiness. A promise or appointment should never be made with the clients unless the counselor knows full well that she or he can keep it. Authenticity and candor also are excellent antidotes. Nothing feeds and expands this defense as much as game playing.

Clients who project are exquisitely sensitive to verbal nuances, body movements, a simple sigh. If a usually engaging client asks the counselor if the latter is anxious to terminate an interview when the counselor is, he or she can answer honestly. "I am but it's got nothing to do with you. I found out a half hour ago that I'm the one who has to pick up my son at the sitter's because my spouse got hung up in town." An honest explanation punctuated with a chuckle and even a compliment, "I thought I was hiding my nervousness. You're very perceptive," will help the client to see that her perception is accurate and to express it under such circumstances is OK.

Regression

Regression as was noted in Chapter 2 is characterized by immature behavior and is often manipulative. The counselor's task is to communicate that the behavior affected by her defense is seldom attractive and more often than not will alienate other people. The illustration which follows exemplifies a situation which has occurred a number of times with the author.

Illustrative Excerpt: Counselor Ralph

CO: *I'm sorry. Jean, I can't do it. I'm not going to serve as your job agent. You'll have to make the call yourself.*

CL: *What's the big deal?*

CO: *It's a big deal. You'll have to set up the interview yourself.*

CL: (Yells) *I thought you were here to help me.*

CO: (Quietly) *I am. I'm here to help you help yourself.*

CL: (Sulking) *What a fraud this place is. All they tell you here is that they want to help. You ask for help, and you get a lot of half-baked explanations.*

CO: *Not half-baked. It's true. We're, I'm here to help you help yourself.*

CL: (Cries out) *So! Help me!*

CO: (Quietly) *Jean, a woman who whines like a baby does not endear herself to people.*

CL: (Grimly) *Ralph, you can take this place, your psychology too, and roll it up into a big fat ball and shove it, you know where!*
(Slams out)

Next day

CL: (Sheepishly) *I made the call. I got an interview at two o'clock today.*

CO: *Good!*

CL: *I'm scared, Ralph. I'm scared.*

CO: *Aren't we all. Let's talk.*

Repression

Repression is the defense which clients may well have employed immoderately in their past. Too often the effect has been to leave them scared, immature, and unsure of themselves. Rather than attempt to deal with the whys and whens of the repression, this counselor has found it more productive to help the client build other defenses. Two defenses which seem to address themselves to the debilitating effects of repression are *compensation* and *sublimation*. In the former, clients are encouraged to look for and identify with situations, hobbies and/or events where they can find some reward and demonstrate some measure of success to their own selves. Similarly, sublimation involves directing energy in the service of others and one's own healthy self. Alcoholism programs especially provide ample opportunity for the development of both defenses.

SILENCE

Silence is often threatening to counselors, even thoroughly competent ones. They became anxious, seeing a protracted pause as a symptom of their ineptitude. Not understanding the many excellent reasons for it, they break it clumsily and thereby communicate their anxiety and in turn increase the client's discomfort.

Why Silences Occur

Silences may occur for various reasons. The following seven reasons are the most common causes.

1. Embarrassment is a major reason silences occur especially at the initial contact. Clients do not know what to say. The initial contact with the alcoholism counselor may well be their first experience with counseling. The most alcoholics know, and this in a dim way, is that they are supposed to confide and share innermost feelings, fears, and fantasies. Clients might be willing to do this, but do not know how. Simply, they are too embarrassed to begin.

2. Resentment, hostility, and anger are all reasons why silences occur. This is especially true in the mandated referral. The counselor is perceived as an agent of the person making the referral. What the alcoholic sees is that she is being victimized by the court, the parole office, or whomever. The client, then, releases her hostility in a passive way — by keeping mum.

3. Testing of the counselor is another reason for silence. The alcoholic woman, it will be remembered, often has a disposition toward paranoia. The silence may well be a response to that. By keeping silent, letting the counselor do the talking, the client can size up the counselor better. In addition, the client can evaluate the counselor's reaction. This client knows that she has some kind of responsibility to talk and share. The client knows that the silence can precipitate a variety of reactions in the counselor: impatience, anger, embarrassment, etc. So she tests the counselor. This interpersonal stance by her may well be habitual and not even conscious.

4. Conflict is another reason for silence. More often than not, alcoholic women are emotionally betwixt and between. They don't know what to say, where to start, precisely because they have so much to say. So clients sit tongue-tied and helpless, victims of their emotional conflicts. Such clients often perspire, fidget, twitch.

5. Fear is a major reason for silence in alcoholic women, especially at the initial contact. The counselor finally is just another stranger. Typically, these women have learned that most people are simply not that caring. Moreover, at some level all clients understand that a purpose of the counseling is to change them, and note, no human being ever delights in that idea. On the contrary, most people are scared by any potential change in themselves. They know what they have. Who knows what change will bring? This kind of feeling is a major reason alcoholics persevere in their drinking.

6. Integration by the client of what she or the counselor has said can cause silence. Counseling can be painfully emotional, even traumatic at times, and some clients need time to absorb it all. A silence for some clients is simply a manifestation of that need.

7. The end of a topic may produce silence. Sometimes a silence occurs because the counselor and the client have finished a long discussion. A pause may occur while the client searches for a relevant topic.

Handling the Silence

Once the counselor understands that the silence is a product of complex client dynamics it should be less threatening. In any case she or he should be better equipped to deal with it. Some of the specific reasons for a silence (at times several reasons may exist) are easy to discern. Others are more difficult. The counselor's ability to fathom and deal with these more indiscernible reasons will test both his or her clinical skills and perceptual sensitivity. Following are some suggestions for dealing with differently motivated silences.

1. Embarrassment is easy to detect. Confrontation usually aggravates it. The better approach is a comment or question manifestly unrelated to the client's alcoholism but about the client and/or her interests. (A look into her background before the first session is always helpful.) The question might focus on a hobby, her work, family, and so forth.

2. *Resentment, hostility,* or *anger* is very apparent. A gentle like confrontation is appropriate. In the case of the mandated referral, a comment like this might be helpful. "Wendy, I know you were sent here and quite apparently you're not happy. Just know that I'm here to help if you want it. And I know real well I can't make you open up if you don't want to." When a mandated referral is not the reason, confrontation is still appropriate. "Wendy, you're not happy. I'm sorry for that. Just know that I'm here to help if you want it..." and so forth.

3. *Testing* of the counselor can occur for various reasons. This motive for silence is not always easy to detect. When the counselor genuinely is puzzled as to the why of the silence, probing with neutral comments is in order, i.e., "Sometimes it's tough to talk," or "You're quiet today. Do you know why?" Under no circumstances should the counselor launch into chit-chat. If the counselor concludes because of the client's facial expressions, body language, and just feelings that the client's silence is a function of hostility, then the counselor should lean back, smile appropriately, shrug, and say to the client,

"Whenever you're ready is okay with me." The idea is to communicate patience and receptivity.

4. *Conflict* is very apparent. Reassuring comments delivered softly with warmth are usually beneficial and ultimately move the client to talk.

5. *Fear,* once detected and it's not difficult to do so, is dealt with in much the same fashion as one would deal with conflict.

6. *Integration* by the client of ideas, concepts, insights, and personality components often produce silence. This silence is best left alone as the client is in the process of absorbing what she is feeling or has just learned. A comment by the counselor serves no purpose. A question would be even worse.

7. The *end of a thought* expressed by the client may cause silence. The author has let this silence go on with the new client hoping she would break it and thereby assume more of the responsibility for the counseling. He has not let it go on if the client was becoming embarrassed; nor has he let it go on when the rapport and progress are solid. Under these latter circumstances this counselor breaks silence with a comment like, "Well, what thoughts are you having?" If the client responds with none, the counselor will break the silence by referring to something the client said previously.

Activities for Learning to Deal Effectively with Silence

The following activities on learning to deal effectively with silence and those which come immediately after each of the subsequent techniques illustrate activities which the prospective and inservice counselor can utilize to both learn and upgrade counselor skills. These activities are in outline form and can be modified, expanded, or revised to meet local training needs. Any alterations, however, should retain the requisite elements of any effective learning exercise. These are justification, purpose, objectives/outcomes, specific activities, and evaluation methods.

Justification.

Protracted pauses may generate anxiety in the counselor and/or the client. Learning to deal with the silence can abate that anxiety and facilitate counseling.

Purposes.

1. To expand the student counselor's theoretical knowledge about the element of silence in counseling.

2. To develop and sharpen the student counselor's practical skill to deal effectively with silence.

Outcome.

Student counselor demonstrates that she or he can indeed handle silence.

Specific Activities.

1. Student counselor obtains verification that she or he knows theoretical reasons why silences occur in counseling.
2. Student counselor obtains verification that she or he knows possible and varied ways to handle silence.
3. Student counselor views video demonstrations on how to handle silence.
4. Student counselor views live demonstrations by mentor on how to handle silence.
5. Student counselor engages in role-playing with the mentor.
6. Student counselor views videotaping of himself/herself during a counseling session with a new client.

Evaluation.

1. Feedback is obtained from mentor and student colleagues.
2. Activities continue until student counselor and mentor are mutually satisfied with student counselor's performance.

LISTENING

Prefatory Comments

We are enhanced when we feel that people listen to us. Most alcoholic women do not feel so precisely because they have learned that no one listens to them. This feeling has contributed much toward their suspiciousness, their anger, and their penchant for testing others. The counselor who listens, in a word, enhances. Such a counselor provides the alcoholic with a rare opportunity to unfold and expand.

Patterson (1959, p. 168) believed that listening is "the basic, most universal, most important technique in counseling and psychotherapy." If listening isn't the most important technique, it is certainly critical. Without this ability, the counselor will find that meaningful rapport is impossible.

Effective listening is sometimes difficult even for competent, experienced counselors. In the emotionally charged climate of counseling, easily conditions can cause the counselor to ask inappropriate questions; to offer unasked for, unneeded advice; to interrupt with an irrelevant interpretation; or to supply a well intended but unnecessary supportive remark. Behaviors like these communicate a lack of interest, tell the client that the counselor is not listening, and that the counselor is one who is meeting his or her own needs, not those of the client.

Aspects of Listening

The listening counselor not only hears the client's words but also is exquisitely sensitive to her feelings, tones, and sounds made. **Feelings** and **tones** carry the real meaning of words and reflect the emotions of the client. Such tones Westcott (1966) has termed **phasis**. The counselor who is finely attuned to the phasis in client talk is the one who can get close. Thus in his or her responses the counselor can, should address the emotion the client is feeling as well as the verbal content expressed, i.e., "I believe you, Bill. That crackle in your voice tells me real well how angry you really are."

The counselor also should be fully aware of **sounds** that a client makes, like finger drumming, hand clapping, even making the chair squeak with his/his constant shifting. Westcott (1966) has termed such sounds **strepitus**. They speak much about the client's internal anxiety. To respond to them or not would be dependent upon the quality of rapport existing between the counselor and alcoholic. If the rapport is good, a comment whimsically made might be very appropriate; i.e., "That's a regular tattoo you're doing there. It's even got a regular beat." In sum, a response to feeling tones, to sounds made by the client demonstrate in a concrete way how well attuned the counselor is to the client's presence and to everything about her.

Listening Techniques

For the counselor to listen is not enough, she or he also needs to communicate his or her motivation to do so. Following are some practical suggestions to accomplish this communication.

1. How the counselor **sits** communicates much about motivation to listen and is really a function of personality. Some counselors are more formal or casual than others. Simply, one should sit so she or he is comfortable. Counselor comfort will communicate and set a comfortable tone for the encounter. The counselor should sit, of course, so the client can be observed directly. This author who leans back and puts his feet on top of the desk has never been able to appreciate Freud's method to sit behind the head of the lying down client.

2. The counselor should structure the counseling hour so **no** interruptions occur. A phone for incoming calls should be programmed for transfer to another phone. If this isn't possible, a feasible procedure might be to have the phone put on a jack so it can be pulled out for the counseling hour. Hanging out a "Do Not Disturb" sign is eminently appropriate. All these procedures will serve to communicate to the client this important idea—you are the focus of my attention.

3. To listen to his or her best, the counselor should develop the ability to **isolate distracting** thoughts. This idea was

explained fully in Chapter 6 under "Obstacles to Establishment of Rapport." A rereading of that section might be helpful.

4. The counselor will not be able to listen attentively if she or he is not fully cognizant of **topics and words** which precipitate a negative reaction internally. Certain words and subjects are emotionally laden for some people and counselors are no exception. This fact was illustrated in dramatic fashion to this author about a year ago. The woman at the very first session told this counselor an ethnic joke, followed with another about Blacks. The counselor overlooked them figuring they were a function of the client's anxiety, perhaps some kind of testing, and so forth. At the next session, she opened with a particularly tasteless story about Blacks. This counselor let down his guard and winced. The client became embarrassed and asked if she had been offensive. When told she had been, she became angry and left. She returned later that day and apologized, finished with the rationalization, "We're all different." However, she never made another racial slur.

In this instance it all worked out okay. However, had the author better known what his feelings were he would not have winced, would not have had to say he was offended, and thereby come near to losing the client. However strong one's feelings might be regarding the obscenity and stupidity of prejudice, the counseling session is simply not a forum for instruction in healthier race relations.

5. The counselor who asks focused, pertinent **questions** will demonstrate that she or he is listening. These questions should always be derived from the client's comments and should never introduce a new topic. Questions unrelated to what the client is discussing ordinarily reflect inattention, boredom, and general uninterest. This whole topic of questioning is developed more fully in the next section.

Activities for Learning Listening Skills

Justification.

Counseling is not possible if the counselor does not know how to listen. Effective counseling is enhanced mightily by a counselor who is a skilled listener.

Purposes.

1. To increase the student counselor's theoretical knowledge about listening in counseling.

2. To develop and increase the student counselor's practical listening skills.

Outcome.

The student counselor demonstrates that she or he has acquired listening skills.

Specific Activities.

1. The student counselor obtains verification that she or he knows reasons why counselor listening can be blocked.
2. The student counselor obtains verification that she or he knows how effective listening can be enhanced.
3. The student counselor views video demonstration of counselors who are effective listeners.
4. The student counselor views live demonstrations by mentor counselor.
5. The student counselor role-plays with mentor counselor or colleagues.
6. The student counselor views himself/herself on video tape.

Evaluation.

1. Student counselor obtains feedback from mentor, colleagues, and clients.
2. Activities continue until mentor and student are mutually satisfied that the student counselor is an effective listener.

QUESTIONING

Problems

Questions, especially with alcoholics, may have certain problems. Questions by their very nature are designed to elicit information, information which the client can consider too private to share. They may touch on areas which engender fear. In short, a basic problem with questions is that they probe into the unknown.

Questions for some counselors, too often, lead to more questions. Too often, the counselor takes on the spectacle of a courtroom with the counselor playing the role of a prosecuting attorney. A barrage of questions can turn counselor and client into adversaries.

Questions have another potential disadvantage. Clients may become conditioned to think in terms of answering questions, not in terms of sharing, expressing voluntarily, self-examining. In short, their sense of responsibility for counseling may become stultified.

Finally, questioning per se has another major disadvantage — too often it focuses upon the cognitive domain rather than upon feelings. Cognitive understanding is helpful, even desirable, but without emotional appreciation the cognitive understanding has little value for the client. Under such circumstances, meaningful insight is simply not possible.

Positive Aspects

Despite these limitations, thoughtful questioning can be helpful and facilitative. It can serve as a lead into productive discussion. Clear, succinct, gently toned questions ordinarily are not inappropriate if the counselor derives them from the client's comments and discussion.

Questions posed should always be open-ended. After posing the question, the counselor should wait for the client's response. Therein will lie the validity and fruitfulness of the counselor's query.

Following are two illustrations. In this scene the client has been talking nonstop for almost ten minutes.

Inappropriate Use of Questions: Counselor Myrtle

> CL: . . . *anyways, like I was saying, I know I have to take each day at a time, and I'm doing that, but I think I can start making plans to get out of here. I've been sober for two months now, and I want to thank you. You've really helped me.*

> CO: *Why are you banging on the table like that?*

> CL: (Laughs) *I'm nervous.*

> CO: *Why are you nervous?*

> CL: (Shrugs) *I don't know, the way you're looking at me makes me nervous, makes me feel like a goldfish in a bowl ...* (Client's talk continues aimlessly for several minutes.)

> CO: *Why are you talking so much today? Any why are you banging on the table again?*

> CL: *Like I said. I'm nervous.*

> CO: *You're getting ready to blow it aren't you?*

> CL: *You know damn well I'm not.*

> CO: *Then how come I didn't see you yesterday?*

> CL: *I told you about that.*

Comments on Counseling Excerpt. This counselor broke the rules of good questioning. Her questions were not founded on client comment. She asked a second question before she got answer to the first. She sounded a little bit like an anxious but determined prosecuting attorney. Even her observations of client table drumming sounded more like accusations than gently toned comments designed to communicate an accepting confirmation of the client's hyperactive behavior.

Appropriate Use of Questions: Counselor Rosemary

The following scene opens exactly as the first did.

CL: . . . *anyways, like I was saying, I know I have to take each day at a time, and I'm doing that, but I think I can start making plans to get out of here. I've been sober for two months now, and I want to thank you. You've really helped me.*

CO: *That's why I am here. To help. How exactly have I helped?*

CL: (Drumming hand on the desk) *Well you're not like some of the other counselors around here, always on your back, buzzing around, asking questions, trying to get into your head. Al's got a counselor like that, always asking him if he's building up to drink.*

CO: (Smiles) *Should I ask you that?*

CL: *Sure, ask.*

CO: (Seriously) *Are you building up to a drink?*

CL: *No!* (Slams the desk)

CO: *Would you say this beating you're giving this desk today is the same you that you were a week ago?*

CL: (Silent for a moment. Sighs.) *You know, huh?*

CO: (Nods) *I know.*

CL: *I'm dying. Doc.*

CO: (Smiling) *Let's talk about it.*

Comment on Counseling Excerpt. Both counselors are very aware that the client's behavior was symptomatic of BUD. The second one's use of questions aimed at letting the client know of her awareness without making her defensive and getting her to talk. In sum, a counselor's questions should not be merely a reaction to client's specific comment. They should have an ultimate purpose too. In this instance it was to get the client to discuss her craving.

Activities for Learning Questioning Skills

Justification.

The counselor, who questions effectively, demonstrates interest in the client, reinforces rapport, and generally facilitates the counseling progress.

Purposes.

1. To increase the student counselor's theoretical knowledge about the technique of questions.
2. To develop and sharpen the student counselor's questioning skills.

Outcome.

Student counselor demonstrates that she or he has the ability to question effectively.

Specific Activities.

1. The student counselor obtains verification that she or he is familiar with the theory of positive and negative aspects of questioning.
2. The student counselor obtains verification that she or he knows appropriate and inappropriate use of questioning.
3. The student counselor views examples of effective counselor questioning.
4. The student counselor views live demonstrations of effective questioning.
5. The student counselor role-plays with mentor or colleagues.
6. The student counselor views video tape of himself/herself questioning in counseling session.

Evaluation.

1. Student counselor obtains feedback from mentor, colleagues, and client.
2. Demonstrations continue until counselor and client are mutually agreed that the student is an effective questioner.

REITERATION OF CONTENT

Definition

Reiteration refers to a literal restatement or rephrasing by the counselor of what the client said. When the counselor does this restatement, she or he is telling the client that she or he understands. Ordinarily when the counselor reiterates, no attempt is made to interpret the meaning of what the client said.

Explanation

Reiteration as a technique serves many useful purposes. It immediately puts the counselor into an accepting role, thereby facilitating both rapport and communication. It invariably elicits client feelings conducive to better cognitive understanding. Reiteration helps clients to focus and delineate their thinking. It can help clients reconsider both thinking and viewpoint, i.e., when the counselor reiterates with an inquisitive or honestly puzzled look. Another prime value of reiteration is, then, to help clients crystallize their thoughts.

The following two examples illustrate this technique. The client is an alcoholic wife and mother in her early thirties. This excerpt was taken from a tape and was edited by the author.

Illustrative Excerpt, Directivist: Counselor Greg

CL: *You can't help me, not in this.*

CO: *When you open like that, I know you want to talk. So talk and try me.*

(Pause)

CL: *He's having an affair.* (She starts crying.)

CO: *Your husband's screwing around on you.*

CL: *Yes. Bastard. When I really needed his support. Instead of help, I get degraded.*

CO: *The bastard degraded you.*

CL: *God, it's enough to make me want to blow it.*

CO: *You want to get blind, stinking drunk.*

CL: (Screams) *I won't! I won't!*

CO: *You won't if you don't want to.*

CL: *I want to. He said his life was hell when I was drinking. God knows I want to make his life hell again for what he's done to me.*

CO: *You want to make his life hell for degrading you. Drinking will punish the bastard.*

CL: *And it will too!*

Illustrative Excerpt, Nondirectivist: Counselor Joel

The following illustration is a simulation of the preceding excerpt.

CL: *You can't help me, not in this.*

CO: *You don't feel I can help you. You may be right. I'm here to try if you want me to.*

(Pause)

CL: *He's having an affair.* (Cries)

CO: *John is having an affair.*

CL: *Yes. Bastard. When I really needed his support. Instead of help I get degraded.*

CO: *Right in this time that you need support the most, he degrades you.*

CL: *God, it's enough to make me want to blow it.*

CO: *It's enough to make you want to return to drink.*

CL: *I want to. He said his life was hell when I was drinking. God knows I want to make his life hell.*

CO: *You want his life to be hell for what he's done to you.*

Comments on Illustrative Excerpts

Both counselors did a credible job. Joel, the nondirectivist as usual is little less blunt, a little less emotional, and little more literal in his reiteration. Greg, the directivist, tends more toward colorful rephrasing, is more inclined toward the supportive remark, "You won't if you don't want to." Both did well to focus and respond to the client's statement and neither did any interpreting.

Activities for Learning How to Reiterate Content

Justification.

The counselor who can reiterate well is one who facilitates both rapport and communication.

Purposes.

1. To heighten the student counselor's awareness of the effectiveness and benefits of the reiteration technique.
2. To sharpen the student counselor's ability to reiterate content.

Outcome.

Student counselor is effective in ability to reiterate content in an actual counseling session.

Specific Activities.

1. The student counselor obtains verification that she or he knows theory underlying when and how to reiterate content.
2. The student counselor views excerpts of model counselor reiterating on video tapes.
3. The student counselor views live demonstrations of reiterating.
4. The student counselor does role-playing with colleagues with or without mentor observing.
5. The student counselor observes self reiterating on video.
6. The student counselor demonstrates ability to reiterate in live counseling sessions.

Evaluation.

1. The student counselor obtains feedback from mentor, colleagues, and so forth.
2. The student counselor continues activities until counselor and mentor are both satisfied with performance.

REFLECTION OF FEELING

Definition and Value

Reflection of feeling is closely allied to the concept of empathy. When counselors reflect feeling, they communicate that they understand and perceive what clients are experiencing and feeling.

Reflection of feeling is among the least threatening of counselor techniques, because the focus is on emotions and not intellectual content. It involves no questioning, no verbal pushing, the counselor merely mirrors tones and feelings eliciting and clarifying self-referenced emotion.

Counselors who reflect feelings effectively, invariably lead the client into self-confrontation. Clients who hear and feel feelings come back at them are made to realize that their feelings are important, legitimate, and not crazy at all. Why? Another human being has understood and mirrored them.

The major benefit of this technique is not only in clients crystallizing their feelings but in understanding their feelings in relation to people. Feelings which trouble the most, of course, are those which have to do with relationships.

Alcoholics who come for counseling are usually very confused about relationships. They are laden with anger, guilt, and/or fear about them. As their feelings become clarified, self-understanding, in relation to others, becomes more ordered, more logical, and more healthful. The change, though gradual, is usually discernible as it is reflected in client's talk, general manner, even appearance.

Language

The counselor should try to use the language easily understood by the client. This counselor's preference is to use the same words as the client, varying only to avoid sounding like "Little Sir Echo." In any case, pretentious terminology always should be avoided.

Client Enhancement

Clarification of feelings enhance alcoholic women in two important ways. When feelings are reflected to them, they come to see that feelings, more often than not, are causes of much dysfunctional behavior. Frequently they ultimately see something more important—that they can cause their behavior, that they do not have to be victims, and, if they are, the reason is that they choose to be. The development of this way of thinking is vital if they are to begin to recover.

The counselor can be most effective when reflecting feelings if certain points are kept in mind.

Feelings Hide Feelings

The counselor should address only the feelings presented by the client. At the same time, the counselor should bear in mind that the obvious feelings are not always the most important ones. Many clients mask their more debilitating feelings with other ones. The author recalls a female alcoholic, for example, who punctuated every third sentence with a sharp, nervous laugh to mask her anger and guilt.

Timing

Too often counselors wait for a client to finish a rather lengthy verbalization and miss much important affect. Feelings should be reflected as soon as possible after they are expressed.

Once the client has come to see that feelings cause behavior, she invariably begins an examination of precipitating motives. Such an examination can only lead to a better self-appreciation.

Clarification of feeling is essentially a technique of the Rogerian nondirectivist school. The illustration which follows is by a follower of that school. The edited excerpt is drawn from four sessions. These tapes are from a colleague's library.

Illustration of Reflection of Feelings: Counselor Toni

CL: *I'm going to have to stop drinking. I know it.*

CO: *Your tone says that you don't want to.*

CL: *I do. It's just that my husband and my daughter ... but they're right, I know they are.*

CO: *They're pressuring you, making you feel guilty.*

CL: *Yes, especially my daughter. My daughter had such a look of horror on her face when she caught me pouring a drink.*

CO: *And so the guilt. You wanted to die.*

CL: *Yes, I did. And I made it worse. I screamed at her for tip-toeing. I've got a tip-toer for a daughter. She never wears shoes in the house only those damn slipper socks. It's like she haunts the house, always materializing out of nowhere.*

CO: *She tip-toes around, materializes out of nowhere, and makes you feel guilty and angry 'cause you can't have a drink whenever you want.*

CL: *My husband's worse. He just lectures me. I have to account for every damn penny now. It's hard saving money for booze out of the grocery money. And he lectures me right in front of her. How do you think that makes me feel?*

CO: *Humiliated and then angry too, I'll bet.*

CL: *Yes, and the humiliation is hurting my daughter, too. I've told him that. I've told him I've got to want to stop myself and he's only making it worse with his damned sermons.*

CO: *He makes you so mad that you want to keep drinking.*

CL: *Yes, honestly, sometimes when I'm alone and drinking I feel like I hate the two of them for what they're doing to me.*

CO: *Drink makes you feel you hate them.*

CL: *I'm not so sure it's the drink that does it. Sometimes even when I'm sober I hate them. Like right now.*

CO: *Right now you feel you hate them.*

CL: *I think like that a lot. Really it's why I started. I'm convinced of that. You know that old line about being driven to drink? It's not so crazy, not so crazy. They drive me to drink, the two of them, him with his sermons and her watching me like a hawk.*

CO: *I can appreciate how being watched like a hawk would make you angry. It would me.*

CL: *(Crying) God I was so awful. I made a real ass of myself. (Pause) We went to our annual family reunion and I got* drunk. *The whole thing's a blur for me. I don't remember too much only that I tried to dance on a picnic table while people ate and I fell off. I remember looking up and the looks, the awful looks, and a woman's voice saying, "She's a drunken bum." The last thing I remember is driving home in the car and my daughter was sobbing. Right then I wanted to die. I had humiliated my husband, my daughter, and me. Drunk, drunk as I was, I cried. Believe it or not for the first time in my life I got a good look at myself in the awful looks, in that woman's sneer ("She's a drunken bum") and in my daughter's tears. You have to know she never cries. I made her cry.*

CO: *Her tears made you see yourself better.*

CL: (High pitched voice) *It's not them I hate. It's me. I hate me and what I'm doing to them and to me. I hate myself. I hate myself for how I look, too puffy in the face, too big in the stomach all vodka and gin. It's me I hate, not them.*

Comments on Illustrative Excerpt

To fully appreciate this or any effective counselor by the printed word is very difficult. On the tape the counselor's tones jibed perfectly with those of the client. The reader can still learn from this excerpt though. The counselor didn't use the stereotypic lines "What you're feeling is ..." or "You feel..." Instead the counselor focused on the client's feelings and her words by reusing them via paraphrase and by reinforcing the validity of her dramatic self-confrontation. Probably a fair assumption would be that the counselor's knowledge and exquisite sensitivity probably convinced her at the onset that her avowed hate of both husband and daughter was only a mask for her own self-hate and a prop for her denial of the love she really felt for them.

Activities for Learning How to Reflect Feeling

Justification.

The ability to reflect feeling effectively is a critically important skill in counseling because through this technique the counselor is able to communicate empathy.

Purposes.

1. To heighten and reinforce the student counselor's awareness of the importance of emotional communication in counseling.
2. To sharpen the student counselor's ability to reflect feeling.

Outcome.

The student counselor demonstrates his or her ability to reflect feeling effectively in a real counseling session.

Specific Activities.

1. The student counselor obtains verification that she or he is thoroughly conversant with the theory behind reflection of feeling.
2. The student counselor views video excerpts of professional counselors as they reflect feelings.
3. The student counselor views live demonstrations of feeling rejection.
4. The student counselor does role-playing with colleagues and with mentor.
5. The student counselor demonstrates ability to reflect feeling in live session.

Evaluation.

1. The student counselor obtains feedback from mentor colleagues.
2. The student counselor considers progress of his or her real clients.
3. Activities continue until the mentor and the student counselor are satisfied with performance.

ROLE-PLAYING

Requirement

The basic and only requirement in role-playing is that the participant talk, do, and try to feel as the other person whose role she is playing.

Value

The author has found role-playing to be an especially valuable tool in alcoholism counseling. When this technique is utilized, alcoholics have an opportunity to become the object of their very own denials, rationalizations, and projections. This technique provides a unique learning experience for them because they see and hear in a dramatic way how they are perceived and how they relate to others. In turn, they act out the feelings they know others have toward them.

The technique should be used by the counselor and the client only after rapport has been established and participants feel that they know each other well. Role-playing is a novel and even exciting alternative to the regular counseling session. It is especially instructive and emotionally illuminating for the alcoholic when this technique is used with other family members. Alcoholics usually seem to be astounded to learn how much they know about a husband's and child's feelings and interpersonal stance. More often than not, the alcoholic woman and her family usually seem to be emotionally rocked by the experience. Clients have found no technique more effective in promoting cognitive understanding and emotional appreciation of their problems and of the other person's too.

Activities for Learning the Art of Role-Playing

Justification.

Once the counselor has mastered this technique, the alcoholism counselor can help the client to experience feelings which she has denied, projected, and rationalized. Also through this technique, the client experiences how she is perceived and can come to understand why people relate to her as they do.

Purposes.

1. To heighten feeling awareness in the student counselor.

2. To facilitate the student counselor's identification with clients (people) and thereby promote flexibility in counselor personality.

Outcome.

The student counselor demonstrates his or her ability to role-play effectively.

Specific Activities.

1. The student counselor obtains verification that she or he is well grounded on the theory behind the role-playing technique.
2. The student counselor does role-playing with colleagues under mentor observation.
3. The student counselor does role-playing with a mentor.
4. The student counselor does role-playing with a real client with mentor observing or a video-tape of a role-playing session with a client is made for self and mentor evaluation.

Evaluation.

1. The student counselor obtains feedback on previous four activities from a mentor.
2. Activities continue until the mentor and the student counselor are both satisfied that the skill has been attained.

RECAPITULATION

Many alcoholics have a talent for delivering long discourses. This is true especially in the initial sessions but generally abates as the relationship strengthens and they become healthier.

Why the Long Discourse?

Long discourses are usually a function of the usual alcoholic ailments—fear, suspicions, and unbridled anxiety. By giving a long discourse, alcoholics are able to keep the counselor at distance while they evaluate him or her; or again, the discourse may be nothing more than a camouflage for insecurities. No matter. Whatever the reason, long monologues are not uncharacteristic of alcoholics in their initial sessions. What can the counselor do? She or he can recapitulate.

Definition

The counselor who recapitulates responds with a focused, succinct synopsis of the client's discourse. When counselors recapitulate, they should try to use the client's words and phrases.

Value

Recapitulation has three benefits:

- It helps to build rapport because it shows the client that the counselor is listening.

- It helps the client to focus thoughts and keep to a point or theme.

- It reinforces the counselor's own understanding.

Illustration of Recapitulation: Counselor Ann

The illustration which follows is simulated but serves to exemplify this simple but valuable technique. The client in this illustration is a blend of several alcoholics whom the author has treated. The counselor is a directivist. The session is the initial contact.

CL: *Why do I drink? It's easy. It's not a big mystery. My life is awful, just awful. I have no time to myself. I have a witch of a mother-in-law who lives upstairs from us, a husband who's a nag and five kids who are driving me crazy. That's why I drink. All those tests I took, I could have saved you the trouble. You should have asked me. It would have been simpler. So I get bombed. What else have I got? I mean what have I got? I feel like I'm being eaten alive and my bones picked clean. My husband is just not the husband I married. He finds fault with everything I do. I never do anything right. He finds fault with my housekeeping, my cooking, even with how I make the bed. Dear God! He expects a house to be neat when there are five children in it! He gets furious when supper isn't ready when he comes home, furious if it isn't cooked to perfection and, according to him, it never is. This morning after I made the bed, he* spent five minutes criticizing how I'd made it because I hadn't made the sheets squared like they do in hospitals! That man is a compulsive maniac! But it's the kids, the kids who are driving me nuts and having to be with them all the time. Five of them from age one to seven. I told him, I tell him all the time I need to get away from them, I need a break. He won't listen to that. Just takes off to work and leaves me alone with them. Five of them. I wanted to stop after one, two at the most. He had the crazy idea about big happy families. Well, we've got a big, big family alright but it's something less than happy. I'm not, and I don't think he is either. We don't sleep in the same bed anymore. We now have twin beds. I'm just not interested in sex with him and even being near him for that matter. No, I really don't think I'm alcoholic. It's my life, my life is so awful, so dreary that I drink. That's it. Why are you laughing? What are you thinking?

CO: I'm thinking you didn't leave out too much. You're life is awful, a nagging husband whom you describe as a compulsive maniac, kids that are driving you crazy. You have no break from them so you get bombed once in a while. The only thing is you never really finished telling me about your mother-in-law. You said she was a witch and sort of left it at that.

CL: A witch. Yes, she's that. I swear the only thing she lacks is a broom. She nags me too, only sweetly, not sugar sweet, saccharine, disgustingly falsely sweet. She reminds me of him. In fact just like him. Different sexes, same personality. Identical. He really is her son. You know what that witch did and said to me the day we got twin beds? She shook her head and said I should reconsider having them and asked me how could I ever be a good wife if I didn't meet my husband's needs? That witch tried to make me feel guilty about my sex life! God who wouldn't drink, when I have those two on my back. Talk about being between a rock and a hard place. Two days I really had it, so I drank myself into a stupor. As you know I woke up in detox.

CO: (Nodding) Your husband's got the same personality as your mother-in-law. She even intrudes on your sex life or at

*least on what kind of a bed you choose to sleep in. But tell
me, Ellen, was it worth waking up in detox?*

Comments on Illustrative Excerpt

The counselor here is building rapport by showing the client
she's listening. She lets the client vent even more by returning
to an undeveloped theme, the mother-in-law. By recapitulating
so effectively she reinforces the client's understanding.

Activities for Learning the Technique of Recapitulation

Justification.

Alcoholism counselors who can recapitulate effectively
build rapport, help the client to focus thought, and thereby
facilitate the counseling process.

Purpose.

To develop counselor ability to recapitulate.

Outcome.

The student counselor will be able to incorporate this
technique into his/her repertoire of techniques.

Specific Activities.

1. The student counselor obtains verification that she or he
   accepts "justification" previously.
2. The student counselor does role-playing with colleagues,
   under a mentor's observation.
3. The student counselor will do role-playing with a mentor
   while focusing on recapitulation.
4. The student counselor will make audio tapings with one
   or more clients.

Evaluation.

1. The student counselor will obtain feedback from the
   mentor.
2. Activities continue until the mentor and the student
   counselor are satisfied that the skill has been attained.

CONFRONTATION

Research

The research indicates that confrontation as a technique is both valuable and productive. In a study by Kaul, Kaul, and Bednar (1973), clients found that confrontation led them to explore their inner feelings.

Kelly (1975) has expressed that confrontation is more effective and productive than is reflection of feeling. Use of confrontation, he felt, increases self-awareness for both client and counselor and is the technique which most effectively can lead to a client's commitment to change. Koeppen (1972) viewed confrontation as a threatening technique because pain is given and received but she pointed out, a promise to help and grow is in this technique too.

Discussion

The counselor who confronts, threatens. More often than not the alcoholic is scared by confrontation. Why? Because at some level she knows that it potentially can tear down defenses and alter the distorted perception held of others too. Herein lies the promise to which Koeppen alluded. For only when defenses and perception are righted can the alcoholic get back on the road to recovery.

Confrontation is an art. It's effectiveness will be determined by the counselor's emotional astuteness and competence in discerning the correct moment to confront.

Critical in any confrontation is concern, concern which springs from an honest belief that in the threat of the confrontative remark there does indeed lie a potential for enhancement. The most effective confrontative remarks are those which communicate that concern.

To accomplish this communication, the counselor should introduce confrontative questions with words that are neutral and tones that are gentle. For example, with the alcoholic who shows symptoms of Budding, the author has found such comments as these following appropriate.

> With the silent alcoholic who's usually talkative. (Chuckle) *"Seems like I've been doing more than my share of talking today. What's happening?"*
>
> With the irritable alcoholic. *"We all have our irritable days, but seems as if you've really been bitten today. Can you tell me about it?"*

> With the overconfident, euphoric alcoholic. *"You feel like you're definitely recovered. What do you think that means?"*

The real artistry in the previous confrontative remarks lies in the counselor's ability to have affect jibe with words. The counselor must be and sound unaffected and must know the client. The counselor must feel confident that confrontative remarks will not alienate the client but will indeed enhance the relationship.

Illustrative Excerpt, Nondirectivist: Counselor Roselyn

The following two excerpts illustrate this confrontation technique.

CL: *The doctor thinks I ought to go on Antabuse.*

CO: *Oh? And what's your feeling about that, Betty?*

CL: *I don't want to.*

CO: *You don't want to.*

CL: *No.*

    (Pause)

CO: *You want to tell me why?*

CL: *If I haven't learned anything else, I've learned I've got to do this thing myself. I don't want to get hooked on something and I don't want to lean on any crutch. Besides I don't believe in taking any pills. Like I said I got to do this by myself.*

CO: *You don't want to lean on anything or anybody. You want to beat the booze yourself.*

CL: *Yes.*

CO: (Smiling) *You don't want to lean on anybody. Correct me if I'm wrong, but essentially what you're saying is that you don't feel that you need any help?*

CL: *I'm not saying that.*

CO: *You're not.*

CL: *No. There's a difference between leaning and getting help.*

CO: (In an honestly bewildered tone) *What's the difference?*

CL: *Well, I meant like there's a difference between pills and people. You lean on pills, you get help from people. You're a person. I get help from you because you're a person.*

CO: (Grinning) *Seems like I haven't helped all that much now, have I?*

CL: (Grinning back) *You mean just cause I blew it twice in the past month?*

CO: (Nodding) *Yeah.* (Pause) *Do you feel the doctor's a person?*

CL: *He's okay.*

CO: *I guess what you're saying, then, is that you want my help but not his help.*

CL: *No, what I'm saying is that I don't want pills.* (Eyes wide) *They're dangerous. They can kill you.*

CO: (Nodding) *Or at least make you damn sick if you drink.*

CL: (Sheepishly) *Yeah.*

CO: *Maybe what you're saying is that, you still want to be able to choose to get drunk when you want to.*

CL: (Stonily) *What I'm saying is that I don't want to get hooked on a pill.*

CO: (Grinning) *Are you saying that you prefer to be hooked on alcohol?*

CL: (Loudly) *No, I'm not saying that.* (Sighing) *Right now, I guess, I don't know what I'm saying. Let me think about it okay?*

The previous simulated excerpt is an example of the kind of approach to confrontation which this author prefers. The nondirective confronts but does so gently, at times deferentially, but hangs on doggedly, occasionally even dueling intellectually with her client in order to adhere to the main point, helping the client to dismantle her denial defense and rectify her perception.

Illustrative Excerpt, Directivist: Counselor Danielle

CL: *The doctor thinks I ought to go on Antabuse.*

CO: *What do you think?*

CL: *I don't want to.*

CO: *Why not?*

CL: *If I haven't learned anything else, I've learned I've got to do this thing myself. I don't want to get hooked on something, and I don't want to lean on any crutch. Besides, I don't believe in taking any pills. Like I said, I got to do this by myself.*

CO: *What you're telling me, Betty, is that you don't think you need any help.*

CL: *I'm not saying that.*

CO: *So what are you saying?*

CL: *There's a difference between leaning and getting help.*

CO: (Candidly) *What difference?*

CL: *Well, I mean like there's a difference between pills and people. You lean on a pill, you get help from people. You're a person. I get help from you because you're a person.*

CO: (Seriously) *Doesn't seem like it's been all that much. You got drunk twice in the past month.*

CL: *Yeah, but I've been dry now for over a week.*

CO: *What are you saying? Maybe that you're not sure you want to stay dry too much longer?*

CL: *Christ no! I'm not saying that.*

CO: *So what's all this about helping and leaning? Doctors help like they know how, with prescriptions. Me, I help by listening and talking. People help how they can and how they know how. So what are you saying?*

CL: (Stonily) *What I'm saying is that I don't want to get hooked on a pill.*

CO: (Seriously) *You'd rather be hooked on booze?*

CL: *Christ I hope not.*

CO: *Okay, let's go over it again . . .*

This approach is blunt. At times, it is harsh. There is no intellectual dueling. The counselor's affect is serious and reflective. Her genuine concern is reflected in the final comment,

"Okay, let's go over it again." What the counselor means is that the client's denial defense needs to be attacked again.

Which of the two approaches is better? That is for the counselor to decide. The most important criterion is that the counselor must be comfortable with the method employed. Directive, nondirective, or somewhere in between, the method must fit with the counselor's personality if she or he is to confront with artistry.

Activities for Learning the Confrontation Technique

Justification.

Confrontation is conducive to self-exploration and heightened self-awareness by the client. Its special value in alcoholism counseling is that it can serve as a catalyst to restructure defenses.

Purpose.

To develop the counselor's competence to confront.

Outcome.

The student counselor will be able to demonstrate an effective use of the confrontation technique.

Specific Activities.

1. The student counselor obtains verification that she or he accepts and is conversant with the theory behind confrontation.

2. The student counselor makes an observation of video tapes or listens to audio tapes of counselors who use this technique effectively.

3. The student counselor does role-playing with colleagues or mentor.

4. The student counselor demonstrates ability to confront with real client (live or on video tape).

Evaluation.

1. The student counselor obtains feedback from the mentor.

2. Activities continue until the mentor and the student counselor are satisfied that the skill has been attained.

SUMMARY

The frame of reference for many alcoholics is derived from the Twelve Steps of A.A. The counselor who has understanding of these steps finds that rapport comes more easily. Once the counselor has learned how the client interprets these steps, the counselor gains a valuable window into the client's system of thought and emotional life.

An important task of the counselor is to help the client to redirect and restructure her defenses. Explanations and/or illustrations were provided for denial, rationalization, displacement, fantasy, projection, and regression. Repression is a defense better left alone. Its best antidote would seem to be establishment of other defenses like compensation and sublimation.

Silence is threatening even to competent counselors. Silence occurs because of embarrassment, resentments, testing, client conflicts, fear, the client's need to integrate, and the end of a client-counselor topic. A variety of techniques exist to handle the silence.

The counselor's ability to listen is critically important if progress is going to be made in counseling. She or he needs not only to listen to words but also to be exquisitely sensitive to the client's feelings, tones, and sounds. The counselor's motivation to listen is communicated by how she or he sits, by obviating interruptions, by isolating distracting thoughts, by being fully cognizant of those topics and thoughts which can block counselor ability to listen, and by learning to ask focused, pertinent questions.

Questioning as a technique has innate problems because

- it probes into the unknown,

- it can lead to more questions,

- it may cause the client to become conditioned to think in terms of questions and thereby lose her sense of responsibility to share more fully in the counseling, and

- questioning focuses upon the cognitive rather than upon feelings.

At the same time questioning also can be facilitative as it can lead into productive discussion, especially when the questions are open-ended and avoid the noted dangers.

Reiteration refers to a literal restatement or a rephrasing of what the client says. Reiteration is valuable because it puts the counselor into an accepting role, elicits client's feelings, and helps the client to delineate and reconsider his/her thinking.

The counselor who reflects feeling communicates that she or he understands and perceives what the client is feeling and experiencing. The values of reflecting feelings lie in helping the client to crystallize her feelings and in understanding those feelings in relation to people. When reflecting feeling, the counselor should use simple language and be concerned about timing. This technique enhances the client by helping her to learn that feelings cause behavior, that feelings hide feelings. The ultimate benefit of such knowledge is to help the client explore the motives of her behavior.

Role-playing involves talking, doing, and trying to feel as the other person whose role one plays. Role-players become the object of their own denials, rationalizations, and projections. Role-playing is an especially valuable technique in counseling the alcoholic intrafamilially.

The counselor who recapitulates responds with a focused, succinct synopsis of the client's long monologue. Recapitulation helps the client to build rapport, to focus thoughts and to keep to a theme. Recapitulation also reinforces the counselor's own understanding.

Confrontation is a valuable and useful technique as has been reported by researchers. The counselor should be fully aware that confrontation can be and often is threatening. Counselors can mitigate this threat if they are emotionally astute, if they genuinely are concerned and can communicate that concern, and if they introduce their confrontative remarks with neutral words and gentle tones. In addition, they must be and sound unaffected, know their client, and feel confident that their remarks will ultimately enhance the counseling relationship.

FOR REVIEW AND REFLECTION

1. Articulate your position on the *Twelve Steps of Alcoholics Anonymous.*

2. Is your penchant toward the directivist or toward the nondirectivist style of counseling?

3. Which of the alcoholic defenses do you believe will be most difficult to restructure?

4. With which of the techniques described do you feel you will experience the most difficulty? With which the least?

5. Do you find client silence a threat? If so, reflect on the why of it.

6. Is the ability to listen to both tones and words part of your make-up? If not, do you feel the need to develop such an ability?

7. Are you one who can mirror feelings? Do you agree with the author on its importance?

8. Role-playing involves a "let's pretend" attitude that often becomes very reality oriented. Do you expect to role-play in your work with clients?

9. Confrontation with some clients can be embarrassing. Will you be able to do it?

10. Learning practical techniques in counseling requires the expenditure of much time and energy. How willing are you to do so?

Chapter 8

COUNSELING
THE ALCOHOLIC
WOMAN IN A GROUP

The basic and general goal of counseling the alcoholic women in a group is the same as counseling her individually: namely, *to help her achieve and maintain sobriety.*

Although the goal for both treatment modes are identical, many of the theoretical and practical concerns with group counseling (from six to ten individuals) are substantially different. The nature of group counseling will be discussed under these four topic headings:

Benefits,

Behaviors of Alcoholic Group members,

Functions of the Group Alcoholism Counselor, and

Stages and Techniques.

BENEFITS

Counseling the alcoholic woman in a group has inestimable value. In a group the alcoholic woman learns

1. to accept help,
2. about herself,

3. interpersonal skills, and

4. tolerance of self and others.

Learning to Accept Help

The socialization process teaches many women to become dependent. As seen in many contexts and discussed in preceding chapters, many become so dependent that they lose their self-respect and turn to alcohol and away from people. Yet, for most of these women the socialization process, perverted as it might have been, especially regarding closeness and warmth and the value of relationships, remains ever ready to be nurtured.

The alcoholic woman, like the alcoholic man, entering a group wants help. Unlike him, however, she needs very little in interactive warmth to come to accept it. The reason for this is that the same process of socialization which made her feel emotionally violated now serves her in the therapeutic climate of alcoholism counseling. The physical presence of peer alcoholics, male and female, their closeness and nearness, combined with the emotionally intense sharing through talk and behavior in a group invariably lead her to give of her own self.

She finds that the mere act of listening not only gives her a sense of giving but also provides her with feelings of reward for doing so. It is precisely these feelings which let her do now what she's not been able to do heretofore; namely, accept help from others.

Learning about Self

For most alcoholic women the inevitable effect of learning to give and accept help from others is to learn about their own selves. In the receptive and caring climate of a group, these women learn that despite the unfortunate socialization process that they underwent their addiction finally is a function of their own choice.

As they listen to the moving and authentic self disclosure of peer alcoholics, as they tell their own stories, and as they question and are in turn questioned, they learn to look inside. They learn to do this with the new-found need to learn about the workings and control of their own selves instead of the narcissistic preoccupation which precipitated and maintained their alcoholism. They learn that their own mislearnings and consequent dysfunctions are not unique or strange but are part of the alcoholic condition. They learn that their problems stem from within and not without, from their own choices and judgments and not external manipulation. In short, these women learn to do what they have never done — to take responsibility of their own selves.

Learning Interpersonal Skills

Most alcoholic women feel uncomfortable interpersonally. In most cases, the apparent warmth and expansiveness which some are able to display are a veneer and a thin one at that.

A basic reason for their interpersonal discomfort is the latent but constant nag that most people cannot be trusted. The inevitable effect of this is that they are quite unable to let others get close emotionally. This inability, in turn, keeps their interpersonal skills stunted.

Their general discomfort with people has another reason, common among alcoholics, a low self-esteem. In general, the alcoholic woman feels she has little to offer, little to give in a relationship.

Feelings of suspicion dissipate, self-esteem is enhanced and inevitably bettered in a group. Membership obligates participation, and participation militates against suspicion. And so as they proceed to give and accept help they naturally come to feel better about themselves. The combination of a diminution of suspicion of others combined with an enhanced self-esteem inevitably leads to increased interpersonal involvement and improved interpersonal skills.

Tolerance of Self and Others

The inevitable derivative of the three benefits previously described is the development in the alcoholic woman of a trait alien to them—namely tolerance. As noted in prior context, the alcoholic is beset with a conscience which could be fairly described as scrupulous. The common effects of scrupulosity are obsessiveness, hyper-cynicism, a nagging disposition, and a general intolerance of self and others.

If any specific learning accelerates and facilitates the acquisition of this trait of tolerance in the new alcoholic woman, it has to be finding out that her peers in the group suffer, experience, and display many of the foibles and weaknesses which harass her. Such learning is a positive revelation. More often than not, this revelation precipitates and facilitates the giving and loving of self by these new members.

It should be understood that this giving and sharing are not maintained exclusively by feelings of altruism, but they are generated in these women by the need to understand and become comfortable with their own respective selves. Whatever the motive, the effect is enhancing both for new members and for their peers.

BEHAVIORS OF ALCOHOLIC GROUP MEMBERS

Group sessions are characterized by both healthful and unhealthful behaviors. The healthful behaviors are those which facilitate the emotional growth progress of the alcoholic woman and/or of a fellow member. The three most important among these are

1. attending,
2. sharing, and
3. facilitating.

The unhealthful behaviors are all those which produce self-destruction, which emotionally stultify another member, or which impede the collective progress of the group. Among those behaviors are included

1. hostility,
2. nonparticipating,
3. absenteeism,
4. buffoonery,
5. psychologizing,

6. housekeeping,
7. manipulating, and
8. seducing.

Healthful Behaviors

Attending. The critical ingredients of attending are *listening* and *communicating*. When we feel listened to, we are enhanced. Conversely, when we feel no one is listening, we feel demeaned.

Most alcoholic women feel that no one listens to them. They are probably right. Because of broken promises, procrastinations and elusive and cynical ways, they have lost credibility. For whatever reasons, being a member of a counseling group affords a wonderful opportunity to feel listened to, with a consequent sense of importance previously unknown.

As is true of most human behaviors, listening is learned. In a group the counselor is in the best position to teach it. Leader words, actions, and general demeanor are invariably modeled by members.

Leader posture and expression tell the speaker whether she is being listened to or not. In a group the effective counselor sits as if she or he is motivated to hear everything said by everybody. Face and body bent tell the person talking not only that she is being heard but that her words are being processed. The counselor can accomplish this easily by reiterating her comments, by questioning, and by *not* introducing new thoughts or ideas, i.e., thoughts and ideas not raised by group members.

By adhering strictly to these ideas of the listener role, the counselor lets members know not only that they are important as people but also that a behavioral model is present with whom members can identify.

The woman communicates in a group when she talks *to* and not *about* another member. Very little ever occurs in human interaction which is more awkward or stilted than to hear oneself being discussed. This is true even when the talk is complimentary. Please note: in a group, this is often not so.

Accordingly, an important first issue with an all new group or with the woman newly arrived in an ongoing group is to inform her that *any and all talk about another is to be addressed to that member.*

In a group, members communicate when their words, their emotions, and their body languages all fit together. Most people find it difficult to process the meaning of words per se. Words in and of themselves can be and often are boring. For most, *the emotion upon which words ride is what makes them interesting, even captivating.* Most people are more likely to laugh uproariously when they hear funny dialogue than when they read it. Students are more likely to be bored by a monotone-like delivery than with one filled with affective peaks and valleys. In sum, *most people are not touched by the cognitive (words) alone but by a blend of words and emotions.* When the words and emotions jibe with the speaker's body language then their intention is indeed "grabbed." Their attention is grabbed for the very simple reason that the message delivered *communicates*—its words, emotions, and body stance fit and complement each other. Such are the requirements of authentic communication.

When appropriate, effective group therapists model these ideas. Members should see that it's not only O.K. but also desirable to smile a happy or complimentary thought. When members accompany an angry statement with a glower or when they lacrimate a sorrow, the counselor's reaction should tell them such reactions are perfectly O.K.

Sharing. Sharers in a group are those who have come to trust. Trust is a rare trait among newly recovering alcoholic women. It is even rarer among alcoholic women who are drinking. Their paranoid perception militates against its development.

Newly recovering women more often than not have had no experience with group counseling. They are fearful and suspicious of a process which obligates trusting; especially is that true because their socialization process taught them that they can't trust anybody.

Such women can be understood as being still in the throes of projection and denial. Not having been exposed to a situation or an experience where they could or had to learn it, they do not know sublimation. Put another way, they have not yet been able to learn to find reward in giving or that the road to health can be eased much by the development of emotional relationships. Sad but true, in the giving of self and in interpersonal relations in general, *alcoholic women function with the emotional wherewithal of children.*

In a group, trust comes to the newly admitted woman only after she has had an opportunity to become acclimated. As she begins to identify with the talk and behaviors of individual members and of the group collectively, she begins to sense the warmth and mutuality that are the essentials of rapport. Of course, this new-found rapport precipitates the trust needed to get on with her own rehabilitation.

Once she begins to find emotional reward in trusting others, she shows it—in her talk and in how she looks. Why? Because trusting raises self-esteem, both of the trusted and the trustee.

A principle obstacle to learning to trust is confidentiality. Group members have to know that anything and everything said in the group is inviolate. It behooves the counselor to explain and reiterate this to the whole group whenever a new member is admitted. The author's explanation always includes the idea that confidentiality is an indispensable prerequisite to group process. My line delivered with conviction is that, *"If there is no confidentiality there can be no group."* My sense is that group members have always honored the confidentiality dictum. In no case can I recollect an instance where it has been violated. My sense, too, is that the group's apparent respect for confidentiality has facilitated trust in the newly entering member.

Group leaders would do well to let the new woman to the group know that they recognize the difficulties involved in trusting a number of strangers. A statement in this regard can be helpful only as it confirms and reinforces what the new member knows, i.e., albeit dimly, that participation in a group is premised upon trust.

Trust leads to self-disclosure which ironically, in turn, promotes more trust. This promotion and expansion of trust in a group is probably why counselors find that group members invariably reward and often do so generously that first fumbling attempt at self-disclosure by newer members.

The wonderful thing about self-disclosure is that once alcoholic women have come to trust, they learn to do it quickly. A very strong, positive correlation exists between self-disclosure and improvement of emotional health. The more they share and confide their most acute anxieties, frustrations, and past embarrassments, the healthier they become. Their self-perception and perception of others become more optimistic. Their ability to listen improves and increases. Thus, they are able to share the anxieties and frustrations of other members.

With increased self-disclosure, the defenses with which these women insulate themselves — projection and denial — begin to crumble. As they share more and more, these defenses are replaced slowly but inevitably by sublimation.

The author is pleased most when self-disclosure comes at the beginning of a session. What he has learned is that if alcoholics have time to mull over what a member has shared, they are likely to be moved themselves to share. Self-disclosures early in a session generally precipitate self-disclosure by other members. These subsequent precipitates can be understood as supportive statements to the initial discloser. Whatever the reason, the effect is usually a happy one. Interaction invariably becomes warmer and more tolerant.

Facilitating. Initially the counselor is the prime facilitator. As the group progresses, facilitating behavior becomes the choice behavior for most members. A point to note is that not uncommonly, alcoholism counseling groups include one or more women who because of prior group experience are quite knowledgeable about facilitating. Not uncommonly too, some members because of disposition and/or inclination are natural facilitative types. The danger with these last, discussed under the heading "Unhealthy Behavior, Psychologizing," is that some of these women might be facilitating consciously or unconsciously at the expense of their own needs. Such facilitators are of course in denial. That is, they are facilitating to avoid dealing with their own problems. Member facilitators not psychologizing but who are themselves progressing toward health and termination from the group can be understood as being in accelerated recovery. The especially active member facilitators are usually those who have most recently discovered the emotional pleasure to be found in the sublimation defense.

Alcoholic women find a special reward in facilitating because they learn, and quickly, that it is not purely an altruistic activity. What they learn is that the feeling effects of facilitating enhance the self as much as they enhance others.

Facilitators move group members toward health. They do this by listening like they meant it. They respond only to what is said and question and probe with nothing more threatening than authentic concern and curiosity. Their words, their effects, and their body language, when they do, all *communicate* a need to help—sans strings.

Indigenous to facilitating is giving ***feedback***. When a group leader or a member gives feedback, she or he focuses on words or behavior of a particular member. The one giving feedback tells her or his own feelings about what the member has said and/or done. Giving feedback never involves nagging, carping, or criticizing. Rather, its cardinal rule is that it be couched in deference, if not humility, and its emotional by-play are tact, diplomacy, and simple kindness. The author tells his group that giving feedback is a purely subjective process. I am very fond of saying that, "*What is true in a group depends upon who is lookin'*." Ergo, feedback has value only if the recipient thinks and feels it's so. *Feedback finally is one person's reaction to another. Feedback is not objective truth.* With these statements as a frame of reference then the one giving feedback should preface the words with "My personal feeling is that ..." "I'm not talking for anyone else when I say that ..." "My reaction and mine only is that ..."

Such prefaces not only make it clear that feedback is just one human's opinion to another, but they inform and elucidate. More importantly, they minimize the risk of hurt.

Feedback's most important effect is to expose the recipient of it to another view of herself. Couched with good will only, the feedbacker's view is usually accepted thereby enhancing the member's and the group's movement toward growth.

Unhealthful Behaviors

Hostility. As has been noted in this text in a variety of contexts, the prime defenses for alcoholic women are denial and projection. The effect of denial usually is to put them on a different emotional and perceptual wave length from those with whom they come in contact. More often than not, the effect of all this on these women is bewilderment and anger, compounded typically by the fantasy defense.

The defense of *fantasy* in alcoholics, both in women and men, is characterized usually by a sense of victimization. While in the case of women this sense can be more readily understood and evokes sympathy, this sense of victimization helps these women to develop and cultivate tableaus where they can function as the focal point of attention, if not adulation. These women spend such a disproportionate amount of time in fantasy, find such an inordinate amount of reward in it that too often they ultimately come to lack in interactive skills and are beset with an acutely low self-esteem. Encounters with strangers, it should be noted, are the situations that raise the most anxiety both with interaction and with their self-esteem.

Every alcoholic displays her or his hostility differently. This is true not only because of the genetic uniqueness of human personality but also for the obvious and simple reasons that hostility varies from person to person in kind, amount, and intensity. With men, it also is often manifested via sarcastic and demeaning *humor* which more often than not is personably rather than generally directed. In men, it also is expressed more often in *rudeness*. This expression may be due to some perverted understanding of what it means to be a man or, more simply, may be due to the fact that these men were never exposed to role models from whom they could learn socially appropriate ways.

Alcoholic women generally do not express their hostility with cruel humor or rudeness. Their method rather, is via *testing*.

The woman, newly admitted to a group, by definition encounters strangers. Invariably, she feels compelled to test them. Testing can be understood as one of the more salient symptoms of the alcoholic's suspiciousness if not paranoia. Its rationale, while simple, can be exasperating. Central to the testing is the alcoholic woman's perverted idea that how much hostility a person will tolerate from her is a measure of how much she or he cares. The testing can take any of a variety of forms—vitriolic teasing, temper tantrums, mimicry, etc. Unfortunately, ironically the more people put up with the abasements, the more they fuel the hostility. If and when they react with anger, the hostile testing woman has a ready response, *"See, I knew you didn't care!"*

The only happy note about testing in a group is that it declines rapidly as members become acclimated to each other (and pass each other's tests).

No specific or simple techniques can be outlined for dealing with the alcoholic woman's hostility. Confrontation, in any form, is not a good idea as it reinforces her basic notion that hostility is justified because everyone else is hostile. The best way for the therapist to mitigate hostility in a group is to communicate to all the members that they are all accepted unconditionally. Therapists can best provide antidotes for hostility if they model and promote the qualities outlined under the preceding heading "Healthful Behaviors," i.e., attending, sharing, and facilitating. Inevitably these alleviate, or at least ameliorate, the unpleasantness generated by hostility.

Finally, it is not naive and it should be pointed out that patience is an indispensable prerequisite in counselors who deal with hostile alcoholic women. They need to remember that the hostility these women vent toward them and their peer members is never personal but is an emotional trait sown in them early by neglect, indifference, and cruelty. This trait took more than a while to grow and develop in them, and the reality is that it is a part of their personalities. Quite apparently, the therapist and the group members can not surgically remove this undesirable trait, but both can contribute an emotional climate conducive to developing insight into the why of it. This insight combined with the acquisition of healthful behaviors mentioned can help such women better control their hostility.

Nonparticipating. Interpretation via defenses does not effectively explain the why of nonparticipation in a group by some alcoholic women, because the defenses associated with nonparticipation are many and varied. The reasons for it in a group include those reasons for silence detailed and explained in Chapter 7 under "Practical Techniques." A rereading at this point might prove helpful. Now, while these reasons for silence may explain the whys for individual nonparticipation and silence in an individual and even in a group, they do not explain why a whole group may become silent.

The three following reasons are fairly common ones. Other reasons may indeed exist but these three are the most common. The author's experience is that group nonparticipation often occurs because

1. the group does not want to deal with an anxious or embarrassing issue,
2. the group and the leader are not communicating, and/or
3. the group feels affronted and wants to get back at the leader.

What group leaders know is that silence in a group precipitates a lot more tension than it ever does in individual counseling. Happily and not uncommonly, alcoholic counseling groups include a member who has very little tolerance for such tension. A tense silence broken by an anxious alcoholic, however, does not explain the why of the silence. If the reason is that the group is reluctant to deal with an anxiety provoking issue, confrontation through questioning by the therapist is in order. The one to question first would be the one who broke the silence, as that member is probably the one interested in abating the tension.

When the reason has to do with communication, the author has discovered that confrontation by questioning is again the best way to resolve the issue. Questioning each member in turn or selecting articulate members has been effective for this author. The answer(s) which come out of a group have been both startling and amusing. For example, early in the author's career, when he was employed in a psychiatric hospital, he was leading a new group. In its several early encounters, the group was beset with protracted silences regularly. Frustrated, bewildered, and not a little threatened, I questioned the group. The answer which came back readily was simple and not a little pointed. What I learned was that my questions, probing, and interpretations had been couched in language more appropriate for a graduate school setting than one where the average length of education for members was seventh grade. Mildred, the little woman who sat directly opposite to me looked me right in the eye and summed it up simply and succinctly, *"Big words, doc. Too many big words!"*

The third reason for group nonparticipation is usually due to hostility. If an entire group is angry or resentful, the therapist is probably in some measure responsible. Several approaches for resolution can be considered.

1. Careful and intense self-examination by the therapist focusing especially on his or her perception of the group.
2. Discussion with a colleague, again focusing on perception of the group and consideration of new strategies.
3. If the therapist can honestly admit to inadequacies, then an apologetic, deferential discussion about these inadequacies with the group is very much in order. Quite apparently, no group has ever been offended by an honest admission of fault. After all, it is the essence of very effective self-disclosure previously described.

Absenteeism. The prime defense for absenteeism is denial. Absentee members are absent, because, for whatever reason, they need to hold on to the illusion that they are not alcoholic. Absence from the group demonstrates that illusion.

Reasons for an absence may be legitimate but they are few and dire—death, a contagious illness, and/or a crippling accident. No other excuse can and should be tolerated by the therapist or the group. The point, *attendance at every single session is mandatory.* It is an indispensable requisite. The therapist should make this point and with conviction when the alcoholic attends her first meeting. Many groups have rules about absences, i.e., one, two, or more absences for reasons other than those indicated and a member is expelled. Such rules should not be imposed by the therapist imperiously as they might engender hostility unnecessarily. Rather they should be issued as policy from the group so that it can have more meaning, more force, and more easily identified with.

Unjustified absences hurt not only the absentee but the group as well. Every group has a palpably unique personality just as do individuals. When a member is absent from the group without explanation, then the group's personality is different. The difference is rarely a healthier one, for the absence, always painfully obvious, engenders talk which is rarely complimentary to the absentee and even more rarely to the members who discuss her.

The author's position is that absence without justification needs to be discussed. Why? Because unjustified absence invariably engenders much, much hostility. Like it or not, justified or not, it is perceived as rejection of the group by most if not all members. The reason for this is simple. Rejection is in the background of virtually all alcoholics. Indeed, for many it was precisely rejection which contributed to, often precipitated, the alcoholism.

Even though some steam needs to be let out by the group, an effective leader will not let discussion about an absentee deteriorate into just a complaining, belittling session about her. Such a leader will help the group develop a constructive plan to help the absentee. Each plan will necessarily be different as its design will be determined by both the needs of the group and the absent member. Even so, every plan should include ideas about communicating to absentees that they are needed, that they are important to the group personality, and that they are missed. An important point is for the plan to provide time for the group to discuss with the absentee her motivation, commitment, and readiness for the group.

Buffoonery. From time to time the group might include a woman who is genuinely funny, whose jokes are only ironic and not directed personally. Such a woman is perceived as a *clown*. She is loved by all the members not only because the humor is devoid of hostility but because the jokes and buffoonery entertain and relieve group tensions.

Alcoholic women, especially in the treatment center, are generally not perceived as sources of entertainment. But this is exactly what a clown is—an entertainer. When the clown is in especially good humor, she can precipitate honest belly laughs.

Clowning like most human behavior serves a purpose. In group therapy, it hides the denial defense, and, more often than not, it does so exceedingly well. Effective clowns make people laugh, and, ironically, every laugh feeds denial. Effective clowns make members forget that clowns are in a group for the same reason as the rest of the members — namely to achieve and maintain sobriety.

The alcoholic clown is an **anomaly**. Alcoholism and clowning are really like oil and water, they don't mix. Why? Because alcoholics ordinarily are preoccupied with their own selves, are inclined to emotional isolation or, at least, they structure their lives to keep people at a distance. Clowns, on the other hand, are emotionally attuned to others and enjoy being with others (how else can they get laughs?). The clown who is an alcoholic, then, is as conflicted as any alcoholic and probably more than most.

The actual buffoonery of the clowning woman can be understood as nothing more than a sophisticated veneer.

After having provided the usual moments of entertainment the clown can sit back comfortably and let others take over to interact therapeutically. If the therapist is not vigilant, the clown can stay quite uninvolved in the actual attending, sharing, and facilitating. The sensitive and conscientious therapist will not let this happen. The problem is not especially difficult to remedy. All the counselor needs to do is to direct an occasional simple question or remark at her. In this way, the therapist is able to remind both the clown and the rest of the group why she is there.

Psychologizing. Today, more people than ever have sophisticated vocabularies in psychology and psychotherapy. Words like defenses, rapport, transference, and countertransference are, if not part of every day usage, then at least readily understood. This is probably due to the popularization of psychology and of counseling group process through literature and television, and to the substantial increase in the number of people with some college education during the past generation. Whatever the reason, today we meet people who love to interpret the whys and wherefores of human behavior in general and in particular of the people they know. We call these people *psychologizers*.

Psychologizers are to be found everywhere and too often in the counseling group. Like the clown, psychologizing women deny their alcoholism and engage in idiosyncratic behavior to divert attention from themselves. An important difference exists between the two however: clowns usually are lovable and psychologizers usually are not.

Psychologizers effectively support their denial defense with intellectualization. Thus they engage in analyzing, interpreting, and explaining the motive and behaviors of other group members both when appropriate and when not. Given free rein they can do so ad nauseam.

At the same time it should be noted that their long intellectualized defining of peer behavior can be, often is, smooth and cogent. Usually a response to their fantasies regarding being powerful, these monologues are controlling because of the amount of time they demand of listeners.

Many of the psychologizing women one encounters in the alcoholic group learned to be so in past groups and in individual counseling. Even though they may need more treatment, they display a remarkable knowledge of both the language and the techniques of counseling.

How much of a problem psychologizers pose is determined by just how much they need to control. An especially controlling one can indeed be an unfortunate burden for the group. Those psychologizers, who are especially adept, can and do impress the newer, more naive members with their cognitive expertise. The psychologizers win them over and ally with them against another member or other members, thereby creating a subgroup within the group. In short, some psychologizers, especially the hostile ones, make themselves out to be rivals of the group leader. Understandably the inexperienced therapist can be threatened by such people.   More unfortunately still, these controlling psychologizers are very much aware of the threat felt by such a therapist and, consciously or unconsciously, thoroughly enjoy the prospects of vying for group leadership and control.

The best way that the therapist can obviate the possibility of such an embarrassing prospect or eventuality is to meet with the psychologizer alone.   At the meeting the therapist should point out in the clearest fashion what the respective roles and responsibilities of each of them are and that rivalry for the leadership role is not one of them.

The behavior of psychologizers can strain the patience threshold of the best therapist.   The constant temptation is to confront.   This may or may not be a good idea.   It is as if the psychologizing has been going on for some time and the therapist sees that the group collectively or particular members are being silenced or alienated.   It is not a good idea to confront the psychologizer or any member for that matter if the therapist is not emotionally and cognitively convinced that she or he understands the member's dynamics.

Housekeeping.   Occasionally the counseling group includes a very active woman, one who constantly is busy doing for the group.   This person will set up chairs and make coffee before the meeting on a regular basis and on occasion will provide snacks.   While the group is in session this busy bee will buzz around the group pouring the coffee and serving the snacks. Such an individual is called a housekeeper.

Housekeepers keep busy for the same reasons that buffoons buffoon and psychologizers psychologize—namely, to divert attention from their alcoholism.   Like others previously described, housekeepers are in denial. Also, they cultivate a rich fantasy life.   In their fantasy world they are nurturant, servant-like, and enhancing. Thus the image they project fits pretty much with the image they hold of themselves.

Basically, housekeepers are likeable people.   As with the clown, to not like them is hard for the simple reason they seem (and do) find much pleasure in doing for and giving to others.

The personality of the giving, active, serving individual that they display in the group counseling is consistent with the one they display prior to entry and pretty much the one they display after they terminate.

Although exceedingly private in disposition, housekeepers are usually people beset with strong submissive and acceptance needs. By doing, doing, doing for group members they are able to meet both needs. Their busy frenetic ways can and often serve as a camouflage for their alcoholism and obviate their involvement during the more intensely dramatic moments of a session.

If their dynamics are understood and appreciated, housekeepers are usually excellent candidates for group counseling and invariably profit much from it. Guided by the counselor, the members should be encouraged to praise and reward the housekeeper's physical efforts for the group. What the author has discovered is that questioning after being verbally rewarded by the group makes the housekeeper receptive to self-disclosure and a rapid movement toward emotional growth.

Some housekeepers, however, are more complex in nature. These are the ones whose fantasies go beyond nurturance and service to others and include a maternal-like role. These housekeepers on some level see themselves as protector types and they try to expand the housekeeper role to fit that self-image.

Their own submissive streak notwithstanding, and/or perhaps because of it, they are able to detect those members who have dependency needs. Finely attuned to such needs in the group session they anticipate and act ahead of the therapist or peer who is about to protect a member from the verbal abuse of another or of a clique. The dependent prone members, male or female, are usually grateful to the housekeeper and quickly come to perceive her as a kind of emotional crutch.

Housekeepers who continually try to function as protectors can be likened to over-protective mothers, and, like the overprotective mother, the protector-housekeeper seeks not to nurture but to control. Unrestrained in the group, housekeepers could become destructive.

If just plain told this, the housekeeper would be astonished. She would not understand. Such astonishment would be a good thing because it would mean that she is oblivious of the demeaning nature of her protector need and that her penchant for it is unpremeditated.

A most effective technique for the author with this kind of housekeeper is to lead the group in a discussion of the traits of the controlling alcoholic enabler. Most of the members know the enabler type only too well. This topic invariably precipitates a discussion which gives off a lot of heat but light too. Not only the housekeeper, but all the members who incorporate even remotely comparable qualities find they can suddenly become the objects of more than a few acerbic comments. More often than not the session seems to have a healthful sobering effect (no pun intended!) on the enthusiastic housekeeper.

Manipulating. In a therapy group composed of alcoholics, the participant most likely to accuse the housekeeper or anyone else about being controlling is the person guilty of the same. This person is termed the *manipulator*.

If one understands the defense structure underlying it, one can better understand the why of manipulator behavior. Denial is foremost. Manipulators continue to adhere to the notion that they are not alcoholic. Projection is a strong prop for denial. Manipulating women feel they are themselves constantly being manipulated and not uncommonly view the group leader, man or woman, as one out to brainwash them.

A common streak in the manipulator personalities, blatant or latent, is *blaming*. Manipulators tend to look out, not in, for the reasons for their problems. They justify their feelings and behavior upon attitudes, talk, and actions of others. In their own view, their misfortunes, especially their alcoholism, are a function of the dark motives and manners of other people. Simply put, they are quite unable to take any responsibility for their own lives.

Shastrom (1967) has developed a comprehensive description of manipulator types. Two types may be considered, those who operate from a position of strength and those who operate from a position of weakness. The list reworded to fit the woman, is provided in Figure 8.1.

From a position of weakness	
baby	sensitive to hurt
clinging vine	dependent
nice gal	warm
From a position of strength	
the judge	critical
the shrew	aggressive
the calculator	controlling
the queen bee	strong
the governess	supportive

Figure 8.1. Manipulator behavior from two positions: Weakness and strength. Modified from Shastrom (1967) with permission.

The most effective way to deal with the manipulator woman is to address her perception of herself and others. Openness, candor, and authenticity may confound the manipulator but ultimately and inevitably lead her to a realistic self-view of her life.

Seducing. The *seducer*, woman or man, is that person who uses words, emotional charms, and body to obtain sexual favors. The successful seducer is the manipulator par excellence. She or he demands, from a position of weakness. Seducers can be, to put it delicately, emotionally flexible if not ambidextrous. To them, from where they are coming does not matter. What matters to them is where they're going and, most importantly, what they expect to get.

The description here is of seducers and the seductive process in general. Add alcohol and the whole manipulative process becomes exacerbated. Now, though they be inveterate manipulators, the dynamics of the alcoholic seducers are very different from those of the alcoholic manipulator not interested in seduction. Alcoholic seducers are not necessarily blamers, nor do they usually hold an especially victimized view of themselves or of life. In fact, effective seducers who are alcoholics, especially when in their sober states, operate with a fairly adequate self-esteem.

The defense which helps to explain them best is not denial or projection but *fantasy*. Male seducers fantasize most about being in control of others, especially of women. Females fantasize about being the focal point of attention, having their proverbial simple wishes treated as commands and dispensing favors sexual and otherwise with discrimination.

The addiction to alcohol for a disproportionate number of both these males and females is related in no little way to their inability to make a long term emotional commitment to the opposite sex. Their heterosexual stance rather is promiscuous.

Despite their apparent sophistication and sometimes "smooth" interpersonal ways, heterosexual alcoholic seducers are a confused and terribly vulnerable lot. The following story illustrates not only how confused and vulnerable they can be but even more just how destructive mutual seduction in a group can be.

Case Example. Jack had been in the group for almost a month when Connie entered it. Quiet and essentially still nonparticipating he had attended every session (six of them) faithfully. The group was one I led for a local branch of a major industrial concern which at the time had a little over fifteen hundred employees. The group including Connie, consisted of nine alcoholics, seven men and two women.

This was Jack's second time in a group with me, both times self-referred. The first time he had been forced to withdraw after two months (eight sessions) because he had been sent by the company to a new plant in a nearby state to set up payroll procedures. Such was the respect in which he was held by central headquarters. Of average height, balding, and more than a little overweight, Jack had been twice married—the first time for three years and the second time for three months. In the middle-manager classification he earned seventy-five thousand dollars a year and paid no alimony.

During his membership in the first counseling group, Jack had displayed a quiet but affable, easy-going disposition. His questions and general responses to group members and his self-disclosures toward the end of his first counseling group, while few, had been thoughtful. These had shown not only that he listened well but that he was interested, wanted to help others, and wanted to learn about himself. Even though a waiting list existed, I had been pleased to skip over it to admit him, rationalizing that his was a *readmission.* My conviction was that he was serious about achieving and maintaining sobriety.

Connie had been on two waiting lists besides mine when she was admitted to the group. Twenty-eight years old, divorced, and with three children, Connie worked as an assembler and earned a little over sixteen thousand dollars per year. Blond and average of both face and figure she came in wearing a shy, wistful look.

Connie started in the group and Jack's demeanor changed. The quiet, nonparticipating member the group had known suddenly became very involved if not assertive, even displaying apt if not skillful counseling skills. At her very first session, he questioned several members with thoughtful questions, made a couple of astute observations, and an interpretation I totally concurred with at the end of a long monologue. He even cracked a joke!

Reflecting on the first Connie session afterwards, I had to conclude that Jack had participated very appropriately and had accomplished something else. He'd made himself noticed. That realization led me to watch the interplay between the two. One didn't have to be especially keen to discern that Connie was attracted to Jack. Her eyes never left him. Jack's tell-tale signs were even more transparent. Even though he continued to be active, if not dynamic, he addressed no comments or questions to Connie. He didn't have to. His way of looking at her had begun to become embarrassing.

Up to the time Connie started in the group, members had been openly warm, encouraging, and active. Within three sessions of her arrival, the talk became strained. At the end of the following session the only person talking besides me was Jack. Connie meanwhile, despite several questions by me and a couple by other members, had smiled with apparent uninterest.

Then I got an unsurprising bit of news. As a consultant counselor on a part-time basis (four to six hours per week), I've neither access nor interest in gossip about plant personnel. Access and interest notwithstanding, I learned from an anonymous message on my telephone machine that Jack and Connie were dating.

As I saw it, the problem was not just mine or Jack's or Connie's or Jack's and Connie's together. It was the group's problem. At the next session I confronted the group with comments and questions such as these. *"I used to look forward to this group. I find myself dreading it now. What has happened to alter my feelings? What changes have taken place in this group during the past couple of weeks?"* This last question precipitated a veritable storm of comments, all very pointed, very bitter and all directed at Jack and Connie. The substance and emotional sum were that the members were resentful. The only other woman stated it succinctly: *"I don't mind what you do with each other before and after but I really wish you'd both stop making goo-goo eyes here!"* More than a few told Connie that they thought and felt she was not ready for the group.

The session was Connie's last. After her second absence the group voted to drop her. Jack stayed. With her departure he returned to the more quiet listener type he'd shown himself to be prior to her joining. He progressed healthfully and terminated from the group four months later.

P.S. A month after his termination he and Connie were married and he adopted her children. Within a year, she left him. He now pays alimony.

FUNCTIONS OF THE
GROUP ALCOHOLISM COUNSELOR

In a prior work (Perez, 1986) the author outlined the functions of the group therapist. These functions are of two categories:

1. administrative, and
2. therapeutic.

The author's experience since describing those functions has only reinforced his belief in their validity. These functions together with their specifics are summarized in the following paragraphs.

Administrative Functions

The first decision the therapist needs to make is to decide what the *size of the group* will be. As so much else about counseling work and particularly group work, the ideal size depends upon the therapist's personality. A group with a minimum of six members and a maximum of nine seems to work best for this therapist.

A second administrative duty is to *screen candidates*. This can be done by interviewing members individually. The group composition that works best for this author is a group made up of both men and women with at least two individuals of the same sex. The author's experience has been that the more he knows about a potential member's past the better he is able to facilitate interaction between and among members. He has found it especially valuable to know about a member's past counseling experience, if any, and especially if the member has or has not been in trouble with the law. The author's experience is that potential members who are arrested for D.U.I. (driving under the influence) are not the best candidates. This is precisely because they are ordered into counseling. They are usually resentful and hostile. As participants, they go through the motion, complete their "sentences," and, in most cases, return at a later date. The best potential candidates are the self-referred. These individuals are usually motivated to achieve sobriety.

A third administrative function has to do with **hosting and launching the group**. This duty involves arranging and coordinating the session times. This is an enterprise which the author has found at best tedious and more often frustrating. Another function is to explain to each member, either during screening or at the first session, the therapist's basic rules regarding interaction among members, i.e., to talk to and not about each other and policy regarding absence from a meeting. Many rules members make themselves. These usually have to do with eating during the group, smoking, and walking around. All of these behaviors, the author permits. A group should not be launched unless members hear what their roles and obligations are in the group especially regarding attending, sharing, and facilitating.

Therapeutic Functions

The four therapeutic functions are defending, supporting, observing, and intervening.

How much **defending** the therapist does is determined by the emotional climate, context, and vitriol and the counselor's personality and disposition.

Supporting involves rewarding and encouraging the shy, inhibited, and fearful member — the one who has more than the usual difficulty involved in the counseling group.

Observing is what the therapist does all the time. It has to do with being exquisitely sensitive to the dynamics of each and every member. Observing is perhaps the most draining of all the therapeutic functions as it is constant.

Intervening means sharing. When the therapist intervenes, she or he is essentially modeling counseling skills, i.e., questioning, listening, clarifying, reflecting, etc., the skills outlined in Chapter 7.

The alcoholic woman passes through stages in the treatment process. Only with a clear knowledgeable frame of reference will the group therapist be able to understand what is happening and why it's happening and be in a more effective position to help her. Each of the stages will be described in terms of dynamics, defenses, and the techniques which seem to be most effective to facilitate treatment.

STAGES AND TECHNIQUES

Prefatory Notes

Counseling groups are of two kinds: the open or on-going group and the closed group. The **on-going group** is one where members come and go. They enter, go through the stage in the treatment process to termination and discharge.

The **closed group** begins with all new members. It may be run in one of two different ways. Thus the group members stay together until all members terminate. This is rare. More commonly, members terminate in terms of their own particular motivation, speed, and needs but no new members are introduced into the group until all the starting members have terminated. The type the author had in mind in the descriptions which follow was the open group.

The alcoholic woman passes through stages in the treatment process. Only with a clear knowledgeable frame of reference will the group therapist be able to understand what is happening and why it's happening and be in a more effective position to help her. Each of the stages will be described in terms of dynamics, defenses, and the techniques which seem to be most effective to facilitate treatment.

The stages as listed and described here do not usually occur in nice, sequential order. The stage concept was adopted here so that the therapist can know all that can and usually does take place. The dynamics and defenses described are all exhibited in a group and usually occur in the respected stage described. At the fourth session, a member may seem to exhibit the dynamics of one at the third stage. Then at the next session, she may have regressed back to the first stage and stay there for the next half dozen sessions! Thus, in the same way alcoholics do not adhere to a neat stage process of progression into and recovery from alcoholism, neither do they proceed neatly and logically through group process. Quite apparently, neatness and logic are not indigenous to human dynamics.

With the exception of the first one, stages do not begin with any clear indicator. They never end clearly either. Rather they meld and merge. For this reason to determine on what stage a member is in the treatment process is difficult. Only when she is close or at the termination stage can we know. Even then, the knowing (both by counselor and the member) is fraught with more than a few doubts. Finally, we are discussing alcoholism recovery!

The length of time necessary to pass from the first to fifth stage is a function of much: the energy and motivation of the alcoholic woman, how well she gets along with the group, how articulate she is, not a little the skill of the therapist, and, finally, the reality of the administrative circumstances in which the group work is performed, i.e., if a city, country, or state locale, what length of treatment time is prescribed, etc.

The five stages are

1. adaptation,
2. rapport,
3. conflict,
4. progression, and
5. termination.

Adaptation

At this stage the only thing the alcoholic woman knows is that she is embanking on a new experience and with strangers! Even for normal people a new experience can be perceived with embarrassment, shyness, and not a little bit of fear. Add strangers to it and all these feelings become stranger.

To an alcoholic woman, beset as she is with a perception which leads her to effect distance rather than closeness with others, normal feelings become exacerbated. Simple fear may become latent terror.

The defense most women new to group use to defend against this terror is **denial**. At this stage the most common supports for it are **projection, fantasy**, and **rationalization**. The best way to deal with these defenses at this early point is simply not to. Even gentle and kindly couched questions might be perceived as challenges and conceivably could result in a stranger—like sense of estrangement and even dropping out.

A woman's interaction at this stage is best understood in terms of her emotional immaturity and her acutely fearful perception. Acutely uncomfortable then, she relates with silence often, with hostility sometimes, and, not uncommonly, with awkwardness.

An important point to note is that whenever a new woman is introduced her personality will change the personality of the group. A critically important point, then, is for the therapist personally to do anything and everything to help her to feel welcome and comfortable. Truly as this new person feels and goes so will the group. Members usually know this and are usually exceedingly helpful.

At this first stage when the new member talks initially she does so about externals, little or nothing meaningful about herself, but rather about the weather, the physical setting, current political events, etc. Not uncommonly, she makes many contradictory statements about her opinions and feelings even about these externals. Such contradictions can be understood as a function of her emotional discomfort and her fear.

The techniques explained and described in Chapter 7 and most effective at this stage include the following:

1. listening
2. questioning
3. reiterating

4. recapitulating

5. reflecting

These techniques can be utilized by both counselor and members.

Rapport

At this stage the new member begins to perceive herself and the group more kindly and more realistically. This is due to her new found feeling of acceptance by them and of them. Blended with this feeling is one newer still—trust.

In this emotionally sheltered but still alien climate the alcoholic woman wants and begins to explore her dynamics through group interaction. These first fumbling attempts are precisely that—fumbling, awkward. The reason for this is simple. While she might be feeling more accepted and accepting and more trusted and trusting, she still has not learned how to self-disclose, even though she may have been privy to the self-disclosure of others.

By listening to these others, she begins to accept, trust, and realize that her problems are not external but internal, that they are the cause of her own discomforts and dysfunctions. Before the end of this stage, for many women the longest of the five, she begins to make little comments about the pain she has felt and is feeling.

This second stage, rapport, is a learning one. At this stage the woman begins to learn who she is. This she *learns by listening* and *becoming emotionally attuned* to the self-disclosure of the other members. The mutuality, the warmth, and the sense of relationship and membership in the group help her to *clarify her sense of self*. This clarification comes from the first time realizations of where she is coming from emotionally and where she is. At this stage she *learns to stop drifting emotionally*. She learns to do what she has never done: *to make goals and resolutions* for her interpersonal life. Remember, however, much of this learning is in an embryonic phase. The woman new to the group is still far more familiar with alcoholic than with non-alcoholic ways of perceiving and interacting. In most people, old perceptions and behaviors die hard. This is especially true for alcoholics and most especially for scared alcoholics, as are all women new to group counseling.

Denial and **projection** are still operating, albeit more weakly. **Regressions** and **minor relapses** occur at this stage. **Group warmth and identification** with that warmth, however, help the majority of new women to continue their rehabilitation.

All the techniques used in stage one continue to be of value. At this stage, the focus of the leader and peer members (via leader direction) should be to **reward** all fumbling behavior and movement toward growth.

Especially valuable as a technique at this stage, besides those alluded to, is **reflection of feeling** because it is so non-threatening and because more than any other technique it seems to facilitate self-disclosure.

Conflict

At this stage the woman accelerates her search to discover who she is. The honest **ventilation of emotion** is common. The ventilation is both in response to others and is part of her own **self-disclosures**. This ventilation includes the spectrum of emotion from hostility to empathy. Now while ventilation of hostility via testing is fairly common in the alcoholic woman, **expression and communication of empathy are not**. Since it is learned in the group, this behavior ordinarily is a brand new one for her. It is one with which she quickly comes to identify and learns to incorporate into her personality.

This **ventilation of feeling** by the woman is of course what characterizes this stage as the conflict stage. Ventilation facilitates periods of **countertransference** and the **empathy of transference**. Both of these are expressions of her needs and movement toward trying to build and **develop relationships**.

During the first two stages, when and if she expressed and shared, she did so in terms of *past* experiences. The feelings she expressed also were described as past feelings, i.e., how she felt long ago when she was a child or early adolescent. At this stage, feelings are expressed as *now* feelings. *The feelings are owned now.* In other words, she is admitting to whom she feels she is presently. These kinds of self-disclosures are the ones which communicate the ultimate in authenticity and which bring people close, again something she has not been able to do with these kinds of self-disclosures.

Her self-perception of victim begins to erode and a new concept of herself begins to emerge. Her sense of self takes on new meaning. She begins to see that she contributed to her sense of victimization by bland acceptance of the injustices and unfairnesses foisted upon her. She begins to see that her life can be in her control *if she so chooses.* Concomitant with this new sense of self comes a most healthful attitude; namely, to *take responsibility* for her own behavior.

Sessions where she has shared and experienced in these authentic ways are the ones which she leaves feeling like she is just now experiencing life.

The denial defense diminishes at this stage. Interestingly, the projection defense continues to hold on. This is seen in the fact that most women continue to show that they are very angry people. Indeed, those who previously were not displacers of their anger become so. However, neither the woman who was displacing habitually nor the one who suddenly begins, persist in doing so. Both types of women stop doing it. The cessation of displacement is a kind of marker indicating the end of the stage for most alcoholic women. Sudden displacement by non-displacers should be read as an encouraging sign, as much as an unfortunate one, as it reflects a comfortableness felt with peers that they had not felt before. Also it may reflect a period of emotional transition in their movement toward sublimation (channeling other energy into enhancing behavior).

At this stage the two techniques most effective are **confrontation** and **questioning**. Both can be effectively employed now because members at this stage have a surer sense of themselves and are solidly identified with the group.

Progression

At this stage the alcoholic woman perceives confidently and optimistically. Her interactions reflect an honest geniality and **interest in others**. Among other things what this indicates is a dramatic diminution in her narcissistic preoccupation with self so typical of the alcoholic. Because she is not preoccupied with her own self, she has the emotional wherewithal not only to *enhance others* but to *want* to do so.

At this stage, when she gives feedback, she feels free to express any and all feelings. She is still awkward when she tries to enhance feelings, but ones which might hurt she expresses with gentleness and tact. At this stage she admits easily and freely to past and present contradictions in her behavior.

Perhaps the most important change in her behavior is indicated by a *questioning of her own self-perception* which she harbored prior to and on the way to becoming alcoholic. At this stage among the most examined aspects of self has to be her sense of victimization. Now that her sense of victimization has pretty much eased she begins to understand the why and wherefore of it and how she herself might have contributed to it. And as she explores all this with her peers, she begins to discard *old values and attitudes* and to begin to *investigate, new ones.*

This is a stage when the phases of transference and countertransference are resolved. Such resolutions inevitably precipitate healthful changes because they provide previously unshown *insights into the self.*

Termination

When the woman reaches this final stage, she looks as she feels—healthy. Her perception and expectations of others, while optimistic, are far from naive. (Her experience with alcohol and the group obviate any possibility of naivete.)

Devoid of threat now, her perception facilitates and promotes interactions which are generally rewarding. Her system of *communication is congruent.* Words, emotions, and behavior all jibe. At this stage the alcoholic woman gives and gets messages easily.

Most importantly, she realizes full well that continued good health is contingent on the maintenance of sobriety. She knows that maintenance is premised upon constant, *persevering self-examination.* Why? Because she is in a process of **recovery** which is non-ending, ever-continuing.

This woman in termination has learned to *accept herself* and to *believe in her ability to improve and grow.* This self-perception leads her to *accept and tolerate the differences and idiosyncracies of others.*

Finally, the learning of trust begun at the second stage and strengthened throughout the group process leads her to achieve the confidence that she can **risk**, risk trusting and loving; risk the trauma of rejection; the joy of acceptance.

SUMMARY

The goal of group counseling for the alcoholic woman is **to help her achieve and maintain sobriety.**

The benefits of this kind of counseling for members include learning to help, learning to accept help, learning about self, learning interpersonal skills, learning tolerance of others and of their own selves.

Two kinds of member behaviors in a group can be considered—the healthful and the unhealthful. The healthful ones include attending, sharing, and facilitating. The unhealthful ones are hostility, non-participating, absenteeism, buffoonery, psychologizing, housekeeping, manipulating, and seducing.

The functions of the group counselor can be categorized into two—the administrative and the therapeutic. Administrative functions include determining size of the group, screening candidates, and hosting and launching the group. The therapeutic functions include defining, supporting, observing, and intervening. It was noted that counselors can either move forward toward excellence or regress. They can not stand still.

The kind of counseling considered here was that of the open group. The five stages considered were adaptation, rapport, conflict, progression, and termination.

FOR REVIEW AND REFLECTION

1. After studying the group approach to counseling the alcoholic woman, do you think you would prefer to work with her in a group or individually? Why? Why not?

2. Among the benefits listed for group counseling, which one do you think has the most value and why?

3. Among the healthful behaviors listed, can any of them be learned more effectively in individual counseling than in a group? If so, which one(s) and why?

4. Are there any unhealthful behaviors listed in group counseling which are also apparent in individual counseling? If so, what are they?

5. Which one(s) of the counselor's therapeutic functions would be the most difficult to learn? Why? Which one the least? Why?

6. Do you believe that a group containing women only would work better for you than one composed of both sexes? If so, why? Why not?

7. Which technique(s) among the stages considered will be the easiest to master? Which the most difficult? Why?

8. Whenever a new member is introduced into the group, the personality of the group is changed. Explain the why of this.

9. What personal qualities do you possess which will promote rapport in a group?

10. Will you go out of your way to contact individuals who have gone through formal termination process from the group?

OTHER READINGS PERTINENT TO THE ALCOHOLIC WOMAN

1. Alcohol Alert. (1990, October). *Alcohol and women.* (Reprints available from the National Clearinghouse for Alcohol and Drug Information, P.O. Box 2345, Rockville, MD 20875.)

2. Blume, S. (1989, January-February). Why we are concerned: An overview of women and alcohol. *Counselor, 20,* 14.

3. Blume, S.B. (1990). Alcohol and drug problems in women: Old attitudes, new knowledge. In H. B. Milkman & L. I. Sederer (Eds.), *Treatment Choices for Alcoholism and Substance Abuse.* (pp. 183-198). Lexington, MA: Lexington Books.

4. Braswell, S.P. (1989). *Job stress and alcohol use among black and white working women.* Ph.D. dissertation, United States International University, San Diego. (Reprints available from UMI, 300 North Zeeb Road, Ann Arbor, MI 48106. Refer to order no. DA 8824068.)

5. Brown, O.M. (1990). High blood alcohol levels in women. *New England Journal of Medicine, 323* (8), 553.

6. Charette, L., Tate, D.L., and Wilson, A. (1990). Alcohol consumption and menstrual distress in women at higher and lower risk for alcoholism. *Alcoholism: Clinical and Experimental Research 14* (2), 152-157. (Reprints available from Lina Charette, PhD, Program Coordinator, Youth Alcohol and Drug Program, Addiction Services, The Royal Ottawa Hospital, Ottawa, Ontario, Canada K1Z 7K4.)

7. Chatham, L.R. (1987). Women's Health: A course of action. Issues Related to Alcohol, Drug Use and Abuse, and Mental Health of Women. *Public Health Report, 102* (Suppl. 4), 16-18. (Reprints available from the National Clearinghouse for Alcohol and Drug Information; P.O. Box 2345, Rockville, MD 20852, 301-468-2600 or 1-800-729-6686.)

8. Cole-Harding, S. (1990). *Men, women and alcohol: An analysis of gender differences in drinking and responses to intoxication.* Ph.D. dissertation, University of Colorado at Boulder. (Reprints available from UMI, 300 North Zeeb Road, Ann Arbor, MI 58106. Refer to order #DA9013666.)

9. Fellios, P.G. (1989). Alcoholism in women: Causes, treatment, and prevention. In G. W. Lawson & A. W. Lawson (Eds.), *Alcoholism and Substance Abuse in Special Populations* (pp. 11-36). Rockville, MD: Aspen Publishers.

10. Flanigan, B., McLean, A., Hall, C., & Propp, V. (1990). Alcohol use as a situational influence on young women's pregnancy risk-taking behaviors. *Adolescence, 25* (97), 205-214. (Reprints available from Beverly Flanigan, University of Wisconsin-Madison, School of Social Work, 425 Henry Mall, Madison, WI 53706.)

11. Frezza, M., DiPadova, C., Pozzato, G., Terpin, M., Baraona, E., & Lieber, C.S. (1990). High blood alcohol levels in women: The role of decreased gastric alcohol dehydrogenase activity and first-pass metabolism. *New England Journal of Medicine, 322*(2), 95-99. (Reprints available from Dr. Charles S. Lieber, Alcohol Research and Center, Veterans Affairs Medical Center, 130 W. Kingsbridge Road, Bronx, NY 10468.)

12. Gomberg, E.S.L. (1989). Suicide risk among women with alcohol problems. *American Journal of Public Health, 79* (10), 1363-1365. (Reprints available from Edith S. Lisansky Gomberg, PhD, Professor, School of Social Work and Professor of Psychology, Alcohol Research Center, Department of Psychiatry, School of Medicine, University of Michigan, 2091 Frieze Building, Ann Arbor, MI 48109-1285.)

13. Gruchow, H.W., Barboriak, J.J., & Sobocinski, K.A. (1989). Alcohol consumption and abuse among women and the elderly. In R. R. Watson (Ed.), *Diagnosis of Alcohol Abuse* (pp. 217-230). Boca Raton, FL: CRC Press.

14. Hagan, T. (1987, June 14-19). *Retrospective search for the etiology of drug abuse: Background comparison of a drug-addicted population of women and a control group of non-addicted women.* Proceedings of the 49th Annual Scientific Meeting. The Committee on Problems of Drug Dependence, Inc. Monograph No. 81. Philadelphia. (Reprints available from Teresa Ann Hagan, Family Center

Program, Thomas Jefferson University Hospital, 11th and Chestnut, Philadelphia, PA 19107.)

15. Halliday, A., & Bush, B. (1988). Women and alcohol abuse. In M. Lipkin, Jr., H.N. Barnes, M.D. Aronson, & T.L. Delbanco (Eds.), *Alcoholism: A guide for the primary care physician* (pp. 176-180). New York: Springer-Verlag.

16. Hamlett, K., Eaker, E.D., & Stokes, J., III. (1989). Psychosocial correlates of alcohol intake among women aged 45 to 64 years: The Framingham study. *Journal of Behavioral Medicine, 12* (6), 525-542.

17. Kravetz, D., & Jones, L.E. (1988). Women reaching women: A project on alcohol and other drug abuse. *Administration in Social Work, 12* (2), 45-58.

18. Lex, B.W., Teoh, S.K., Lagomasino, I., Mello, N.K., & Mendelson, J.H. (1990). Characteristics of women receiving mandated treatment for alcohol or polysubstance dependence in Massachusetts. *Drug and Alcohol Dependence, 25* (1),13-20.

19. Lundy, C. (1989, December 1). *Women and Alcohol: Moving beyond disease theory.* Conference Paper, Third Biennial Health Conference on Health Futures, Wilfrid Laurier University, Waterloo, Ontario, Canada, and the 31st Annual Meeting of the Institute on Addiction Studies, Hamilton, Ontario, Canada, July, 15-20, 1990.

20. McNair, L.D. (1990). *Alcohol use and stress in college women.* PhD. dissertation, State University of New York at Stony Brook, Stony Brook. (Reprints available from UMI 300 North Zeeb Road, Ann Arbor, MI 48106. Refer to order #DA8918949.)

21. Mello, N.K. (1988). Effects of alcohol abuse on reproductive function in women. In M. Galanter (Ed.), *Recent Developments in Alcoholism* (pp. 253-276). New York: Plenum Press.

22. Mello, N.K., Mendelson, J.H., & Teoh, S.K. (1989). Neuroendocrine consequences of alcohol abuse in women. *Annals of the New York Academy of Sciences, 562,* 211-240.

23. Penniman, L.J., & Agnew, J. (1989). Women, work and alcohol. In C. Wright (Ed.), *Alcoholism and Chemical Dependency in the Workplace*, (pp. 263-273). Philadelphia: Hanley and Belfus. (Reprints available from Jacqueline Agnew, MPH, Division of Occupational Health, Department of Environmental Health Sciences. The Johns Hopkins University School of Hygiene and Public health, 615 N. Wolfe Street, Baltimore, MD 21205.)

24. Rohan, T.E., & Cook, M.G. (1989). Alcohol consumption and risk of benign proliferative epithelial disorders of the breast in women. *International Journal of Cancer, 43*, 631-636.

25. Ross, H.E. (1989). Alcohol and drug abuse in treated alcoholics: A comparison of men and women. *Alcoholism: Clinical and Experimental Research, 13* (6), 810-816. (Reprints available from Dr. Helen Ross, Clinical Epidemiologist, Psychiatry Program, Clinical Institute, Addiction Research Foundation, 33 Russell Street, Ontario, Canada M5S 2S1.)

26. Schenker, S., & Speeg, K.V. (1990). Risk of alcohol intake in men and women: All may not be equal. *New England Journal of Medicine, 322* (2), 127-129. (Reprints available from Steven Schenker, M.D., University of Texas, San Antonio, TX 78284-7878).

27. Seitz, H.K., Egerer, G., Simanowski, U.A., Phillips, M., Sweeney, G.D., Zedeck, M.S., York, J.L., Alpert, J.J., Zuckerman, B., Frezza, M., DiPadova, C., Baraona, E., Lieber, C.S., Schenker, S., & Speeg, K.V. (1990). High blood alcohol levels in women. *New England Journal of Medicine*, 323 (1), 58-62.

28. Thorne, F.C. (1950). Principles of personality counseling: An eclectic viewpoint. *Journal of Clinical Psychology, 233*.

29. Wilsnack, S.C. (1989, January-February). Women at high risk for alcohol abuse. *Counselor 20*, 16-17 . (Reprints available from The Counselor, 3717 Columbia Pike, #300, Arlington, VA 22204.)

30. Wilsnack, S.C. (1987). Drinking and drinking problems in women: A U.S. longitudinal survey and some implications for prevention. In T. Loberg, W. R. Millers, P. E. Nathan, &

G. A. Marlatt (Eds.), *Addictive behaviors: Prevention and early intervention*, (pp. 1-39). Amsterdam: Swets & Zeitlinger.

31. Witteman, J.C.M., Willett, W.C., Stampfer, M.J., Colditz, G.A., Kok, F.J., Sacks, F.M., Speizer, F.E., Rosner, B., & Hennekens, C.H. (1990). Relation of moderate alcohol consumption and risk of systemic hypertension in women. *American Journal of Cardiology, 65* (9), 633-637. (Reprints available from Graham A. Colditz, MD, Channing Laboratory, 180 Longwood Avenue, Boston, MA 02115-5899.)

REFERENCES

Axelson, J.A. (1967). The relationship of counselor candidates empathic disposition and rapport in small group interaction. *Counselor Education and Supervision, 6*, (4) 287-292.

Baldwin, R. O. (1984). Stability of masculinity-femininity scores over an eleven-year period. *Sex Roles, 10*, 251-260.

Bart, P. B. (1971). Depression in middle-aged women. In V. Gornick & B.K. Moran (Eds.), *Women in sexist society* (pp. 99-117). New York: Basic Books.

Beckman, L.J. (1978). The self-esteem of alcoholic women. *Journal of Studies on Alcohol, 39*, 491-498.

Beckman, L.J., Day, T., Bardsley, P., & Seeman, A.Z. (1980). The personality characteristics and family backgrounds of women alcoholics. *International Journal of the Addictions, 15* (1) 47-54.

Bepko, C. & Krestan, J. A. (1983). *The responsibility trap.* New York: The Free Press.

Bersak, C. (1990). Enhancing self-esteem as a strategy for treating female alcoholics. *Alcoholism Treatment Quarterly, 8* (3) 105-111.

Bucheimer, A. (1961, March 28). *Empathy in counseling.* Paper delivered at APGA convention.

Butterfield, F. (1986, July 13). The class of '61 offers some dissertations on itself. *New York Times*, E30.

Chaikin, A.L., Derlega, V.J., & Miller, S.J. (1976). Effects of room environment on self-disclosure in counseling analogue. *Journal of Counseling Psychology, 23* (5), 479-481.

Cheng, A., & Hsin, H. (1973)   Rapport in initial counseling interview and its impact in effectiveness.   *Acta Psychologica Taiwanica 15*, 31-40.

Cook, W.L., & Goethe, J.W. (1990, March). The effects of being reared with an alcoholic half-sibling; a classic study reanalyzed. *Pam Process, 29* (1).

Curlee, J. (1970). A comparison of male and female patients in an alcoholic treatment center.   *Journal of Psychology, 74*, 239-247.

Denzin, N. K. (1987). *The alcoholic self.* Newbury Park, CA: Sage Publications.

DeRivera, J. (1977).   A structural theory of the emotions. *Psychological Issues, 10* (4), 34.

Ekman, P., & Friesen, W.V. (1969). Non-verbal leakage and clues to deception. *Psychiatry, 32*, 88-105.

Elpern, S., & Karp, S. A. (1984).   Sex-role orientation and depressive symptomatology. *Sex Roles, 10*, 987-992.

Fletcher, K. D., Price, D. K., & Cook, C.H. (1991, October). Problem drinking and family history. *British Journal of Addiction, 86*, 10, 1335-1341.

Ford, M.R., & Lowery, C.R. (1986). Gender differences in moral reasoning: A comparison of the use of justice and care orientations. *Journal of Personality and Social Psychology, 50* (4) 777-783.

Freud, S. (1949).   A general introduction of psychoanalysis. *Perma Giants*, New York, 25-71.

Galanter, M., Talbot, D., & Balleqos, K. (1990, January). Combined alcoholics anonymous and professional care for addicted and physicians. *American Journal of Psychiatry, 147* (1), 64-68.

Gilligan, C. (1982) *In a different voice: Psychological theory and women's development.* Harvard University Press.

Glatt, M.M. (1959). A chart of alcohol addiction and recovery. *British Journal of Addictions, 54* (2).

Glenn, S. W., Parsons, O. A., & Stevens, L. (1989). Effects of alcohol abuse and familial alcoholism on physical health in men and women. *Health Psychology, 8* (3), 325-341.

Gomberg, E. L. (1989). Alcoholic women in treatment: Early histories and early problem behaviors. *Advances in Alcohol and Substance Abuse, 8* (2), 133-147.

Gove, W. R. & Tudor, J. F. (1973). Adult sex roles and mental illness. *American Journal of Sociology, 78*, 812-835.

Goodyear, R.K. (1981). Termination as a loss experience for the counselor. *The Personnel and Guidance Journal, 59* (6), 347-350.

Gross, H., & McCaul, M.E. (1990). A comparison of drug use and adjustment in urban adolescent children of substance abusers. *International Journal of Addictions, 25* (4A).

Haase, R.F. (1970). The relationship of sex and instructional sex to the regulation of interpersonal interaction distance in a counseling analogue. *Journal of Counseling Psychology, 17* (5), 233-236.

Haase, R.F., & DiMattia, D.J. (1970). Proxemic behavior: Counselor, administrator, and client preference for seating arrangements in dyadic interaction. *Journal of Counseling Psychology, 17* (7), 319-325.

Haase, R.F., & DiMattia, D.J. (1976). Spatial environments and verbal conditioning in a quasi-counseling interview. *Journal of Counseling Psychology, 23* (5), 414-421.

Harburg, E., & Gleiberman, L. (1990, September). Familial transmission of alcohol use, III. Impact of imitation/non-imitation of parent alcohol use on the sensible/problem drinking of their offspring. *British Journal of Addiction, 85* (9), 114-115.

Harford, T., & Spiegler, D. (1982). Environmental influences in adolescent drinking. National Institute on Alcohol Abuse and Alcoholism. Special Population Issues. *Alcohol and Health Monograph, No. 4*, D.H.H.S. Pub. No. (ADM) 82-1193. Washington D.C: Supt. of Doc., U.S. Gov't Printing Office.

Harford, T.C., & Spiegler, D.L. (1983). Developmental trends of adolescent drinking. *Journal of Studies on Alcohol, 44* (1), 181-188.

Hobbs, N. (1962). Sources of gain in psychotherapy. *American Psychology, 17,* 741-747.

Hurley, D. L. (1991, May). Women, alcohol and incest: An analytical review. *Journal of Studies on Alcohol, 52* (3), 253-268.

Israel, A. C., Raskin, P. A., Libow, J. A., & Pravda, M. D. (1978). Gender and sex-role appropriateness: Bias in the judgment of disturbed behavior. *Sex Roles, 4,* 399-413.

Jackson, D. (1957). The question of family homeostasis. *The Psychology Quarterly Supplement, 31* (1), 79-90.

Kanner, L. (1963). The scope and goal of psychotherapy with children. *American Journal of Psychotherapy, 17,* 366-374.

Katsuhiko, S. (1969). An analysis of the change in rapport during counseling. *Japanese Journal of Child Psychiatry, 10* (3), 180-188.

Kaufman, E. (1990). Critical aspects of psychodynamics of substance abuse and the evaluation of their application to a psychotherapeutic approach. *International Journal of Addictions, 25* (2a).

Kaul, T., Kaul, M., & Bednar, R.L. (1973). Counselor confrontation and client depth of self-exploration. *Journal of Counseling Psychology, 20* (2), 3, 132-136.

Kelly, B.J. (1975). Concerned confrontation: The art of counseling. *Social Journal of Educational Research, 9* (3), 110-122.

Kendon, A. (1972). How people interact. In A. Ferber, M. Mendelsohn, & A. Napier (Eds.), *The book of family therapy.* Science House: New York.

Knight, P.H., & Blair, C.K. (1976). Degree of client comfort as a function of dyadic interaction distance. *Journal of Counseling Psychology, 23* (1), 13-16.

Koeppen, A. (1972). Confrontation: A threat and a promise. *Texas Personnel and Guidance Journal, 1* (1), 9, 39-43.

Konovsky, M., & Wilsnack, S.C. (1982). Social drinking and self-esteem in married couples. *Journal of Studies on Alcohol, 43* (3), 319-333.

Kress, M. K. (1989, Summer). Alcoholism: A women's issue, a disability issue. *Journal of Applied Rehabilitation Counseling, 20,* 2, 47-51.

Kuhn, D., Nash, S. C., & Brucken, L. (1978). Sex role concepts of two and three year olds. *Child Development 49,* 443-451.

Lerner, H. G. (1988). *Women in therapy.* Northvale, NJ: Jason Aronson.

Lips, H. M. (1993). *Sex and gender, an introduction* (2nd ed). Mountain View, CA: Mayfield Publishing.

Lott, B. (1987). *Women's lives. Themes and variations in gender learning.* CA: Brooks/Cole.

Luepnitz, D. A. (1988). *The family interpreted. Psychoanalysis, feminism, and family therapy.* N.Y., N.Y.: Basic Books.

Luza, J. (1990, November). Drinking behavior as it relates to relationship with parents, parental drinking behavior, and gender. *Free Inquiry in Creative Sociology, 18* (2), 213-217.

Lyon, D. and Greenberg, J. (1991, September). Evidence of co-dependency in women with an alcoholic parent: Helping out Mr. Wrong. *Journal of Personality and Social Psychology, 61* (3), 435-439.

Maslow, A.H., & Mintz, N. (1956). Effects of aesthetic surrounding: Initial short-term effects of three aesthetic conditions upon perceiving "energy" and well being in faces. *Journal of Counseling Psychology, 41,* 247-254.

Mintz, W.L. (1956). Effects of aesthetic surroundings: Prolonged and repeated experience in a "beautiful" and ugly room. *Journal of Psychology, 41,* 459-466.

Morgan, C. S. (1980). Female and male attitudes toward lie: Implications for theories of mental health. *Sex Roles, 6,* 367-380.

Nakamura, K., Takano, T., & Iguchi, T. (1991, October). Family involvement for improving the abstinence rate in the rehabilitation process of female alcoholics. *International Journal of the Addictions, 26* (10), 1055-1064.

Nespor, K. (1990). Treatment needs of alcoholic-dependent women. *International Journal of Psychosomatics, 37,* (1-4).

Orford, J., & Velleman, R. (1990, June). Offspring of parents with drinking problems: Drinking and drug taking as young adults. *British Journal of Addiction, 85* (6), 779-794.

Patterson, C.H. (1959). *Counseling and psychotherapy: Therapy and practice* (p. 168). New York: Harper and Row.

Patterson, C.H. (1963). Control, conditioning and counseling. *The Personal and Guidance Journal, 41,* 680-686.

Perez, J.F. (1979). *Family counseling: Theory and practice* (pp. 47-51). New York: D. Van Nostrand.

Perez, J.F. (1986). *Counseling the Alcoholic Group.* N.Y., N.Y.: Gardner Press.

Perez, J.F. (1992). *Alcoholism: Causes, effects and treatment.* Muncie, IN: Accelerated Development.

Radomsky, N. A. (1992, July). The association of parental alcoholism and rigidity with chronic illness and abuse among women. 19th Annual North American Primary Care Research Group. *Journal of Family Practice, 35* (1), 54-60.

Rogers, C.R. (1961). The place of the person in the new world of the behavioral sciences. *The Personnel and Guidance Journal, 39* (6), 442-451.

Schaefer, R. (1984). The pursuit of failure and the idealization of unhappiness. *American Psychologist, 39*, 398-405.

Shastrom, E.L. (1967). *Man the manipulator: The inner journey from manipulation to actualization.* New York: Abingdon Press.

Skinner, B.F. (1956). Critique of psychoanalytic concepts and theories. In H. Fergl & M. Scriten (Eds.), *Minnesota Studies in the Philosophy of Science,* Vol. I, 85. Minneapolis: University of Minnesota Press.

Smith, L. (1992, January). Help seeking in alcohol-dependent females. *Alcohol and Alcoholism, 27* (1), 3-9.

Smith, M. L. (1980). Sex bias in counseling and psychotherapy. *Psychological Bulletin, 87*, 392-407.

Stake, J. E. (1983). Ability level, evaluation feedback and sex differences in performance expectancy. *Psychology of Women Quarterly, 8*, 48-581.

Stone, G., & Morden, C. (1976). Effect of distance on verbal productivity. *Journal of Counseling Psychology, 25* (5), 486-488.

Szasz, T.S. (1961). *The Myth of Mental Illness.* New York: Harper & Row.

Tahka, V. (1966). *The alcoholic personality: A clinical study. 13.* Helsinki: Finnish Foundation for Alcohol Studies.

Tannen, D. (1990). *You just don't understand — Women and men in conversation.* New York: Ballantine Books.

Tarasenko, Y. I. (1990). Specific features of social regulation in the clinical picture of alcoholism in women. *Soviet Journal of Psychology, 11* (4), 79-87.

Thoma, S.J. (1986). Estimating gender differences in the comprehension and preference of moral issues. *Developmental Review, 6* (2), 165-180.

Thompson, J. R. (1978). *One male psychotherapist's pilgrimage into his sexism.* Paper read at APA Meeting in Toronto.

Tilby, P. J., & Kalin, R. (1980). Effects of sex-role deviant lifestyles in otherwise normal persons on the perception of maladjustment. *Sex Roles, 6,* 581-592.

Tinsley, E. G., Sullivan-Guest, S., & McGuire, J. (1984). Feminine sex role and depression in middle-aged women. *Sex Roles, 11,* 25-32.

Turnbull, J. E. (1989, June). Treatment issues for alcoholic women. Special Issue: Treating the alcoholic: A social work challenge. *Social Casework, 70* (6), 364-369.

Walter, D., Nagoshi, C., Muntaner, C., & Haerzen, C.A. (1990, October). The prediction of drug dependence from expectancy for hostility while intoxicated. *International Journal of Addictions, 25* (10).

Westcott, R. (1966). Introducing coenetics. *American Scholar, 35,* 342-356.

Whitley, B. (1979). Sex roles and psychotherapy: A current appraisal. *Psychological Bulletin, 86,* 1309-1321.

Widgery, R., & Stackpole, C. (1972). Desk position, interviewer anxiety, and interviewer credibility: An example of cognitive balance in dyad. *Journal of Counseling Psychology, 19* (5), 173-177.

Wilsnak, S. C. & Wilsnack, R. W. (1991). Epidemiology of women's drinking. Special Issue: Women and substance abuse. *Journal of Substance Abuse, 3* (4), 133-157.

Wolberg, L.R. (1954). *The Technique of Psychotherapy.* New York: Greene and Stratton.

INDEX

A

Ability to persevere 66
Absences 218
Absenteeism 217-8
Abuse 63
Adaptation 231-3
Addiction
cycle of, *Figure* 94
Adler, A. 122
Adult daughters of alcoholics
(ADOA) 63-76, 77
Agnew, J. 242
Alcohol alert 239
Alcoholic families
climates 64
daughters 63-76
Alcoholic woman
in the family 57-78
Alcoholic woman in group
counseling 205-38
behaviors of alcoholic group
members 208-27
benefits 205-8
functions of the group
alcoholism counselor 228-30
stages 230-7
techniques 230-7
Alcoholic women
See Women, alcoholic
profile 49-52, 53-4
Alcoholics
relapse 90
Alcoholism
course of 81-91
progression 81, *Figure* 82
progression stages 84-5, *Figure* 82
recovery levels 85-6, *Figure* 83
relapse 87-90
Alpert, J.J. 242
Amaro, H. 49
Anomaly 219

Approval

Approval
constant need 65-66
Aronson, M.D. 241
Attending 209-10
Attuned 233
Axelson, J.A. 134, 245

B

Baldwin, R.O. 31, 245
Balleqos, K. 161, 246
Baraona, E. 240, 242
Barboriak, J.J. 240
Bardsley, P. 46, 57, 245
Barnes, H.N. 241
Bart, P.B. 32, 245
Beckman, L.J. 45, 49, 51, 52, 57,
245
Bednar, R.L. 196, 248
Behaviors, avoiding 143-4
Behaviors in group counseling
healthful 237
unhealthful 237
Behaviors of alcoholic group
members 208-27
healthful 209-14
unhealthful 214-27
Behaviors, healthful in group
counseling 209-14
attending 209-10
facilitating 212-4
sharing 210-2
Behaviors, unhealthful
absenteeism 217-8
buffoonery 218-9
fantasy 214-5
hostility 214
housekeeping 221-3
manipulating 223-4
nonparticipating 216-7
psychologizing 219-21
seducing 224-7

Intellectualization
  counseling excerpt 148-9
Interaction 31, 53, *Figure* 30
Interest
  in others 236
Interpersonal skills
  learning 207
Intervening 229
Investigate
  new values and attitudes 236
Israel, A.C. 32, 248

J

Jackson, D. 57, 248
Jardine, R. 5
Jayle, M.S. 5
Jellinek, E.M. 81, 90
Jones, L.E. 241
Jones, M.C. 50
Jung, C. 122

K

Kalin, R. 32, 252
Kanner, L. 126, 248
Karp, S.A. 33, 246
Katsuhiko, S. 134, 248
Kaufman, E. 161, 248
Kaul, M. 196, 248
Kaul, T. 196, 248
Kelly, B.J. 196, 248
Kendon, A. 147, 249
Knight, P.H. 146, 249
Koeppen, A. 196, 249
Kok, F.J. 243
Konovsky, M. 58, 249
Koradoff's syndrome 126
Kravetz, D. 241
Kress, M.K. 38, 249
Krestan, J.A. 33, 245
Kuhn, D. 31, 249

L

Lagomasino, I. 241
Launching the group 229
Lawson, A.W. 240
Lawson, G.W. 240
Leads

repertoire of 135
Lerner, H.G. 119, 120, 249
Levels
  bottom 125
  communication 145
  recovery 85-6, *Figure* 83
Lex, B.W. 241
Libow, J.A. 32, 248
Lie 67-8
Lieber, C.S. 240, 242
Life
  frantic way of 72
Lindbeck, V. 50
Lipkin, M. Jr. 241
Lips, H.M. 32, 249
Lisansky, J.M. 50
Listening 175-8, 202, 232, 233
  activities for learning skills 178
  aspects of 175-6
  prefatory comments 175
  techniques 176-7
Loberg, T. 243
Lott, B. 31, 32, 249
Lowery, C.R. 35, 246
Luepnitz, D.A. 33, 249
Lundy, C. 241
Luza, J. 49, 249
Lyon, D. 63, 249

M

Malliday, A. 5
Manipulating 47, 223-4
Manipulator 223-4
Marlatt, G.A. 243
Martin, N.G. 5
Maslow, A.H. 140, 250
McCaul, M.E. 57, 247
McGuire, J. 33, 252
McLean, A. 240
McNair, L.D. 241
Meaning 31, *Figure* 30
Mello, N.K. 5, 241
Mendelsohn, M. 249
Mendelson, J.H. 5, 241
Milkman, H.B. 239
Miller, S.J. 140, 245
Millers, W.R. 243
Mintz, N. 140, 250
Mintz, W.L. 140, 250

ABOUT THIS BOOK
AND THE AUTHOR

Joseph F. Perez, Ph.D.

The author has known for a long time that the dynamics which make for alcoholism in a woman are markedly different than those which make for alcoholism in a man. Writing and doing research on alcoholism gave the author the knowledge cognitively. It was the many heart-rending, empathic moments in therapy with the alcoholic woman, however, which convinced him that the dynamics of the story told by any alcoholic woman were quite unlike any told by any alcoholic man.

Alcoholics of both sexes harbor a victimized view of society, a view with elements of suspiciousness if not paranoia. The woman's view, however, is founded in the reality of a socialization process which demeans, deprives and emotionally flagellates her sense of self and esteem. Her perception, her conscience, her system of psychological defense are all molded to fit the needs of society and the institutions it serves, not hers. Protestations about the injustice of her lot are met with a curious mélange of reaction—frequently with surprise, sometimes with amusement, occasionally with anger, and not uncommonly with vindictiveness. Some women shrug and just plain accept their victimization. Some women deny it. Some women dedicate their lives battling it. And some women, whatever their reasons, exquisite sensitivity, frustration, despair, try to escape it—via alcohol. It was precisely to help therapists come to appreciate the dynamics of these last that the author wrote this book.

A licensed psychologist in Massachusetts, Joseph F. Perez is Professor and Chairman of the Department of Psychology at Westfield State College. He took his bachelor's degree Magna Cum Laude at the University of Connecticut in 1954, and five years later he obtained a Ph.D. from the same University. In recognition of his scholarly achievements the University in 1987 inducted him into Phi Beta Kappa as an alumnus.

Dr. Perez's initial exposure to alcoholism counseling began in 1961 when he was a staff psychologist at the V.A. Hospital in Northampton, Massachusetts. Although he continued his counseling work for the following two decades he did not focus his attention upon alcoholism until the early 80's. Since then his abiding professional interest has been the theory and practice of alcoholism counseling as a teacher, a practitioner, and a researcher.

As a teacher, he teaches courses and conducts seminars both at the graduate and undergraduate levels. As a practitioner, he facilitates groups and conducts workshops in private industry for recovering alcoholics. As a researcher, he has been something more than involved and occupied. *Counseling the Alcoholic Woman* is the sixth book he's had published on alcoholism counseling since 1985.

On the lighter and personal side, Joe Perez loves all his work. Teaching permits him to fulfill his need to be a ham. Writing, particularly his efforts in the pure trade market, lets him translate his fantasies into reality. His counseling work give especial meaning to his life. His other loves include tennis, scrabble, the New York Yankees and cooking (soups, squid, and tripe).

He lives with Gerri, his wife of 39 years, and Mimi, his youngest of their four children, in Northampton, Massachusetts.

Other Books
By Joseph F. Perez

Counseling: Theory and Practice

The Initial Counseling Contact

General Psychology: Selected Readings

Mom and Dad Are Me

Family Roots of Adolescent Delinquency

Family Counseling: Theory and Practice

Family Counseling

A Father's Love (A Novel)

Counseling the Alcoholic

Counseling the Alcoholic Group

Coping in the Alcoholic Family

Relationships: Adult Children of Alcoholics

Tales of An Italian American Family (Short Stories)

Alcoholism: Causes, Effects, and Treatment